William J. Sowden

The Northern Territory as it is

A Narrative of the South Australian Parliamentary Party's Trip

William J. Sowden

The Northern Territory as it is
A Narrative of the South Australian Parliamentary Party's Trip

ISBN/EAN: 9783337143428

Printed in Europe, USA, Canada, Australia, Japan

Cover: Foto ©Suzi / pixelio.de

More available books at **www.hansebooks.com**

THE

NORTHERN TERRITORY

AS IT IS.

A NARRATIVE OF THE

SOUTH AUSTRALIAN PARLIAMENTARY PARTY'S TRIP,

AND FULL DESCRIPTIONS OF

THE NORTHERN TERRITORY;

ITS SETTLEMENTS AND INDUSTRIES.

BY WILLIAM J. SOWDEN.

WITH AN APPENDIX, CONTAINING REPORTS ON THE GENERAL
RESOURCES OF THE TERRITORY BY PROFESSOR TATE, F.G.S.

Adelaide :
W. K. THOMAS & CO., GRENFELL STREET.

1882.

TO THE

HON. J. LANGDON PARSONS, M.P.,

MINISTER FOR THE NORTHERN TERRITORY,

AND

HEAD OF THE PARLIAMENTARY PARTY

WHO VISITED THE TERRITORY,

THIS BOOK IS RESPECTFULLY DEDICATED

BY KIND PERMISSION.

INTRODUCTORY.

THE writer offers no apology to his readers, for to such of them as were self-sacrificing enough to follow his sketches, published in the *South Australian Register*, detailing the movements of the Parliamentary Party in the Northern Territory, is due the appearance of this little book. They asked for it, knowing what they were committing themselves to; and they have it. Those who have read the descriptions of the Northern Territory as they appeared in the *Register*, reading these also will find some additions and a good deal of re-arrangement. If they discover, moreover, a little revision let them not marvel. An occasional verbal inaccuracy crept into the original publication; and that there were so few and that these few were so trifling—these are legitimate grounds for wonder. Consider, pray, that a good deal of the "copy" was written on shipboard when gale-tossings caused cabin furniture to turn somersaults; or—worse than that—in odd corners of some bush publichouse, 'midst sweltering heat and in an atmosphere thick with insect life; the writer enlightened by the feeblest of feeble candles, and entertained by the strongest of strong festive demonstrations from elated patrons of the host; that it was written, too, on paper which was suffering from the effects of frequent wet-season soakings, and which ever and anon reduced a folio crammed full of facts and figures to a hopeless smear. Consider what legibility the copy would be likely to retain by the

time it reached Adelaide, after it had run these gauntlets, and
then say, prompted by your conscience, that the printer has not
excelled himself and excited your astonishment. For one very
valuable addition the courtesy of the Hon. J. Langdon Parsons,
Minister for the Northern Territory, must be acknowledged. That
addition is the official report presented to the Parliament by
Professor Tate, F.G.S., which Mr. Parsons permitted me to
include in the Appendix. To that honourable gentleman I am
indebted for his permission to allow me to dedicate this little book
to him. To make that dedication was my duty as it was my
pleasure, for Mr. Parsons as official head of the Parliamentary
party was as energetic as he was courteous and affable as a private
gentleman. I acknowledge too, my obligation to the Editor and
Proprietors of the *Register*, who generously gave me the copyright
of these sketches, which were written whilst their writer was
representing the *Register* in the Northern Territory as its Special
Reporter there. Of the history of the Northern Territory itself
nothing need be said here. Of the Parliamentary visit thither
there follows detailed information. Let it be sufficient to preface
it by saying that the idea of the trip was first made public by the
Minister when he brought down the Northern Territory Estimates
in 1831, and when he was able to announce—what not one of his
predecessors had had the good fortune to announce—that the
accounts of that Territory showed a balance on the right side.
It was on the last day save one of January, 1882, that the
Minister, with Messrs. H. E. Bright, L. L. Furner, and J. H.
Bagster, left Port Adelaide, after their fellow-workers in Legislative harness had bidden them a hearty good-bye. It was on the

thirteenth day of April that they were welcomed back again to the colony. What they did in the meantime the following pages reveal. What I saw of the country after the Party left they also show. If the reader who shall plod faithfully through them be not too overpowered by the relief which comes with a sense that a disagreeable task has been overcome, he will be convinced that that extreme northern country of ours, which we have called by courtesy the Northern Territory, but too often, with bitterness, our White Elephant, is a rich possession which other colonies well might envy us. And if he be not convinced of this, the fault is mine, and not the country's.

W. J. S.

CHAPTER I.—EN ROUTE.

ADELAIDE TO MELBOURNE.—MELBOURNE TO SYDNEY.—DEPUTATIONS AND
ENTERTAINERS.—A TRIP ROUND SYDNEY HARBOUR.—A PRACTICAL
OPINION THEREANENT.—THE BEGINNING OF THE REAL VOYAGE.—
THE UNCONQUERABLE MAL DE MER.—A STORM.—WHAT ORIENT-
ALLY-MANNED SHIPS ARE LIKE.—THE FIRST ANCHORAGE.

THE purpose in this partial republication is not so much to
slavishly follow in the lines of the original reports of the
movements of the Parliamentary Party as to describe the
more interesting and least known of the points along the
route. The reader, confronted or affronted with this
warning, will therefore not expect more than a passing reference to
the sister metropolitan cities, Melbourne and Sydney, which were
necessarily visited. At the first the Party arrived on February 1,
leaving it after having been formally deputationized and informally
interviewed by representative men, intent equally upon doing their
visitors honour, and with true Victorian business promptness
getting information from them respecting the Northern Territory,
which, truth to tell, they more highly accounted than South
Australians did at that time. Sydney was reached on February 4,
after the 571 miles' dreary ride along the two railway lines which,
except for a gap of three miles, give unbroken and rapid communication between the two capitals. We were introduced to Sydney
proper when that City was in a sullen humour, and when we felt
travel-weary. We saw it from the railway station at early morn,
amidst a light, vapoury rain, which made the streets cloggy, and a
heat which, with the humidity, gave the sensation of a vapour-bath.
The cabmen were quarrelling over the luggage; bustling people
were pounding away at our corns; we had not had breakfast; news-
boys were thrusting papers in our faces; the street we could see
some distance into gave us a perspective of steaming dreariness;
the hansom, going to the hotel, threaded through so many
windings of the road that we were more than half-inclined to believe that the driver had gone mad, and was trying to describe
with his cabwheels some intricate crochet pattern. And we felt
savage. But a change came. Personally I had discovered an
honest cabman—a man who asked me only double what the fare-
list in my hand authorized him to ask. I was soothed. I felt
that I had not come to Sydney in vain. A subsequent study of

the excellencies of an early breakfast-table strengthened the conviction. A quiet inspection of the city led to a revision of the first
hastily-formed estimate of it, and brought to light many beauties
to compensate for the numerous uglinesses—the uglinesses principally of marvellously crooked streets, some with gradients too fearful to be contemplated by the nervous.

"We're slow—r-a-a-ther, I grant," drawled a prominent New
South Welshman with whom I entered into conversation—"Yes,
we're slower than even you Adelaide folks; but, leaving alone our
harbour, we've got peculiarities—advantages, too—about our
streets that *you* don't own."

"And they are——?"

"Well; so confoundedly up-and-down that each end has a
different climate. F-a-c-t !"

But the harbour was unanimously voted by the Party—as indeed,
it must be of right—the chief glory of Sydney. Our travellers,
moreover, saw it under especially auspicious circumstances, from a
special launch, specially fitted, on a specially fine day, with a
special company, headed by a no less distinguished personage than
the veteran Sir John Robertson, who "runs" New South Wales in
the absence of Sir Henry Parkes.

I shall not attempt to detail the many beautiful sights Sir John's
South Australian companions saw. As practical Mr. Bright said when
asked by his entertainer for an opinion :—"Words and pictures
can't give a correct idea; people must see it." An almost perfectly land-locked bay, Port Jackson; its entrance guarded by
cannon sufficient to make irondust and splinters of the biggest
war-vessel which ever floated or aye will float. Within, for many
miles, vista upon vista of beautiful Rhine-like scenery. Trees
clothing numerous glacial hills. Atop of many of these and
likewise on their sides rise jutting crags, flint-like and sombre,
throwing out in strong relief the pretty wee white cots, the
ponderous towering mansions and the gleaming land-marks (guides
to the incoming mariner) which alternate with them. If all the
indentations of the bay from head to head were measured, the
distance would be proved to be considerably more than a thousand
miles, and in the area that represents you get some of the grandest
natural graving docks to be found in the world; in that harbour
you could float in perfect safety vessels of all sizes, and in number
practically unlimited. A grand place altogether this Port Jackson
—beautiful as Naples—useful as any port in the world. Where
Watson's Bay laps the shore at the foot of Baron Maclay's Bio-
logical Laboratory the Party landed and rambled awhile. Calling
at the Baron's quarters, they discovered that the enthusiastic
scientist had gone away, leaving his card beneath his knocker.

Each of the visitors left his also, and took a lively satisfaction in imagining the model of astonishment the Baron's face would be when he next lifted that knocker, and let the distinguished card-shower fall upon him.

Sydney was left early on the morning of Wednesday, the 8th February, and from that time till the night of the 11th, the voyage was of such a nature that it will doubtless long be remembered—by the members of the Parliamentary party, at any rate, for they were particular sufferers. At one time, and that a long one, it seemed as though history would repeat itself—that the Menmuir disaster would be a companion for the Gothenburg catastrophe, when so many honoured public men and prominent officials of South Australia went down beneath the surging waters; for the oldest navigator along the coast avowed that he never experienced there before such a continuance of baffling winds and waves as we had. When the Menmuir had got outside the Sydney Heads at about 10 o'clock on Wednesday morning, she was met by a raging host of waves each with the white-cap mischief-badge, and as they were safely buffetted, others—perfect swells—spray-wreathed by a strong east wind, had to be contended with. They worked themselves up during the next few hours into mad fury; they leapt on deck and knocked about the movables; they rushed impetuously from side to side; they dashed themselves to pieces against the vessel's gunwales; and then, shattered, plunged into the sea again to make room for more vigorous successors. All day the wind had howled around the ship in strong intermittent squalls, and rain had poured down in a sheet with fully tropical violence. The hencoops had to be kept on the poop to save their occupants from drowning, and several of the sheep died from the effects of the weather. Towards midnight on Friday the storm began to work up to its climax, and two or three hours afterwards was at its height. The passengers, to most of whom the pleasures of the table had been for days a memory only, had to hold on by the sides of their bunks, and after the Parliamentary party had done this awhile a new subject of attention came in the shape of an inundation of sea-water from a particularly strong wave; and then—a truce to dignity! The legislators of all shades of opinion manifested an instant desire to cross over to the other side of the House, and did so; and while they listened to the howling of the storm, and maybe cogitated on the form in which their obituaries would appear, the propeller of the ship suddenly ceased to move, and on the instant there began a heavy bumping sound. This aroused the other passengers, and the cabin, with almost perpendicular floor and swaying fixtures, presented a spectacle which, reproduced, would make a reputation for a smart caricaturist, but the component parts of which had at the time certainly no thought of comic journalism.

" The vessel has struck!"

This was the popular verdict. All the time the bumping had continued, and the screw still ceased from work, and at last a few eager delegates went on deck to ascertain the wherefore, and found that their trepidation, though excusable, was really unwarrantable, for the bumping was caused by a large boat (lashed amidships) which had parted from one end of its fastenings; and the strain on the other had bent the thick iron davit like a rush, and warped and split the big wood beam. The stern had then got into the water, and with every lurch of the vessel it thumped against her side with almost force enough to start her plates. The order to cut adrift was of course given, and its execution was well-nigh marked by a tragedy, the chief officer being dragged overboard by the boat; but instantly a big wave came and washed him back close to the gunwale, and just as it was retreating a seaman on the deck grasped him by the heel and pulled him in. The stormy weather continued thus till Saturday at noon, when a haze even thicker than the mist we had had before came up. The wind veered round to the south-west and blew in violent gusts, bringing with it torrents of rain. The sea ran high, the sun had not been visible for several days, and the view all round was bounded by the haze beyond a hundred yards. The coast was dangerous, and no landmarks had been seen since Moreton Island had receded on the horizon. The vessel was kept on changing courses, at dead slow speed, and the position was a critical one. The captain's calculations were so perfect, however—his allowances for the strong tide-currents so exact—that at 8 o'clock at night, precisely as he had predicted, the light on Bunker's Head was seen, and he and all the company were naturally much relieved, as the vessel steamed past the light where two poor fellows drag out their lives in perfect solitude, through the Capricorn and into the Barrier Passage which leads to calm water sheltered from storms by the famous Reef.

Then the members of the Parliamentary Party began to gather strength again. From the first two hours at sea till the beginning of the fifth day some of them in common with less distinguished travellers were very, very limp, and full of regret that they had been induced to leave their cosy homes to sail the stormy sea at a season when it is in those latitudes at its very worst. But henceforth till we reached the northernmost point of the continent, we got along pleasantly enough, for we were inside the Passage, with a balmy, tropical breeze, a lightly cloud-veiled sun, a smooth sea, good provisions, and prodigious appetites.

On the Menmuir we had an opportunity of seeing how the Celestials work. The crew were all Orientals—the quarter-masters Malays, and the men Chinamen. The latter also act as cooks and waiters. The sailors work as hard as any British tar, and do their duty quite as cheerfully. The cooks are fully equal, to say the least of it, to an average English kitchen knight ; and the waiters, compared with Europeans in their line, are deficient only in superciliousness. Take this ship altogether, with its coloured crew, including its black firemen, and, try to find another of its size more efficiently manned without respect to numbers, and I promise you will have to own to failure.

As we advanced still further northward the record was—" We are getting into tropical regions now, and silk coats and cool covers are in request. The sun strikes down in thorough business fashion, and the air with each degree becomes less balmy and more furnace-like. We are passing almost constantly close between the different islands of the southern part of the Barrier Reef. Some of them are no larger than a haystack, others boast trees, and rocks, and vegetation, but very few so far have much of natural beauty or any population whatever (though they are occasionally visited by wandering tribes of blacks). These are promised us ahead. As I write we are within pistol-shot of the sunken rock on which the Singapore grounded on Ell Island four years ago. It was unknown till she discovered it, and her first discovery was her last. . . . . It is interesting and cheering to contemplate the solicitude which the fact that the Parliamentary party were doomed to go through the tropics caused some Adelaide and provincial chemists to manifest. A representative man sent to various members samples of all sorts of medicaments for curing all manner of ailments ; and as I see a portly, well-esteemed honourable member making himself good-naturedly an envelope for each compound day after day, I am almost tempted to give the ingenious makers of these medicines a free advertisement. But our anchor has just introduced itself to the muddy bottom off Townsville, and mail carriers are inexorable, you know ! "

CHAPTER II.—EN ROUTE.

THE arrangements for boarding upgoing steamers at Townsville were not absolutely perfect. The people were too
meditative, perchance. The authorities, moreover, manifested a faith pleasing to contemplate when they omitted to
send off a medical officer to enquire whether passengers
leaving smallpox-infected Sydney were well or not. This lack of
inquisitiveness saved a good deal of trouble, and in this instance,
as we landed half a dozen of our company at Townsville, it indis-
putably demonstrated the possession of a confiding nature by
Townsvilleans. Of course we did not land; and so we lost the
pleasure of a close inspection of the lions of the place, just as we
had missed overnight a sight of the beauties of the most romantic
scenery along the route—the scenery on either side of Whitsunday
Passage, with its lonely but "stately" lighthouse, pioneering other
habitations. Seen two miles off, however, the part of the township
which the hills hide not looks pleasant enough, though it straggles
over the ground like a distorted centipede. It stretches itself
along the sea, which shallows near it; and towering high above it
on either hand are overhanging crags of respectable altitude.
Away in the background is a wooded range, cloud-capped on this
occasion, and decked with a changeful border of light haze, now
white, now bluish-grey, and, when the sun shone out, looking more
like a congregation of pale-faced rainbows than anything else
deponent wots of. There seems to be an anchorage at some little
distance from Townsville; and within easy sail are pretty little
islands, perennially intensely bright-verdure-clad, and some with
neat white-sand beach-fronts, but most with rocks and undergrowth
constantly lapped by the water, which generally speaking is
shallow, and, when we saw it, at different points was streaked with
earth colour, marking the presence of freshets from the swollen
rivers which have their outflow thereabout. We remained two

hours off Townsville, and then weighed anchor, steaming till 7 at night through narrow winding passages, with smooth sea and no sun. Old Sol's face had almost all along been hidden by a thick veil of cloud and mist, and generally the beauties of the islands peered out at us through a vapour bath, which began to make us fear our sight was becoming defective. Occasionally, however, the sun's rays glint on the rocks and trees ; and, though the hills are scarcely high enough to warrant the adornment, their tops are covered with a cloud-hood, frayed out into delicate irregular edges, and looking surpassingly beautiful. At 7 o'clock we anchored. It is not safe to steam all night, unless the moon shine brightly out ; and during the trip there might as well have been no moon at all, for heavy tropical downpours paled its light. With the first glow of dawn next day, we were under way again, and passed all day through the same kind of scenery as we had seen before. There is a wearying sameness in the landscape during this part of the trip. Before you reach Cooktown, however, you notice points which have an interesting history. After the beautiful Fitzroy Island—till recently the Cooktown Quarantine Station, and before the head-quarters of some bêche-de-mer collectors—there is Cape Tribulation, for instance, aptly named by its great discoverer as the point at which a notable gale arose ; and just beyond you see the reef on which Captain Cook's good ship Endeavour came near her end in the same gale, only escaping by the adoption of the advice of one of the middies that a tarred sail should be passed around her hull to stop the leak which a bump on the reef had caused.

The place where the Endeavour refitted—Cooktown—was our next stopping place. We anchored early on the 15th, and, while the health authorities were deliberating for some time when it would suit their convenience to come off to us, we had an opportunity of seeing by the effect on the sea of a break in the Barrier Reef, of how great value that reef is to the mercantile interests of the colonies. Inside it ships can always ride safely, even when the sea outside is in its stormiest temper. Till the last few years it was considered unnavigable. The water at Cooktown is generally in a rage. It was in a mild one while we were there, but beautiful Mount Cook, standing half its body higher than the average of the hills along the coast, had a white bandage round its head, and frowned down grimly on us. You can't see much of Cooktown from the offing—only (besides some iron stores) a handsome snow-white villa, belonging to the steamer's agent, and the end of a respectable jetty near the Endeavour River, which flows pretty deeply twelve miles or so beyond the town and brings down in barges the station produce of the country through which it passes. These were interesting objects of inspection for a while, but they were filling after the first hour. So most of the passengers fell to fishing, and caught between them a piece of floating gunnybag and mildly chaffed each other on the catch, till by-and-by the Customs people and the doctor came, and guaranteed their healthfulness. Afterwards the saloon passengers, headed by the Parliamentary party, went ashore in a body to see a famous Queensland settlement. That settlement—Cooktown, of course—is not so bad as it is possible for a town to be, but it works hard for the distinction, and will probably gain it by-and-by. With one long street it has made a start with three more on each side at right angles ; but they are not brilliant successes. The people cultivate a healthy grass crop in the main thoroughfare, and flourishing luxuriantly right down to the footpath's edge are beautiful white and pink Vinca and gorgeous red Hibiscus, growing in profusion they never can attain in lower latitudes. There is indeed on every hand a wealth of greenery, amongst it plantain and palm and other tropical growths. The buildings are almost as unsightly as the poorer erections of Sydney; they are all of wood, and the Town Hall is fixed on high piles which the tide plays with when at the full. All that the Cookites have to do when a ratepayer becomes obstreperous at the municipal election meetings is to let the troublesome party down into the river through a trap door in the floor. There was no Cooktown before 1873, when the discovery of the Palmer diggings caused it to spring up like a mushroom. Three years ago their partial failure closed the greater number of the thirty or forty hotels the town held, and shut up some of the stores. Those left, however, find a a good deal to do; for the escorts bring down gold still, and the bêche-de-mer fishers have since last March sent away thence between 300 and 400 tons of fish. This at from £85 to £110 a ton means a good deal of money. The visitors had a melting time, for a hot place is Cooktown, and rather given to fiery trials if one may judge from the number of ash-covered blanks in the street-line. There are two newspapers published there. The editors vary the monotony of things in their little sphere by tilting at each other with somewhat less than Eatanswillian relish, let us hope! There are Chinamen and Chinese women in Cooktown—a good many of them storekeepers, sleek, good-humoured-looking fellows. We met one old gentleman, who strutted along under a thorough cloud of white canvas, and an umbrella like a buggy-hood. He austerely omitted to recognise the salutation of a thin member of our procession. To a very stout one he bowed profoundly and threw at him a really hearty "Good morning." In China the fat men are Mandarins. This Celestial thought the rule held good with us, no doubt. Just before we came in there arrived from

New Guinea a gay-looking junk, built by Chinamen in Cooktown; and it brought a host of "geological, ornithological, and mineralogical wonders," as the paper phrased it. Very good ones some of them, and valuable, too, the Chinese think. Thirteen shillings was what they asked us for the skin of a bird of paradise, which bore unmistakable marks of having been in its time a chronic dyspeptic— its feathers drooped so. It is plucky of these Chinamen to go to New Guinea and get curios—more plucky than it was in D'Albertis to explore the island, because that gentleman knew the Papuans had in war council assembled reluctantly decided that he would be rather too tough eating to make it worth their while to kill him except for amusement, and that even that was risky fun. The Chinese have no such consolation. Before they began a connoisseur near Port Moresby assured them, and also a friend of mine who has a pearl station thereabout, that roasting-cuts of plump Celestial in prime condition, not opium-tinged too greatly, are worth some pence per pound more than the best joints of European. The latter tastes too much of tobacco, they say. Having shipped bêche-de-mer and provisions, it was nearly noon when we saw the last of the mangroves, as the august visitors passed the Mayor of the municipality *incog.* at the head of one of the streets—a street, by-the-by, where a noted alligator named Big Ben holds annual *levée.* On board again, we continued our twelve-knot spin northwards with a sea smooth almost as a mill-pond, running along a channel bounded on either hand by bright green islets and low reefs, with the sun glaring down fiercely from the blue sky unchequered by a single cloud; with the Parliamentary party quite recovered from their *mal-de-mer*; and "all going merry as a marriage bell," if I may be allowed to invent a figure. Indeed, the voyage was now beginning to partake more of the nature of a yachting excursion than a sea trip. We never lost sight of shore—of land exceedingly beautiful, standing out against the waters. The mainland was too distant for observation in this the most highly favoured bit of country passed in the whole journey; but we constantly saw on our beam, big islands, with palms and other vegetation, and pretty little islets. This scenery, even enthusiastic Scots say, has no superior in their own bonny Highlands. If it were ten thousand miles away we would go probably into rhapsodies about it; as it is at our doors we take it quietly and, following the fashion, make Continental tours for recreation. Seriously, however, this scenery—perhaps least known of all the Australian coastline—is the most beautiful, and there is no more pleasant excursion for a fagged-out colonial than a voyage to China along our eastern coast—a voyage which, including three weeks in the Celestial land, occupies only three months and costs comparatively but a trifle. Through the whole six thousand miles the ship is never more than two days out of sight of land. At dusk we passed Lizard Island, where poor Mrs. Watson and her attendant Chinese servants were attacked recently by the blacks, who came in canoes from the mainland and ravaged her husband's sealing station ; and a few minutes afterwards we left behind the barren little islet whither the heroic lady floated in an open tank with her little baby at her breast, and where she (after displaying a heroism beyond all commendation) and her wee charge died for want of water. At night we went within a hundred yards of the lightship near Cape Melville, which was twice attacked by the natives in their canoes ; and in a part of the passage dangerous for navigation in even a night so gloriously starlit and so calm we dropped anchor for a couple of hours, proceeding again with the first blush of dawn. During the day we passed several of the jaunty little lightships, on each of which, away from the mainland, alone in the midst of the waste of waters, three solitary men drag out the weary months. About noon there appeared by the steamer's bows a canoe, paddled swiftly along by two natives, from one of the adjacent islands. The fellows (who wore only a hideous smile, and who were of a coppery-black, and as fierce-looking as it should be possible for mortal to be), clamoured loudly for "bacca" and bread. The officers threw them some trifles, which they picked up nimbly enough and put into their canoe, the while yelling for further favours. The natives, like Oliver Twist, ever yearn for "more." Give them two hundred pounds of flour, and they will importune you for the bag ; or pipe and tobacco, and they will plague you for a lucifer. It was wonderful how nimbly these two fellows —strong, athletic, and more intelligent apparently than those of the southern latitudes—managed their canoe, and how swiftly they sent it through the water in our wake. The canoe is the frailest of frail cockle-shells, but it is almost impossible to overturn it, on account of its being balanced by a wide but light out-rigger. Most of these little craft, I believe, are made in New Guinea and sent down to the natives on the Queensland coast. At 9 at night we anchored till daybreak near the Hannibal Islands, not far from where the steamer Somerset rubbed her back on the reef some time ago. It is about 140 miles from Thursday Island. Next morning we proceeded on our northward course past the 10th degree of latitude, amidst the very fervent heat which alternately fires and boils and steams everything there ; past York Island, to the north of the extreme northerly point of Australia ; and so to anchor by the hulk opposite Thursday Island, about 30 miles from Cape York and three days' sail from Palmerston. On the way various places were pointed out as note-

worthy on account of their being the scenes where many years
since shipwrecks occurred, and shipwrecked folk were killed and
eaten by the natives. Twenty years ago these savages were so
fierce, and the passage of the Straits was so beset with dangers,
that shipmasters loading at Sydney for the route were wont
to wait for each other and to sail in company. One of the most
interesting parts of the natural scenery near the northernmost end
of Australia is the vast congregation of large ant-hills, some
five or six feet high and more, and looking for all the world like
gravestones of redgum and Gothic architecture. Then you see
Albany Island, opposite where so many orgies and native fights
occurred in the old times. The island is divided from the continent by a very narrow channel, where the current runs at the rate
of six knots an hour. You see, too, the remains of the old
settlement at Somerset, the ruins mostly hidden beneath the
luxuriant foliage. You are shown explorer Kennedy's monument,
and the first of the northern pearl stations; and then you pass
the jagged bodkin point, Cape York, which pushes itself of all
continental Australian territory farthest northward, and looks as
though it were trying to hook the York Islet, which is separated
from it by only a little deep passage, with a rock in the very
centre, washed by a stream which flows through at a terrific
rate. And so on to Thursday Island, where the party were welcomed by Mr. Chester, virtually the monarch of the place.

The island is one of the Prince of Wales Group, and there are
six others; but it is the centre. Three or four years ago
what was known as the settlement (which was kept up by the
British, the Queensland, and the New South Wales Governments as a harbour of refuge for shipwrecked folk when Torres
Straits had more storm-victims than it now boasts) was
removed to Thursday Island from Somerset, Cape York.
Of course the first purpose of the settlement has almost ceased
to operate, and the troops who in the early days formed
the most important part of it have been withdrawn. The officials
on the island now have little to do with native or shipwreck
troubles. There is first Mr. Chester, the resident Police Magistrate,
finding enough to do to exercise, in addition to discharging his
magisterial functions, oversight over the duties of collector of
customs, shipping master, and postmaster. There are under his
command a boat and crew, the police sergeant, the pilot, the
signal master; the Government schooner Pearl, carrying two
Armstrong guns and cruising about with no end of pomp for the
protection of fishers in the Straits; and lastly a Government cutter,
which is used as a pilot boat. The officials' residences and offices
occupy the eastern end of the island, and besides private houses

on other parts of it there are two stores and two hotels. (One of the
keepers recently took over the bar in one day not less than £200
for retailing liquors to the pearl fishers. You have only to remember the extent of the population to have a due respect for
their absorbent qualities.) The island has not yet risen to the
dignity of churches or schools, or a gaol. The European population all told is about forty. The island is not a desirable place of
residence. Its mosquitoes and its sandflies challenge competition
for provocation to profanity. Its vegetation is not too prolific, and
just of the ordinary island kind, yet the place is picturesque. A
few bananas are cultivated in the gardens of the various pearl
stations, and sweet potatoes are being grown, but the industry is
only in its infancy yet. The aborigines are very friendly, though
they were none too amiable when first interviewed. They differ
from their sable and savage brethren of the mainland in that their
hair is woolly, if I may make a statement apparently so anomalous.
In personal beauty they resemble the Cape York tribes and—well,
and a disfigured Guy Fawkes. Thursday Island has the shipping
port for all the Straits. It was free till recently, and cost the
Queensland Government a trifle to maintain, but now they collect
taxes on almost everything and book a yearly revenue. There
were a great many pearling stations in the Straits at one time (the
industry has been established about eight years), but two-thirds of
them amalgamated, and the number is now reduced to seven. All
save one belong to Sydney owners. The first cost of a station is
rather heavy. The working expenses on one which has seven boats
average £200 a month. Connected with it on shore there are
several buildings. The one I saw at Friday Island (Captain
O'Hagen's), which may be taken as a sample of the average, consists of the manager's residence—the assistant manager's quarters,
and those of the shore gang, a shell-house, a store-room, a boatshed,
and a place in which the shell-cleaning operations are conducted.
For all these, and the use of their portion of the island, the captain and his partner pay a license fee of about £10
yearly to the Queensland Government. This, with a charge
of £3 a year for each large boat, has only been imposed
since the passage of the Fisheries Act of last year. At
first the fishery was conducted by swimming divers, but now
scientific appliances are universally employed. Then Torres
Straits natives were engaged to dive, and Europeans had charge
of the boats, but the former were found to be hopelessly lazy, and
the latter (who also when the diving apparatus was first introduced
used it) act mostly as managers. Now the work is done by
Malays, Polynesians, Manila men, a few negroes, and fewer
aborigines. The fishing plant includes for each party a sailing

boat of about eight or ten tons register and very strongly made,
and with each of these a dingey; in every boat diving apparatus,
with long air tubes and engines and other fixings. The crews
have six men each, and the diver is in command. Each boat is
provisioned for three weeks, and the diver may fish wheresoever
he will in the whole of the Straits. The duration of the absence
is, however, hardly ever more than a fortnight. Sometimes the
boat returns laden with shell, and at others (very rarely, though)
with none. On its return it is emptied, and the shell consigned
to the shore gang for cleaning. This cleaning is a very easy
operation, and when it is concluded the shell is packed in cases,
and sent either direct to Sydney, where it is worth about £135 a ton,
or to England, where it brings from £160 to £200. The average
weight of each shell is 3¼ lbs. without its contents, which are not
used for food except sometimes by the boatmen. The men who
brave the seas to get it lead an eventful life, the divers especially.
The latter see some strange sights down below the ocean—plant
life and creeping things and sharks innumerable; but the sea-
lawyer fortunately invariably takes fright at the diver's dress, and
rapidly puts as much space as possible between it and him. A
few weeks ago one of the divers saw an immense octopus, and
immediately came up to report an interview with the Father of
Lies in piscatorial shape—his idea (poor ignorant soul) of our
civilized Beelzebub! The divers generally remain four hours
below without returning to the surface, if they are on a good bed.
Each takes down with him a small bag, which, when he fills it
with shells, is hauled to the surface by the people in the boat, who
then lower others as they may be needed. The shells are generally
found in big patches—some are many miles long and containing
scores of tons, but there are numbers of smaller ones. It is a
singular fact that only a few inferior pearls come to the masters'
hands, while they are constantly being bought from the men in
Sydney at high prices. One sold whilst I was there is worth about
£1,000. The explanation is that the boatmen treat them as
perquisites, and sell them when they go down south at the ex-
piration of their term of engagement. Notwithstanding the seeming danger of their work, only very few of the boatmen are lost.
One of the pearl-station owners says that he has missed only
one diver during the last seven years, and not more than four
or five boatmen. Two of the latter were killed by blacks,
near Somerset, on the mainland, and the rest were drowned.
The divers get from £200 a year for the best men, and
the boatmen about £3 a month with rations. All are paid in
commission on the value of their catch and partly in wages. In
stormy weather when they cannot fish (about four days of every week)

the crews belonging to the various stations shelter under some headland, and while the storm rages, or on ordinary nights when they can manage it, and whole days sometimes, play cards for hours, gambling like gentlemen ; tune up the flutina, of which they are passionately fond ; and sing and dance and shout and generally enjoy themselves.

There are 102 pearling-boats in the Straits, and thirty-one employed by " bêche-de-merers." These represent £400 a year in licence fees to the Government of Queensland. There are 800 coloured people and fifty whites engaged in both fisheries, and last year there were 392 tons of pearl, and about 90 tons of bêche-de-mer exported from the island as the produce of the fisheries in the Straits. Pearl shell at £130 and bêche-de-mer at £90 (average)—Figure up the total, please ! This year up to the end of March, the fishers took from an extraordinary bed, 29 miles long, 290 tons of shell which, however, was worth only £100 a ton.

But now a word about bêche-de-mer, the industry second in importance in the Straits, and flourishing most along the eastern coast. The profits are not so large as those the pearlers book, because the trouble is greater, and there are possibilities of the catch being spoilt by bad management. The collecting of the fish is a simple operation. The black-pudding-like sea-slug clings to the reefs, and the fishers float their boats close in at half-tide, and anchor so that when the water goes out they are fast aground. They then collect the bêche-de-mer, and fill the boat with it. When the tide floats their craft they sail away to the station, and hand over their catch to the cleaners. These first, after necessary cleaning, parboil the fish, and then put it in a smoke-house to dry. This drying is an operation necessitating great care and watchfulness. Three different temperatures have to be brought into play, and the least neglect sometimes spoils the whole of the fish being treated. The article in a marketable condition looks like sole leather or thick bark. It nearly all goes to China, where it is esteemed as the main ingredient in a soup, second only in deliciousness—the Chinese say—to birds' nests or plump puppy dogs. You get it sometimes on Straits steamers. I have tried it, and cannot speak enthusiastically of it. Its taste is that of a very feeble mock-turtle. Perhaps our cook did not put forth his best efforts in its preparation, however.

Thursday Island, by the-way, has been a great place lately for "globe trotters." Mr. Chester tells us an edifying little story of one of them. An European traveller the man was, intent on writing sketches of the places he visited or saw through a telescope, and not wholly unacquainted with guide-books. At Thursday Island the steamer was for some reason or other not boarded by Mr. Chester; but there came off a well-known, exceedingly stout, very rough, unkempt sea captain, owning one of the pearl stations. He introduced himself for a joke to the "trotter" as "The High Commissioner, &c.," and the jest was taken in earnest. The scribe published his notes recently, and in them appeared the astounding sentence:—"I was introduced to Mr. Chester, the Government Resident at Thursday Island. He looks more like a fierce buccaneer than the representative of law and order!" There is some perplexity as to who is hit hardest by the joke. Mr. Chester. in point of fact, is no more buccaneer-like than Sir Henry Parkes or Sir William Jervois. And the mention of the latter's name reminds me that an old associate of Sir William's—Colonel Scratchley—left Thursday Island a few days before we visited it. His object there was to see whether the place could be made into a coal depôt for the Imperial Government. His report is favourable, and it is understood that he will recommend the construction of a battery on the big hill over the Residence. The position is admirable. Thursday Island is the key of the Pacific, and the battery, if erected, will command the only really convenient entrance in the North to the inner passage of the Barrier Reef. There are great things in store for the place, which at present is literally a one-horse settlement. There is only one noble steed thereabout, and the owner is more of a charger than the horse is.

You cannot speak on general subjects with old residents of Torres Straits, and more especially the mainland abutting on them, without being impressed with the existence of a great evil there. The evil is the prostitution of the black women. It is a delicate subject to refer to, I know; but it ought to be spoken of and written about more than it has been. When men calling themselves by the name of Britons shamelessly abuse the female relatives of the blacks—buy the hateful favour by bribing father or brother, or take the woman by force against her own and her friends' wish; when these men keep the poor creatures they take as long as they think fit and then turn them loose again; when through their disgraceful conduct they bring down the vengeance of an infuriated tribe of blacks upon them, and then, because they are the stronger, shoot the poor wretches down like dogs—when these things have been done, it is surely not the time for mealy-mouthedness. The evil has decreased of late; so have the blacks. And Christian Governments and Christian men take very little account of the shooting of the natives. The latter murder a man—perhaps a man who, in most of the cases, had brought their just vengeance upon him, or suffered for some one

else who had—and a "revenge party" is forthwith organised to
visit the murderers with retribution. The first camp they come
to they fire upon, regardless of the fact that the natives they
shoot may know no more of the crime than Queen Victoria does.
The Government "official" revenge force may be more discrimi-
nating; I speak of what occurred on the York Peninsula some
years ago. Even now it is considered a joke all along the coast
beyond Cooktown in many quarters to shoot down blackfellows by way of retaliation, and some men pride themselves on
the "row of stiff"uns" they have made in their time, and others talk
pleasantly of "black-crow shooting." The Europeans certainly have
difficulties to contend with in their dealings with the natives, but
the most successful man now in the Straits never shot one of
them, though he has been the pioneer visitor to some of them. I
do fervently believe from my experience in other places, and from
what I hear on good authority here and also of New Guinea, that
if the whites had had one-half the provocation which they had
given the blacks the blood-guiltiness of some of them would have
increased considerably. But the weakest goes to the wall. Oh!
we Christianize the natives, we Europeans; we initiate them by
baptism into the mysteries of religion, but the baptism too often
is a baptism of blood. Mr. Macfarlane's Straits and New Guinea
Mission, the people say, has not been very successful as yet. How
can it ever succeed whilst he and his helpers are so seriously
handicapped?—they propounding a doctrine of peace and goodwill,
and others of their colour trading upon the vices and the lusts of
the natives? There is ample room for other missionaries—missionaries to the whites—on the northern coasts of Queensland, and
the staple text should be "Thou shalt do no murder."

We left Thursday Island on Friday afternoon, February 18, and
the only land passed thence to Port Darwin was Booby Island,
which is now uninhabited, but which was some years ago known
as the "Torres Strait Post-Office." There was a postbox there, and
there was also a provision store, and ships passing by used to land
letters and deliver any which they found addressed to ports to which
they were bound. They replenished the store with provisions for
shipwrecked people who might be cast on the island. After a
while, however, it was found that natives from the islands, as well
as unprincipled Europeans, were in the habit of stealing the food
so charitably left; and so the ships ceased to call, and the Torres
Straits Post-Office suspended operations.

Early on Monday morning, February 26, we had our first glimpse
of the Northern Territory—the point off Port Essington. The
entrance to the adjacent inlet is seven miles wide, and the land
being low on either side the port is difficult to make, and somewhat

dangerous on account of the Orentes Reef (so called because a vessel of that name was wrecked there), which lies off the entrance. Port Essington was "settled" in 1831 by Sir Gordon Bremer for the Imperial Government as a military post and harbour of refuge for shipwrecked sailors. It was abandoned nineteen years afterwards, and the only remains of the settlement now are ruined buildings and an enormous tamarind tree, the wonder of the place. There are numbers of buffalo, the descendants of herds turned loose by the settlement party many years ago. A speculator owning land in the neighbourhood tried some time since the experiment of hunting these cattle, and jerking their flesh for sale ; but he was not very successful, owing mainly to circumstances which could be controlled in future. A number of Adelaide capitalists are about to take the industry in hand. Then you get a glimpse of the Cobourg Peninsula, where a cattle station is, but where little has been done. But chiefest of all sights is that of Melville Island, about thirty-four miles, as the crow flies, from Port Darwin, and separated by Clarence Straits from the mainland about fourteen miles. The island is seventy-five miles long and thirty-eight miles broad. It is said to be fertile, and to possess several good harbours. I was fortunate enough to interview one of the very few Europeans who have visited it, and he assured me that the reports as to the character and number of the blacks there are fully sustained. The island is overrun with them, and they are as fierce as the bulky mosquitoes that congregate in the thick mangrove-lined coasts. For these reasons scarcely any whites have visited the island since 1840, when the military post of Fort Dundas on King Cove was abandoned after having been kept up sixteen years, during which time there were several affrays with the natives. The country for the greater part is low, thickly wooded, and in a great many places fronted by rocks. The highest elevation is 320 feet. The trees and undergrowth stretch down to the coast, and there are two or three rivers on the island—one navigable for a short distance. Separated by Apsley Straits (nearly a mile broad) from Melville Island is another named Bathurst, which is about thirty miles in extent, and which has a grand natural harbour in which a fleet might float. The soil almost exactly resembles that of the adjacent land. In the more open parts the sago, fan-palm, bandana, gum, and other trees grow, and everywhere almost there is evidence of fertility. I have described these islands at such length because they are absolutely unproductive bits of South Australian territory, supporting no one but the swarming tribes of blacks. The hostile Melville natives had better make the most of their opportunities ; ere long we shall have begun to civilize them. If, by-the-way, there is a missionary to spare in South Australia or elsewhere, here is a good opening for him. But he must be hardy and plucky ; as bold in demeanour as in opinion.

At 1 o'clock on Monday, February 21, we passed the entrance to the Adelaide River opposite the Vernon Islands, where the passage is intricate and difficult of navigation, and where the efflux from the river discolours the sea water. We arrived at our destination shortly before 6 o'clock in the evening, when the sun shone brightly and the weather looked as unlike the wet season as it could possibly be. A perfect cloud of vari-coloured flags went up over the Government Residence in sign of welcome, and the leading townsfolk, headed by Mr. Price, S.M., the Government Resident, as soon as possible came off to the vessel, and expressed the welcome gracefully. Mr. Price imparted the cheering information that the District Council and a host of supporters had been marshalled for some time on the beach, to the end that they might fire off an address of welcome to the distinguished travellers ; but the Minister decided not to go off that night, and consequently the eager crowd had to nurse their complimentary sentiments till next morning. The Government Resident remained on board only a few minutes, and soon after he returned on shore bonfires blazed out from various places along the beach, and there was for hours a ruddy glow from the pole which indicates where the end of the jetty is when the sea hides it from view, as it always does when the tide is at the full. In the meantime a grand banquet—the principal incident in connection with which was the presentation of a purse of sovereigns to Captain Ellis in recognition of his conduct during the gale—was proceeding in the saloon. There was so much that was complimentary to be said that it was midnight ere the proceedings closed. It would appear that there was some festivity ashore; for in the early morning there came off to the ship a prominent resident to ask for a light—

"Can't get s-s-hingle dry light 'shore rainy season," was his plaint, "All lightsh damp Deshember to (hic) to May—fact, wholly depen'ent shteamers for lightsh !"

He got a light, and as he went away gravely applying it to the side of the bowl of his pipe, a cynic made some reference to the potency of Northern Territory liquors.

CHAPTER III.—IN THE TERRITORY.

The Official Reception.—A "Dolce Far Niente."—The Start for
the Interior.—Southport.—Gorgeous Cloud Effects.—The
Reception at the Jetty. — National Characteristics. —
"Three Cheers for the Plucky Minister."—A Musical
Melange.—Choice Specimens of Horseflesh.—The Muster.—
"Behold the Party Mounted."—The Blacks.—Largesse.—
"One Big, Big Fellow Feed."—The Start Inland.—Narrow
Escape for Mr. Bagster —Tumbling Waters.—Collett's
Creek.—A Sunstruck Packhorse.—The Rains.—The River
Finniss.—Argument Flat.—Rum Jungle.—A Distance Gauge:
The Price of Limejuice.—Peculiar Ant-hills.

AT ten o'clock on the morning of the 21st February the
Government Resident came off to the ship in the official
cutter, and conducted the Parliamentary party to the
shore, where they were received by the leading residents.
After an inspection of the Government Residence, they
proceeded to the Courthouse, where the principal officials and
about a dozen other folk (Northern Territory musters are not over-
large) had gathered in the hall to witness the presentation of an
address to the Minister by the District Council of Palmerston,
represented by Messrs. P. R. Allen, Joseph Skelton, V. L. Solomon,
Jas. Pickford, and J. G. Kelsey. The address was graceful enough,
and sufficiently in conformity with tradition not to need republication; and what more need be said? The ceremonial trouble was
soon over, the Minister by a thoroughly hearty little speech
winning at once the regard of the Palmerstonians. That regard,
to their honour be it said, they freely extend to all eligible
strangers in the most practical manner. The next three days the
party spent in preparations for the exploration of the interior, and
in a deserved *dolce far niente*, if the *dolce* qualification may be
allowed by the critical reader, when consideration is given to the
fact that eager deputations of sandflies and mosquitoes made with
embarassing importunity the most perplexing demands. There
were demands, too, by human deputationists, the most tempting
being that the party should attend a "welcome" banquet ere they
entered upon their adventures; but the Minister bravely resisted
all their blandishments, deciding to do the work first and the
feasting afterwards.

Well; the start was made on the 23rd. The heavens were
sullen and wept copiously as the Parliamentary party accompanied
by Mr. J. G. Knight (Special Magistrate, Goldfields Warden, Clerk
of the Court, and a dozen other things besides) and Mr. David Lindsay (Government Surveyor) left the apology for a jetty in Palmerston
and boarded the steam-launch which was to convey them to South-

port, amidst the cheers of the Government Resident and his satellites from the shore. To reach Southport the steamer had to go straight down the centre of the harbour and through the Middle or South Arm, which is the most extensive of the inlets from Port Darwin. Its entrance is about three miles wide, but an islet two and a-half miles south makes it bifurcate. The branch we followed trends south-east eight miles from the inlet and seven miles nearly due south, when the channel narrows down to a mere creek at its end, dignified by the name of the Blackmore River, on which the township of Southport is situated, about twenty-six miles from Palmerston. We did the distance in less than three hours, but then we had a swift current with us. There is nothing particularly inspiring about the trip. Save for a little patch of open land and one hill 250 feet high or thereabout, you see little change from swampy flats densely covered with mangroves; though when—after an hour's broiling below, backs to the engine-boiler to escape the rain—we came on deck well-steamed to sizzle in the sun, a few verdure-clad hills were overlooking us in the distance. The water, which varies in depth from six to thirteen fathoms, was muddy but salt, and carried a heavy timber drift, which stuck in the roots of some of the mangroves rising a long way from the water's edge like tangled stake fences. Sheets of galvanized iron stuck between some of them were the official notifications of the presence of rocks or reefs, but a more unmistakable intimation at one point was the top of the mast of the Dawn, a small vessel which foundered off the Channel recently. The best sight of all—and that was poor enough, in all conscience—was Storm Point, about eight miles in a straight line from Southport. It has a few sickly trees upon it, and it deserves lots of credit for having kept them alive so long under such discouraging circumstances. Though it seems absurd to talk of cultivating any of this boggy, swampy land, when you come within half a dozen miles of Southport you are at once struck—if you have any of the utilitarian element about you, and if you are not too disgusted by the eternal sameness of the mangroves to draw upon it—you are at once struck with the thought of what a grand provision Nature has made for future wharf-owners. The river for a very long distance thence varies from two to three chains in width, and the depth of water in many places is as great as that in the new dock at Port Adelaide at ordinary low tide. All that would be needed, besides population, to make this a great shipping place, would be to drive down piles and reclaim a little land. Vessels of three hundred tons could come down and take away without lightering the produce of all the plantations and the output of every factory the circumjacent land is likely to contain for half a century. Speculations were

being uttered in glowing terms and pat periods on the future of
this river, when the smoke of many factories should begrime the
scores of thousands of toiling mechanics, etcetera., when an
enthusiastic sky-gazer called attention to one of the most beautiful
cloud effects to be seen anywhere.   It was not gorgeous, but
the combination of colour was grand.   Minarets of light-blue
cloud shot above a mass of chocolate-and-slate and red-and-brown,
all ever inter-blending; and athwart the whole two rainbows
glanced.   And as they paled away and gradually lost themselves
the sun retired to rest, and the clouds first modestly blushed at
the performance, and then fast-coming darkness kindly put a
veil upon their faces, and the lamps came out in the sky; and a
ferocious horde of mosquitoes imitated them on the land; and
whilst their allies, the sandflies, scratched the surface of our skins,
they dug beneath and gorged themselves with blood.   Thus
were we when we saw towering over our heads the water-end of
Southport Jetty, and heard thereon, and from the land the whizz
of rockets and the clatter of Chinese crackers, the while our nos-
trils were offended with the odour of the powder.   We clambered
up the substantial jetty some fifteen feet or so—for it was low
tide—with the aid of ladders, and as our heads emerged above the
highest piles a loud harsh jabber and an unmistakable guttural
apprised us of the presence of blackfellows and Chinamen
—mutual antagonists—and a good round oath pronounced the
nearness of some of the sons of old John Bull.   All had, to do
the party honour, drawn themselves in two lines, leaving the
centre clear for the passage of the visitors, and as the courtesy
was accepted there rose the cry "Three cheers for the plucky
Minister."   The cheers were given.   Did you ever hear blackfellows, Chinamen and Europeans cheering together?   In this case
you could "analyse" the sounds readily.   They were mixed so.

"Y-e-e-ah! Y-a-h!" Thus the blacks.   *They* didn't know what
on earth all the fuss was about, but felt that anyhow they *must*
help in the business going forward.

"E-e-ep—eep—o-o-ol-a-ay!" Thus the Celestials, with memories
of the cheering of Californian diggers, most of them, and all with
that mysterious inability to articulate the letter "R."   A Chinaman
could no more say "Rogue" than some of them could help being
one under auspicious circumstances.

The Europeans, of course, gave voice to the inspiring old " Hip,
hip, hooray!" which no one knows the origin or age or meaning of,
but everybody *so* likes to hear given heartily.

Mix all these sounds and try to realise the ear-wounding product·
But though the audible tokens of welcome were mixed, the feeling

they were born of was very warm and respectfully appreciative—
much more so than even that displayed by the purely European
gathering who met the Minister at Palmerston.   Mr. Parsons at
once won their hearts by starting a sonorous "Three times three
for Southport," which we visitors gave with full lung-power, though
with not half the effect the welcoming cheers had.   The opposite
party had the advantage in numbers, you see.   Nevertheless the
Chinamen with that aforetime-referred-to notion about Mandarins,
looked humbly—aye, even wistfully—at Mr. Bright, as that good-
hearted, portly gentleman put in his share of our cheer.   The
party then, followed by the still cheering little crowd, went under
other rockets and through more powder-smoke to host Hopewell's
hotel, and had a dinner, which, though laid so far from civilization,
was fit to feast an epicure upon.   But there was a drawback afterwards.   As the party lounged beneath the verandah enjoying the
cool breeze from the river, and waging warfare against the mosquitoes, there came from out the bar-room the sounds of revelry
by night—of music.   I say "music," because I have the authority
of the host for calling it by that name.   The intention was good,
doubtless, but the effect with invisible choruses from outside was
a "sweet commingling," which was confounding—a commingling of
the protests of a bad fiddle against a worse fiddler, the notes of a
bass singer trying to achieve "Come into the garden, Maud" an
octave too low, the croak of bullfrogs, the tinkle of horse-bells, the
gurgle of a Chinese melody, and the profanity of some hilarious
teamsters near at hand.

Southport is pleasantly situated, considering the character of
the surrounding country.   It will not be on the route of any
intercolonial or other railway, probably, but it will ever be the
port of shipment for the south-western hundreds—Clyde and
Milne and Hughes at least.   In public institutions it boasts a
Telegraph Office, a Police Station, and a cemetery.   The Telegraph Station is one of those in connection with the overland line,
and its keeper is Mr. J. W. Johnson, who has also to act as Postmaster and Sub-Collector of Customs.   There are two public-
houses and a couple of stores—branches from the importing
establishments at Palmerston.   The only other English places are
the smithy and the saddler's shop.   Twelve stores are owned
by Chinamen, of whom there are about a hundred in the township—more than three times as many as the European total.
There are a good many blacks—Wilwonga and Larrakeeyah.
There is neither doctor nor chemist.   There are a few flourishing
Chinese vegetable gardens, and plenty of fish—rock cod and a
sort of bream, mostly—is got in the river, which has a tidal rise
and fall similar to that at Palmerston.   Public religious services

are unknown in the township, and private dittos almost so, I should judge ; and there is no school in which the children can be educated. But in the dry season Southport—though in the wet a dull, shambling, dingy, fifth-class, disordered, commonplace little village—is an actively important centre. Thence all the diggers' supplies go down to the goldfields, and thither comes all their gold. The horse and bullock teams, that do no work from December to April, make it their terminus, and the mail contractor has his head-quarters there, getting the post-bags from Palmerston by steamer, which runs down one day and returns the next. The farthest Post-Office south is Pine Creek, but the Catherine, further still, will soon probably be the final point at which the mailman will call. By the coach in the dry season, and by it and pack-horses in the wet, a weekly mail is carried between the terminal point and Southport.

The previous day the pack-horses provided for the convenience of the party arrived at Southport, and next morning the first grand muster came off by the Telegraph Station. Altogether, there were twenty-two horses in the cavalcade ; and the order was—*they must only be walked!* Arab steeds are not plentiful there ; and our collection—though one of the best to be had for love or money, or anything else in the Territory at short notice—would rather have impelled a retired bone-mill owner to reminiscences than have inspired a horse-jockey with pleasure. Mr. Lindsay—indefatigable as a white ant—superintended the selection, if selection you may call a purchase where there is no choice. They were knock-kneed and lame, and bruised and spavined, and flea-bitten, and—in short, everything but what they should be. The half a dozen roadsters for the party stood proudly out from amidst the rest like Hercules amongst pigmies ; but even then before we mounted we had to seriously wrestle with the suggestion that our horses, like another worthy's, would be constantly wanting to lean up against something or to lie down and roll upon us ; our only consolation was that, with the thermometer at 97° in the shade—equal to 116° in Adelaide—they would not have energy enough to do either.

Behold the party mounted ! The Minister in a slashed slouch-hat with veil—*a la* bushranger—light tweed trousers, with singlet, black umbrella, and long white oil leggings, on (as was fit) the best horse of the lot—a horse that, judging by an occasional caper, evidently indulged sometimes in youthful reminiscences ; Mr. Bright (with his seventeen stone distributed over a disheartened-looking nuggetty roadster), with a wideawake brown hat, a tight light singlet, trousers and brown leggings, and a light umbrella ; Mr. Bagster like the Minister, save for a dustcoat ; Mr. Furner

ditto, with slight deviations; the Professor with leggings which
left a white blank above his shoe-tops, and buccaneer-like in look
but for a good-humoured semi-cynical smile; and Mr. Knight somewhat like Mr. Bright.   And each laughing heartily at the grotesque
appearance of the other; and all immensely amused at the sight
and sound of the cavalcade, with its halting packhorses, their vocife-
rous drivers, and the loud crack and wild flourish of the stockwhips,
which oft and again interviewed the steeds' raw backs and sides.
Thus the auspicious start.

I should have recorded before an interesting event—the distribution by the visitors of largesse to the blacks, in public half-
circle assembled in front of the hotel.   The gift was in the shape
of flour—next to tobacco the best-esteemed native luxury—
doled out in a grocer's scoop in anything but grocer fashion by
Mr. Knight.   The sight was certainly the most interesting seen
on this trip.   Oh, such degraded specimens of humanity!—less
manlike some than a grinning and chattering monkey looking
at them from the hotel door.   I question whether, on the whole,
any beings bearing the semblance of humanity could be found
more low-sunk than these.   Physically the men were well-
made, though disproportionately light of tibia; but the women
were lank and puffy and distorted, and, for the most part, ugly as
the Father of Mischief.   Some few, however—the young ones—
were well-looking comparatively.   'Twas pitiful, though still
amusing, to see these people as they came for flour—came with
old tins, and bits of dirty paper, and rags, and leaves.   First an
old lubra (unanimously voted a living skeleton—thin and wizened
and dried beyond belief), holding a chubby child on her
shoulder; then an obese woman—the only stout one I had seen
here yet; then a matron with twin children, the one cross-legged
upon her shoulder, the other affectionately supported by the neck
under her arm; then an "angular parallelogram" in the shape
of a man 6 ft. 4in. high; then some of these sneaking back again
for more; and at the end an ugly woman with a pretty child,
who grabbed a handful of the flour and made its face a
perfect piebald, and rubbing it into its eyes and crying with the
pain caused little milky rivulets to flow adown its nose.   And then,
quarrelling over the food as pigs quarrel over a bone, and quite as
thankless to the donor, with a profuse spitting (not to have seen a
tobacco-chewing native salivate is something to be thankful for!)
and a screeching and jabbering and a discordant whirr like the
alarm-note of a quail, but more discordant—the dusky crowd
moved off to their camp to put their different lots of flour together
and to have for once, at least, "one big, big fellow feed," the while
their benefactors went upon their journey.   That journey began at

about 10 o'clock on the morning of the 24th, when the sun shone down with great fervency. The horses bore the infliction with great fortitude for the first hour, which was engaged in going through rather poor-looking flat country, little different from an ordinary bush landscape in South Australia proper, in point of vegetation, save that the grass was higher and more rank, and the road bore deep water-channels—mementos of recent wet-season rains. At the end of that time Mr. Bagster's horse determined to stand the conveyance of that honourable gentleman no longer, and without any notice took the bit between its teeth and galloped off the road in amongst the thickly-planted trees, winding in and out in such an erratic fashion, and so nearly colliding with them that it was by nought else but a miracle that the Parliamentary party were not under the necessity of leaving one of their number behind them. The first sign of civilization besides the road met with on the journey was Tumbling Waters, as to which its name is the most romantic feature. A little body of water attempts a feeble fall thereabout, and hence the high-sounding title. The only visible erection is a small house to the right of the road—a house in which is vended limejuice, with copious aqueous dilutions, at $7\frac{1}{2}$d. the tumbler. Just beyond this aspiring place is a little rivulet, clear as crystal, which runs down and gives a hand with that ponderous waterfall ; and a mile further on there stands a solitary bark hut, whose proprietor this wet season loses money, and in the dry when teamsters are about makes some, by selling limejuice and baking bread for the Chinamen in the neighbourhood. There is a vein of quartz cropping up here, and the Tumbling Waters Gold Mining Company started a few years ago had good prospects, but stopped at that, of course. Most gold companies do.

Thence to Collett's Creek, and indeed from Southport thither, the country is of an uninteresting and, I should say, a comparatively unfertile character for the most part. The road in the main traverses with wearisome levelness a formation of ironstone conglomerate, which, worn by traffic, forms light gravel or nodules, which make a road-surface equal to macadam. At Collett's Creek, eighteen miles from Southport, the travellers stopped for a sort of siesta and a lunch. A picturesque little place, watered excellently, with a light-brown loam—notable in history chiefly because a white man was murdered by the blacks there for too great attention to a lubra. There was an hotel in the palmier days of the Territory, but it now serves as a private habitation. Some Chinamen have a large and flourishing garden in which they grow all sorts of vegetables. "The soil will grow anything," the oldest resident assured me as the result of his experience. There is little doubt that Collett's Creek will be the westernmost point of the transcontinental railway.

Ere we had reached this point on our journey the heat had struck down one of the packhorses, and (so uncertain is the climate) while the poor beast was rolling about in the blaze of the sun there came down a tremendously heavy rainstorm, which, though it lasted only about half an hour, put in so much work in that time that the journeyers found themselves wet to the skin when it ceased. And as they left Collett's Creek it was pouring in torrents, converting trees into trickling fountains, and the roadway into a rapid river bed. Seeing much of the country right past Mount Fitch and Burton up to the eastern branch of the Finniss was, under these circumstances, impossible. The land, however, is more elevated, and the most prominent geological features are the vast boulders and "runs" of granitic rock. As granite country is generally associated with tin ore, it is not unlikely that there may be rumours of tin discoveries there some day. Just before dusk—following the course of the telegraph line—we forded the east arm of the Finniss, which ran rather swiftly, the water in the centre being about three feet deep. Of course its volume was swollen by the floods. Over the river the country changes somewhat in character. Instead of the tall not too succulent grass is a more dwarfed and richer herbage, and in place of the poorer soil is a rich chocolate, which is fit for anything in the way of cultivation. The misfortune is that, so far as I can learn, there is not very much of it. Till dark we saw ourselves surrounded by this kind of level country, only broken at rare intervals by an unpretentious ridge or two. As we went over Argument Flat—a rather sodden flat, by the way, and called by so odd a name because of the camping teamsters disputing there in the dry season—a thunderstorm, with fierce lightning, came up; and on jogged the dispirited horses, staggering under the weight of the weary bedraggled party, with no sign of habitation or habitant to cheer them, till the lights of the Rum Jungle public-house infused some little hope into them. The jungle had its peculiar prefix because an overland telegraph party fell foul of a cask of rum secreted there.

Next morning, dressed in a robe of bright green raindrop-sprinkled verdure, the place looked picturesque enough. The jungle on the west is, when the sun comes out in the early morning, beautifully checkered with lights and shades such as you cannot see much lower south. The only habitation in the place—the public-house, though unpretentious, and indeed dingy, sets off the view; and its proprietor has added to the effect by establishing a small plantation in which he grows a little sugarcane and some sweet potatoes, both of which yield plentiful crops.

We gauged our distance from hotel competition by the price of limejuice. It was a shilling a nobbler here—50 per cent. advance in twenty miles. These little public-houses must, in the dry season, make enormous profits. They provide, generally speaking, only a mockery of accommodation, and in the place here—and this was one of the fair ones—an honourable member, waking in the morning, found that the population of his sleeping place had been increased during the night by one blackfellow, a Chinaman, a dog, and a pig. Society was decidedly promiscuous, you observe. I have left till the last mention of one of the most peculiar features of the scenery passed through so far, and continuing throughout—I mean the anthills. For hundreds of miles the landscape is relieved by these erections. The busy little ants are fond of fantastic designs. The Gothic they follow most. The forms are of six or seven turreted columns, triple pinnacles, gables twenty feet high, sugar-loaves of two feet, and apparently shapeless masses, yet perfect in their mathematical proportions. One was almost exactly like a bust of Shakespeare, only the immortal Will's face, thus portrayed, looked as though the cast had been taken after he had been battered somehow. Others of the hills run in nearly regular succession due north and south, and the builders of these are called the magnetical ants. Their houses are an unerring guide—a compass to the traveller. The anthills are so hard that they are used, when the position is convenient and the inside is scooped out, as chimneys, and it takes a great deal of heavy battering to break them in, though the shell be not thicker than your palm. The ants mortar together the different lumps of clay of which the hill is composed with a glutinous substance, which hardens more rapidly and effectively than the most valuable coagulation which ever quack puffed. Outside the hill you find only a few hundreds of blackish ants—doing very little : on 'Change when shares are at a discount, I should say, judging by their leisurely look ; but break a piece off it, and you see myriads of the oft-cursed white ants in a section of what looks like nothing else so much as a huge rough sponge. The white ant is a puffy, fat, contented little creature, with a round head like the pink top of a lucifer match ; and collectively you will see him in this broken section, after he has cooled down his disgust at your intrusion—you will see him sitting in council in the cosiest, cleanest little cells or rushing to others—the granaries—to protect his wet-weather stock of grass-seeds and stalks, and other food. Then, if you wait an hour, you will be a witness to the readiness with which he sets about repairing the damage you have done to his tenement. Some of the ants, instead of building independent houses for themselves, cut their way into the heart of trees ; raise a tiny mound outside and sometimes a little way along the trunk, and then actually eat nearly the whole of the firm wood of the tree, leaving as they advance higher and higher, earth deposits in lieu of the timber. By-and-by the tree falls, and then it makes, and is used as, a capital water-duct. This is one of the effects of the ant nuisance. When I come to describe Palmerston, you shall hear a much worse account of them.

CHAPTER IV.—THE INTERIOR.

Rum Jungle to the Stapleton.—Rich Soil.—Banyan Creek.—The
Difficulties of Road-Travel.—Paqualin's Hump.—Iron Ore.
—Stapleton Creek.—A Flowering Bamboo new to Science.—
The Township of Stapleton.—The first of the Gold Country.
—The Virginia, Dean's, and Terrible Mines.—A Versatile
Cockatoo.—Mounts Shepherd and Carr.—The Adelaide River.
— A Disappointment: "No Crocodiles."—Some Studies in
Natural History. — Animal Life and its Variety. — The
Difficulties of the Special Reporter!—Mr. Bright Over-
come. — A Natural Recreation Ground. — Curious Thunder-
storm.—Burrell's Creek.—Bridge Creek : the Reception.—A
Celestial Cracker Fusilade.—A second Eden.—The Howley.
—Yam Creek.—Port Darwin Camp.—A Corroboree.—Femi-
nine Black "Boys."—Port Darwin Camp to the Twelve Mile.
— Eccentric Mile-posts. — A "Pre-Adamite Fossil." — The
Inevitable Deputation.—A Tremendous Memorial.—From the
Twelve-Mile to Pine Creek.—The Turning Point in the
Journey.—Peculiar Geological Formation.—The McKinlay
River.—The Record of the Trees.—Copperfield and its
Copper.—Liberal Gift to the Minister.—Gold Deposits Ex-
traordinary. — Pine Creek and its Plucky Pioneer. —
Sanders's Rush.—The Rainfall and its Effects.—One Scribe
the Less : Almost.

WE were disappointed next morning. The latest recollections of the most sleepless of the party on Friday night
were of rain pouring down as rain pours only in the
tropics, and the prophecy was a flood for the morrow.
But when the time came, as we left the ramshackle
public-house at Rum Jungle the sun was frowning witheringly
upon us as though he intended to grill us offhand. The profuse
jungle vegetation, rain-sprinkled, glittered like diamond rests ; a
select few of the comparative scarcity of birds—the jungle
pheasant, the pigeon, the bower bird, the cockatoo, a sort of
magpie, and others—piped out cheerily, those that could pipe;
and gaudy butterflies—bright-yellow, and mauve-and-black, and
one like an animated pansy, and a good pansy at that—fluttered
gaily about atop the long dazzling white seeding grass.
Nature-lovers in the party were moved to music, and for once the
prospect was that the trip would be a pleasure excursion. Just
behind the starting-point the telegraph poles begin to alternate—
wood and iron—the intention being to make them all of metal
eventually. They are burnt down now very often in the dry season, when the natives and the teamsters periodically fire the
grass to secure a succulent growth immediately after the late
rains and to make it possible to walk through it. The soil for
some distance beyond Rum Jungle is a rich brown loam, sprinkled

with ironstone gravel in places—soil similar to that on McKinnon and Poiett's plantation, three miles due west. The country is beautifully fertile and undulating, and there are some pretty peeps of scenery; the grass tall, but less rank and more succulent; the trees stringybark, ironbark, white gum, and other kinds of eucalypti, as well as the screw palm, all twined round with different members of the convolvulus family. All the way along the road—and also as far as I could cross it while the other horses were perforce going along at a walk—the country is of the sort which would make the fortune of a stockowner holding stock in it. It is grandly watered and grassed, and, of course, is thickly dotted with anthills. This holds good more particularly with regard to the land north of Banyan Creek. Beyond, we had an experience of the difficulties of vehicle traffic on the road. Half a dozen Chinamen, with five horses attached to a small dray, were struggling to extricate their property from the boggy road—a light stiff clay. They had only about eight hundredweight of rice, and they had been six days coming thirty-six miles from Southport. When the bogs cease the country becomes rugged and stony; less useful for pasturage or tillage, and more valuable mineralogically. Several quartz-reefs crop up, and there are ironstone and greenstone in plenty. The most striking upland is Paqualin's Hump—two miles from Stapleton. On it good iron ore has been got, and from its crest you see one of the best views along the whole road. Surrounding hills form an almost perfect amphitheatre, and in the perspective are other elevations rising higher and higher till the last bounds the horizon. The descent of the Hump is long, stony, and winding. Just below its foot is a somewhat pretentious Chinese garden, in which are grown principally the peanut, from which the Chinamen have begun to manufacture oil; the sweet potato, which has been grown luxuriantly after early failures through ignorance of the proper season in which to plant it; and Chinese beans. Then you come to Stapleton Creek—named after poor Stapleton, who was killed by the blacks at one of the telegraph stations—which sometimes foams down more than a quarter of a mile wide, but now rippled over an area of only a few yards in width. The grass all round for some distance has been eaten down, and former rankness has become toothsome herbage. There are high-towering hills around the incipient township of Stapleton, and on the creeks' banks grow, besides bright hibiscus, numerous screw-palm and a thick grove of tall bamboo, which Professor Tate proclaims new to science—a bamboo which flowers periodically on a high stalk, but was not in bloom when we saw it. The township of the future consists now of one public-house, in which wines and spirits and

boots and stores apparently are sold, and the place seems to be a
smithy too. There is a cemetery—the only fenced cemetery on the
goldfields, I am told. About twenty feet square it is, enclosed by
a two-railed fence; the graves now covered six inches with water,
and at time of flood submerged altogether. The place is grass-
grown and neglected. There is no care taken of God's Acre here.
Death is lightly esteemed in the locality. The dead are irreverently
called "worm banquets." On the hill to the east is the first of the
claims marking the actual commencement of explored gold country
in the Northern Territory. The mine is the old Virginia, which
has a twelve head battery, and which an English Company has
purchased. There are two or three other claims—Dean's and the
Terrible—but of them all, and also of the absence of the alluvial,
I shall have more to say by-and-by. The party lunched at the
public-house, after one hon. member had bathed in the future
main street of the future town, under the gaze of the pioneers of
the future inhabitants. A most extraordinarily talented cockatoo,
got from the local bush, beguiled the time—a cockatoo that can
write and talk profanely, beat a demagogue in hi'falutin, and do
everything but speak civilly to the half-dozen Woolwongas who
lazily lounge about the place. From the Stapleton to the
Adelaide River the road runs over mountainous country, with huge
outcrops of ironstone and mica slate. A pretty bit of scenery is
presented at Peter's Creek, and there is at least a suspicion of
grandeur about Mounts Shepherd and Carr, the latter of which
overlooks the Adelaide River. This land, if used at all for
aught but minerals, would be more suited for pasturage than
cultivation ; but close to the Adelaide the soil is rich
enough for anything as far down as I could trace it. The
river was another disappointment. The party were told it was
to be at high flood ; and that if they did not get drowned trying
to cross it they would be snapped asunder by alligators or eaten
up by mosquitos. But the stream was at most only three feet
deep at the strongest running channel, and just as we
entered it, not knowing this, but bracing ourselves for a fearful
struggle, our horses, in the very swiftest of the swift waters,
deliberately stopped and drank. We humbly drove on to the little
hotel on the bank, consoling ourselves with the knowledge of the
fact that not many days before the water was sixteen feet deep,
and that sometimes it is forty. Then the mails have to be slung
over on wires. It was a sore blow to Mr. Knight, our worthy chief
of the commissariat. He had been working up the agony the
whole way along, assuring us he had left behind him an eloquently
couched will and explanatory document concluding:—

Died by drowning for his country's good.

This was rather ambiguous ; and he corrected his first deposition by saying that he *meant* to leave the document. The situation of the little public-house, which, with the exceedingly well-kept police station, make up the little Crown-grant township on the south bank of the south-westerly arm of the Adelaide, is very picturesque. It is on a modest elevation, and around it are foliage-clad hills and abundance of vegetation, with a fine clear view of the stream flowing all the year round. When the railway shall have been made this place, fifty miles from the seaboard, will be one of the most important along its course—a centre for the export of plantation produce from the banks of the river, and gold from the surrounding country. I freely prophesy that land in this locality will ten years hence be sold at £10 a foot ; but the railway must be made within the next five years.

We had plenty of time—for we remained there over Sunday on the downward trip—to rest and look about us. Professor Tate had a special commission for the collection of botanical specimens, duplicates of which were sent to France, and he availed himself of his leisure to pursue his investigations. He was successful. Twenty different heads of grass found he in an area of a few yards, and of his natural history treasures time and space would fail me to speak ; for despite annual devastating fires, the woods are rich in the mantis of many kinds, bugs of various sorts galore, dragon-flies, and other insects in great force. Amongst animals there are the kangaroo, the emu, the native companion, the dingo and several smaller ones. In the river, besides alligators and crocodiles, there are, according to the residents, stingrays or cat-fish, mussel, crab, bream, and turtle 10 or 12 lb. weight. We were to have seen an alligator, but, of course, were disappointed. We had no luck at all—absolutely none whatever !

At night, animal life is—well, various. As I write, in a room whence you can see all the visible celestial luminaries, there comes from the river the croaking of frogs without number and of hoarseness unparalleled. Plaintively mingle with it the cackling of wild geese disporting in the stream, and the shrill notes of curlews looking at the geese, and of an unknown bird, with a voice which would be most like a frog's but that it equally resembles a magpie's. Mosquitoes come in numerical strength, but they seem too sleek and well-behaved to sting. They simply hum harmoniously, and watch the curious beetles and the pretty moths—one of which, crawling out of the ink-bottle, blotting the writing, has close kinship to the death's head—battering themselves to death against the lampglass. A vampire bat flies overhead, the crickets chirp, and a packhorse with hobbles and a bell pokes his head within the open door, and looks enquiringly round with the hungry gaze of a baffled special reporter. The idlers of the party loll about in pyjamas, which are just a little more tangible than the atmosphere; and when they go to rest they lie on hammocks strung up to the fence outside or under the verandah, or else in bedrooms built of the ever-useful bamboo, with apertures through which the wind plays almost uninterruptedly. At home, in the morning the pyjamas are the dress, and in the evening and at noon the dress is the pyjama. Indeed, the problem in this heat with most people—personally I found it less oppressive than that of Adelaide—is how to observe decency with the least possible burden of clothing. The staple salutation is in effect the Egyptian :—" How goes the perspiration?" " Do you sweat copiously?"—and there are nine or ten ditto. Poor Mr. Bright could stand the journey no longer, and no wonder, for it was a rather hard time for unaccustomed physically inactive men. He was counselled not to start, but his pluck was more developed than his endurance; and so at the Adelaide River he fell slightly ill and turned back. A horseman riding nineteen stone is not the man to go through a rough journey in the tropics at such a time of year.

Early on Monday morning, February 27, all the party, save Mr. Bright, who returned by easy stages to the Government Residence at Palmerston, continued their journey, with the sun shining out rather too fervently to be pleasant, but with blessed puffs of cool balmy air, honestly doing all they could to moderate his rays. Almost immediately after starting we found ourselves crossing the Adelaide Plains, which, low-lying, and in the wettest season quite submerged, were now only moderately spongy and sloppy, and opposed but little inconveniences to travel. The country is capitally grassed, and about a couple of miles on the course of the road from the river is one of the prettiest sites for a recreation ground which can be found all Australia over. The ground is a dead level, well drained, big enough for two racecourses, and all round the country undulates easily, being " stopped short" presently by a rugged semicircle of hills, each trying to stretch its head above its brother's, till the tallest, when the clouds are low, is capped with fleecy head-gear.

A group of hills at front and the general ignorance of their names even by experts in the party induce a reference to the elaborate maps and charts, which disappoint us as they have done before. A Northern Territory map is quite in keeping with the place and many of the people—it is rough, superlatively rough. Whilst names of leading ranges are *not* given, surveyor's memos, or akin to that, are reproduced, in imitation of the Nicaraguan chart on which appeared the note by the compiler—

" I have forgotten the name of this place."

And so we eschewed the maps, and when we crossed a creek or skirted a hill unknown, we named it Parsons' Hill, or Bagster's Creek, or Furner's Mount, or Parliament Hill. There are some dozens of each already. Beyond the plains some steep ridges are passed and crossed. Further huge outcrops of mica, slate, and sandstone, and on the roads more ironstone ; anthills thicker than ever, giving a faithful idea by their colour of the different kinds of surface soil. Then the country becomes better drained, and the couch-grass in patches springs luxuriantly. Crossing one of the tributaries of the Adelaide—independently named by us with due propriety Snake's Creek, because not far from it lay a decapitated white-bellied reptile eight feet long—we come into still higher and more rugged country. Big hills rise up on either hand, and the road winds on the floor of a defile between them. The hills are capped with crags, and their surfaces are strewn with slate and sandstone and a little quartz and greenstone. Beyond the defile are more well-grassed plains, which make the rising ranges (not thickly timbered, but clad with tall grass waving in the breeze) look like corn-fields, suspended in mid-air. This on one side ; and on the other rugged rises, rocky, and with gnarled but not big timber. At noon we had our second experience of a fussy thunderstorm and a heavy rainfall. We look for our thunderstorm every afternoon as we look for our river-bath each morning and evening. On this occasion the clouds came up with great suddenness ; peal after peal of thunder—like the falling of a hundred tons of chain a dozen miles upon thick sheets of iron—rattled overhead ; and presently we heard amidst the trees ahead of us a mighty, rustling, rushing noise, and a thick "section" of rain passed by us and whistled through the pass, leaving us untouched. A minute more, and another section hurtled over us, and in five minutes our horses were cowering under a falling sheet of rain, and we were drenched and being further drenched. In an hour the storm had subsided and we were on a dry road. So partial is the rainfall here.

We camped at Burrell's Creek, ten miles from the river, and took possession of a deserted bamboo hut, close by the spot on which a man sometime ago had his life beaten out by the blacks one night whilst sleeping, and about two miles from a new alluvial rush—No. 1 Depôt—on which, however, less than half a dozen men were working then. The land here, like that passed the last three miles or so, is swampy but well grassed. The grevillia and the screw pine everywhere abound. Having lunched under dripping trees and other difficulties, the party crossed the creek and pursued their journey, first passing through strongly marked mineral country—slate, quartz, and iron intermixed, and indicative of gold. All the ridges have strong out-crops of slate. Further on the ground is thickly strewn with quartz pebbles, and further still several well defined reefs cross the road. A swamp 200 yards in width leads up to Bamboo Creek. There are as many bamboo creeks in the Territory as there are colours in the plumage of the strange-looking little mite, no bigger than a humming-bird, which here and elsewhere inquisitively eyed us. From this point to Bridge Creek the land is nicely grassed, but when we crossed it had had no rain for some days. It is capital pastoral country, watered by Sandy, Bridge, and Downey's Creeks, and divided from the other country by Paqualin Mount, at the foot of which good gold is being got. The party marched into Bridge Creek in cavalry form—riders in the van, led by Warden Knight, and the Minister's packhorses in the rear, fronted by our Celestial factotum, Ah Sam. As we approached the bridge—named so by an excess of courtesy—we perceived a hundred Chinamen drawn up in line before a tripod, and immediately afterwards there burst upon our vision a long eccentric triangle of fizzing lights, and our tympani gave audience to a perfect fusilade of crackers—a fusilade so ear-piercing that our horses were inspired to make a sickly attempt at shying. This was the Chinese reception. The Chinamen throughout have been more demonstrative than the Europeans, and after the Minister had acknowledged this courtesy in graceful pigeon-English, they invited him to a Chinese banquet, which he promised to attend on the return journey. Bridge Creek is one of the nearest gold-fields. Its township has had an existence only twelve months, and some of the gold-fields around are not much older. There are of course, an hotel, a general store, with a Post-Office, and several Chinese stores ; but the whole place looks as though it had been set up hastily by an unconscientious contractor, and as if it were in a hurry to get down again. The police camp is a bell tent, which may be removed at a moment's notice. The village is situated near a chain of billabongs, which exhale a malarial atmosphere fruitful of fevers, prolific in deaths. The place is as unhealthy as the Eden of "Martin Chuzzlewit." If the hotel-keeper may be believed, thirty-seven out of ninety people who first came to the gold-field had this fever—a slow, intermittent, prostrating affection, unfitting a man for exercise and robbing him of all energy—and many of them died. He has had eighteen patients lying in and round his house at once, and no doctor has ever visited the place. The poor fellows have no kind nurses to attend to them. The main store—Griffiths's—has the only locally known specific for the disease—tincture of iron, quinine, and the ubiquitous painkiller, not to mention the "drops" of the enterprising Cross, of Gawler—and even the strongest man in the place has lustreless eyes floating in a sea of yellow. A dozen Chinese gardeners round about ward off the scurvy by plentiful growths of vegetables, and others counteract the good by selling opium in stores distributed round the various camps. There is not a white woman in the place—we have only seen two since we left Palmerston—for those who have lived there have had their health impaired, and there is no attraction for the unfortunate dwellers save the excitement of shooting some of the geese and ducks and other waterfowl which swarm upon the billabongs.

We left Bridge Creek on Tuesday morning, February 28, and, ascending the hill at the foot of which the pestilential little place nestles, came upon the first alluvial diggings we had passed on the course of the road. The ground certainly looks promising for gold, and the best proof that it contains the precious metal is that it has been found there in large quantities. The scenery grows less and less tropical, though it has never been much so. The land is higher and drier, and there is an absence of screw-pines and other indications of a wet soil. The road is covered with quartz and iron pebbles, and the hills show the eternal slate formation. There is here almost the first kangaroo grass we have noticed, and there is also a frequent "intrusion of the diorite." An intense heat filtering through no clouds made the gentle fresh zephyrs which came every few minutes welcome as a cool draught to the thirsty, and a few bright-green Chinese gardens gave a home look to a place otherwise wild. Presently we came to a sluggish creek, or chain of billabongs, and halted at the Old Howley hostelry—the most respectable-looking place in a town which seems to have for some time made an effort at respectability of appearance, but to have given it up long since as not in its line. The principal population is a big herd of wiry-looking goats that were successfully reared after many failures. They now thrive well, and are welcome residents in a country where a milch cow is as rare as a sovereign in a church plate. Teams and abandoned drays were drawn up in the township awaiting the return of the dry season, when they might work again, and we had another instance of the partiality of the rainfall in the finely-powdered dust which strewed the roads. The Howley (which is near to the Glencoe cattle station) has been a more important place than it is now. It is not particularly healthy, though it is pleasantly situated on the slope of a gentle acclivity, crowned by a huge quartz "blow." Round about are a few low hills. In a place where screw-palms in plenty and a good loam proclaim rich soil for cultivation, we camped for luncheon, near a puddled waterhole, and, in the abscnce of shade trees, baked in the sun for an hour or so, and then began to drench with one of the heavy rains which fall here with such embarrassing lack of notice. Thus, over country growing higher and higher, and more broken up, and thicker and bigger timbered, with good wide runs of quartz in all directions, we approached the Port Darwin Camp. We crossed the Margaret Creek with its alluvial flats, and Yam Creek with, on its banks, the first diggings, forming part of this " centre." Past the racecourse—for the Territorians attempt races between the animated clothes-horses dubbed equines here—you come to Sailor's Gully, which has been worked out into fragments, and has given up all its gold at shallow depths. Then you pass Stuart's, and other gullies of which the same may be said, and over slaty and sandstony ground and a soft road you come to the Port Darwin Camp, sheltered by a very high hill almost worthy the appellation of mount.

The party drew up, as usual, in cavalry order, and met with a hearty but informal reception under a clothes-line supporting a flag which, shot-riddled, seemed as though it had braved a thousand years the battle and the breeze, &c., and looked all the worse for it. The verandah-posts, clad with greenery, made the otherwise homely publichouse look almost romantic. The place is prettily situated on a flat with hills all round, and thick timber upon them. It is an important mining centre; it contains the ordinary stores, and Chinese merchants' places, and has—unlike any other place in the Territory south of Palmerston—a medical attendant and a Justice of the Peace. In the night the local tribe of aboriginals—the Woolwongas—got up a corrobboree in honour of the Minister, and to earn a good supply of flour and tobacco. The display was not particularly exhilarating, for not more than fifty of the blacks turned out. The men are fine stalwart fellows, and their clothing would hardly cover an area sufficient for a mosquito to exercise himself upon. Most of the women wear a little square of cloth from their loins, and at this corroboree two appeared in the full glory of white Princess robes with gorgeous bright-hued clouds. But when they were asked to enter for a race they did not require many calendar seconds to appear almost in ante-Fall costume. The boys and girls, of course, were *in puris naturalibus*. Their principal characteristic is a wonderful protrusion of abdomen. All of this tribe are circumcised when young; in this respect differing from many of the others. The Master of the Ceremonies—the King—appeared in all the importance of the position and an old battered stovepipe hat and a pair of plaid trousers. The faces of all were streaked with white, and their bodies were striped skeleton pattern. Their appearance

altogether would have been savage if it had not been so supremely
ludicrous. Well; for hours they danced and yelled around a fire
of barrel staves, and shouted war whoops, and trod it lightly and
in capital time to the music of a bamboo-pipe—in sound resembling
a declining blast-furnace—and a couple of sticks beaten kettledrum
fashion. At times their performance was to imitate the wind
whistling through the leaves, and the effect was certainly weird.
But the spear-throwing—propelled from the woomerah, for they
use not the boomerang—was not the best of spear-throwing.
There was one intelligent young fellow, however, with a head like
Byron's, who never missed the mark. As to the others, why, even
Professor Tate, catching up a spear and hurling it haphazard, was
almost as bad as them!

At the Port Darwin Camp there was brought under notice a
custom which is too much in vogue amongst people who drive
cattle over from Queensland. We met one of them who had a
little black, dressed in boy's clothing, travelling with him as servant.
It transpired that this little fellow was really a girl, and what her
life may be I know nothing of. In the particular case I refer to
I suppose it may be comfortable enough, for I believe the master
is a good-hearted man, but in most cases these feminine boys are
the victims of their masters' debasing passions. That is the fact,
and I do not see why the matter should be minced. There has
been too much mincing of it already. Some of these thoughtless
bushmen have, in the stealing of their black servants, had
"brushes" with the male relatives of the latter and shot them down.
The natives make reprisals, and sometimes kill guilty and at other
times innocent men. The whites resident in the district then
have a "revenge" party, and shoot down a score blacks or so, and
call it English justice. The Queensland Government can scarcely
be blamed for this, because in the sparsely-populated districts
they cannot get at the offender. Whether they can prevent the
practice of females going about the country clad in male attire is
another question. Whether we cannot do something in the way
of missionary enterprise is also a question which I will simply
dismiss with the comment that half that we give to foreign mis-
sions would suffice for the work, in the way of which at present
there is absolutely nothing done. These blacks live and die like sheep,
only that their lot is even more degraded. *And the whites degrade
it.* Experienced men throughout both colonies tell you that they
never knew a so-called native trouble arise but that a lubra was at
the bottom of it, and the conscientious will not take part in
"revenge" engagements. How long is this blot on our civilization
to remain? And there is just one more suggestive query—Where
do all the half-caste children go? They are born; the women

remain with their English masters after they are born. Where are
the children? You can't see half-a-dozen the Northern Territory
over. Why?

Wednesday, March 1, witnessed the departure of the party from
Port Darwin Camp midst the hearty congratulations of the biggest
crowd of spectators that the thriving little place could raise. The
country first passed through began gradually to grow higher and
higher, until little hills became rough basaltic broken ranges of
about equal altitude, with deep gullies, bearing marks of heavy
waterwashes, and even now sodden and spongy. The horses off
the course of the road sank knee-deep in rich alluvial flats of brown
soil, and on the road itself were frequent outcrops of sandstone and
quartz, varied occasionally by the diorite. All this untried. Then
the grass grew higher and more rank, and the stringybark prepon-
derated amongst the trees. The anthills disappeared over a wide
area with their fellow-indicators of water—the screw-pine—and
by-and-by both reared their heads again, where the country is
more flat and less thickly timbered, and where the hard stiff grass
makes way for the toothsome "kangaroo." Six miles or so from
the Camp we trod on a strong rich lode of iron ore crossing the
road. Going on beyond the creek we came at once upon land not
even moistened by the rain—upon hills more rugged and precipitous than any we had hitherto met. On one of those hills were
curious stone erections, marking boundaries of natives' tribal
territory—queer cairns, and symbolical geometrical figures "under-
standed" no doubt by the blackfellows, but hopelessly perplexing
in their fulness to any white I yet have seen. Then across
McMinn's Creek, with rich soil on either side, producing the first
yams we had yet seen on the trip. These yams bitten by anyone
when pulled from the ground cause the unlucky one's lips to swell
almost polony-size, and his tongue to throw a detachment out of
mouth ; but when they are cooked after burial underground
the natives consider them a great delicacy. Houschildt's Creek
and its surroundings are as pretty at this season as is Knight's
Creek with its at present wide, dry, flinty bed as void of moisture
as the man who gave it name is void of affectation, but with water-
marks bearing indisputable testimony to the undisputed fact that
when it rains here " pour" is its other name.

" Dry, drier, driest," are the exclamations as the three last mile-
posts leave us past Maggy (with a "y") Jane's Creek, and the fourth
finds us enjoying a sight of the pleasant verdure of the banks of
the McKinlay River. The mile-plates along this road, by the way,
are the only ones in the Territory, and they are peculiar. They
are fixed on trees mostly, and their author and finisher had a free-
and-easy way of arranging them. The desideratum seemed to be

to make a good display of the plate by putting it on a tree of aldermanic girth, and if that upgrowth did not happen to occur at the end of 1,760 yards, well, the figure went up where it *did* occur. That saved trouble ; and it was really done, unless reputedly veracious persons were "dilating." The party thought it not improbable that they were, and the Minister's jocular assurance that Northern Territory miles boasted 2,000 yards each soothed them, as after a hard day's work they drew up greeted by the clatter of a battery—the first they had yet heard—and the cheers of the residents at Tennant's store, the stopping place at the Twelve Mile, the most important gold-mining centre at present. Within the half-hour the party—grave and gay alike—were bobbing about in the limpid stream which runs beside the town, the while Professor Tate eagerly rummaged on the bottom for geological treasures, and presently holding up a nondescript hard piece of blue slate, shouted in all earnestness :—

" Hurrah ! Look ! Why, here's a genuine *pre-Adamite* FLINT FOSSIL !" And he put it with the rest of his treasures.

When the night shades had accomplished their accustomed poetic precipitation the party placed themselves on public exhibition at "gratis" per head, as a miner described it, in an open canvas tent, and whilst they dissected from their perches on candle boxes (for chairs don't come so far south) the inevitable sucking pig, which has all the way through acted as deputy for the fatted calf, they breathed in the pure oxygen of a high elevation, and watched the diggers quoit-playing, and witnessed the usual nightly thunderstorm, the principal feature of which is the prodigality of fuss and the dearth of work. And then came trouble. Forth to the airy tent marched a group of miners, with the old unmistakable hungry deputationist look. These pinned the Minister at the head of the table,· ranged the members on either side, and forthwith began the fire with effective ammunition, taking the shape of the longest memorial I have yet seen — a memorial stretching itself over sixteen pages of foolscap ; and yet so well-compiled as to be interesting reading matter. It was a statement of grievances which have already had sufficient circulation, and need not be repeated here. The Minister's reply was marked by great tact, and it was received enthusiastically, cheers being heartily given for him and his companions, the deputationists keeping up quite a fusilade of acclamation.

There was little time for rest between the late hour at which the importunate deputation with its appalling memorial had finished interviewing the Minister at Twelve-Mile the previous night and that at which the party began their march to Pine Creek on Thursday morning, March 2. But the journey once well begun, the curious road scenery absorbed attention and put an end to lugubrious looks. You pass first the Bamboo Creek—the tenth separate and distinct watercourse of that name we have seen—and then go along a rich alluvial flat from which many Chinese have taken gold, and in which a few are at present doing so. Passing a quartz claim on which two poor fellows with small resources are trying to do great work with the inevitable result of simply scratching the soil to keep the cupboard stocked, we came to the McKinlay River, and crossed it without difficulty, though a few days before a police-trooper was washed some distance by its swift current, swollen by heavy high-land waterfalls. The McKinlay is partly a torrential stream, and at this point it laps the feet of high craggy hills. These hills bear by far the strongest evidences of minerals that we saw. The formation of the country is most peculiar. Huge outcrops of hard slate, broken up into shingled masses, bound the road on either side and cross it again and again, and in scores of places are thrown out big quartz excrescences from the metamorphic slate. All this land would be of no use for cultivation and of little for pastoral purposes; but if it does not produce tin and gold in quantities which shall astonish even people who are not over-susceptible to the emotion of surprise, I beg to be put down as a false prophet. Gold it is yielding now to several reef-fossickers, but they will never lance deeply enough the "million golden veins" with which the "bursting earth" is blessed. Capital and skilled labour must do the business. Then we proceeded over greener hills and verdant deep-soil plains, until we were in the midst of capital land, fit for any kind of cultivation, for grazing, or for gold if its wet-season face does not belie it. In this region waterlilies—rather sickly-looking, it must be confessed—adorn the surface of the marshes. Crossing the Lady Alice Creek, we lunched under the shade of a spreading bloodwood tree, overhung almost by a peaked promontory of slate and sandstone, within the boundary of the Lady Alice Mine. And here let me say that Professor Tait carried out his entomological and botanical collecting with great zest; and the moment we halt and take our cans and pannicans out we detect in one or other some uncanny-looking insectivorous mite or monster that he has imprisoned within them. Turning to the Professor to remonstrate, we descry him on a clifftop or in the grass gleefully administering cyanide to some unfortunate specimen—a Tatii amongst them, is the general hope, in deference to the collector's enthusiasm. Ere we struck camp the initials of the distinguished journeyers had been deeply graven in the impervious bloodwood, and the

𝔓. 𝔍. 𝔅. 𝔗.

(Mr. Bright being absent was not thus honoured) will boldly confront the traveller for generations, if only the woodman and the lightning will spare that tree. Hitherto we had passed several candle-box holes and trenches, called by courtesy gold-mines, and each worked by one or two men ; and almost immediately after starting we found ourselves in rather extensive alluvial gullies, tried by only a few Chinamen—virtually abandoned, indeed. In their time they were rich, and the ground was so valuable that even the roadway has been washed by the irrepressible Celestial—washed in spite of police watchfulness ; for though, as the roads are not surveyed, the law cannot prevent their partial demolition, the policemen justifiably bounce the diggers into protecting them. On the rising ground the surface has been washed in places, and the scene altogether—the vegetation and the physical conformation—is not at all up to the tropical standard. Scaling the Union Hill we come to the Union Claim, of which more hereafter. The place is decaying, though the ground is popularly supposed to be some of the richest in gold in the Territory. A once-flourishing township has dwindled down to about a dozen Chinese bark-and-bamboo habitations and a store or two. The party entered one belonging to the famous Ping Quee, and were received with fully Celestial etiquette by a sleek, well-fleshed, intelligent Chinaman, who obsequiously weighed the gold specimens the Minister bought, and showed—well, to put it mildly—that he had his own ideas respecting gold-weighing. Leaving the Union after an acknowledgment of the courteous bows of all the Chinamen they passed, the party caught their first sight of the striking headland known as McMinn's Bluff, with its surrounding peculiar high broken table-land, flat-topped, and with an immense natural wall bordering its crest all round. Still patches of slate and plentiful ironstone nodules, relieved by veritable oases—as gardens all abloom with vegetation, fostered by Celestial care—in plain English, cabbage and sweet potato gardens. Indeed, almost all the way over the watercourse called Caledonian, after a local abandoned mine, down to Pine Creek, the level land is fit for agriculture or pasturage, and the hills for mineral work as well. We entered Pine Creek at a hand-gallop, painful alike to horses, riders, and onlookers. This settlement is fast declining. It was a very important centre once, and its crumbling and burnt buildings were tenanted and busy with life. But surface-scratching ceased to be paying, and there remain only eighty representatives of the hundreds of Chinamen who some years ago resided there, and contributed many victims to the miasmatic diseases which took so great a company, and to fear of the blacks, who killed one of them and thirsted for others. Instead of two hotels there is only one, languishing, but fairly kept. The Telegraph Station has been abandoned for some time. A trooper combines police with postal duty, and yet survives and fattens. And no wonder, considering that in and all round the town there are only eighteen Europeans, and that for some of them to write or read a letter is as likely as that a bullfrog might thread the windings of the Asses' Bridge, or that a grasshopper might repeat the Litany. The blacks give him but little trouble, and that little comes from the Alligator tribes, who are affected by kleptomania occasionally, and have to submit to a binding dose of iron.

Before breakfast on Friday morning the party started on horse-back to inspect the country, and particularly the copper deposits which the district boasts. Crossing Pine Creek, which had been heavily flooded over-night, and plunging into bog after bog—so deep that the riders had repeatedly to jump off the horses and help to pull them through—they were confronted by a deep gorge and a big range of castellated rocks, wall-like, marking almost the terminal point north of a vast central Australian stretch of peculiar country geologically, and the beginning of a granite formation extending west almost to the Daly. Plentiful quartz outcrops were seen ere we reached Copperfield Creek with its Agrigoolha Camp—some rows of paper-bark mia-mias thrown together anyhow. The generally dribbling watercourse ran deep and clear as we marched through it out of many grievous bogs, and as we reached the ground we were all admonished by fierce brain-protests that hard travel day by day, late retiring, early rising, and no break-fast are not the best things for luxurious members of the Legis-lature, or their more humble followers. Copperfield is distant from Pine Creek seven, six, five, four, four and a-half, and three miles, according to the distance-expert you happen to ask. We had all these figures given oracularly, and to this day I don't know which is correct. The Copperfield, as such, is very much *in nubibus*. About a fortnight's scraping had been done on a couple of strong lodes, which look like "blows," but are not. No trial has been made to test the promise of permanency which the lode gives. The ore to be seen I should value roughly at 40 per cent., and it includes, besides the green carbonates, steel-grey, and red oxides, a little "malleable," and more iron.

In the afternoon the party sallied out to inspect the gold reefs, traversing on the way the shallow alluvial bed, which is nigh worked out in the best known places, and on which not a European is engaged. The first mine visited was that of Manning and Hingham, who work the famed Old Christmas Lead. They perform the stupen-dous task of development themselves, unaided, and they have attained unto the astonishing depth of 72 feet. They have pecu-

liar hard, mottled, blue-and-white quartz, mixed with iron gossan,
and their average yield is two ounces. Strictly speaking, hardly
any trial has been made of the ground. The prospects are
good. The next claim is Michael Mullane's, which is on the south
end of the Christmas. With a staff consisting of one whole
Chinaman, he has paddocked out about 14 feet, and had
two crushings, with a two-ounce average. Scarcely more developed is John Hughes's property, hard by, in which, generally
speaking, the like results have been obtained. Really it seems
almost irony to use the word "mine" in speaking of any of these
claims. They are not developed, and the men working them,
living from hand to mouth, cannot open them out—must have the
gold at once. Capital and skilled labour must be the
watch-word for the Territory. Besides these claims and Jansen's,
to which we paid a lengthened visit, the only one working, in however small a way, is the old Edel Maria, which is down about forty
feet, and from which four men are getting a crushing. This
is the furthest gold-seeking south, excepting the alluvial rush at
Sanders's Creek, twenty-five miles away, worked by 300 or 400
Chinamen, who are making good wages, and who have in
prospect, when they shall have scratched up the surface gold,
another place not far distant. Much further down, the country
has not been prospected at all, on account of the blacks and other
palpable sources of difficulty. On arriving at Mr. Jansen's, we heard the welcome thud of his battery of 15 heads,
with shank-room for five more. It works well comparatively, for
we did not find over-much quicksilver below the blanketings.
There was not much pyrites in the stuff being crushed, however,
or the loss might have been greater. The miners tell us that they
lose fully one-half of their gold; but we shall see later on. Mr.
Jansen, however, considers it necessary to get pulverizers and buddles.
Meantime, after most courteously entertaining the party in his
office, he drew out fully £100 worth of beautiful gold specimens and
presented the Minister with the best, a magnificent one valued at £50.
This grand stone and the others in the collection were taken from
Mr. Jansen's claim—the old Telegraph and the Eleanor. The
former he has purchased about two years. The battery—the
Standard—originally cost altogether £14,000 or £15,000, and Mr.
Jansen bought it and the 10-head at Pine Creek from the Telegraph
Company for £2,000. What two Companies dared not do, a single
man—and he not so rich then as he has deservedly become since—
was plucky enough to undertake, and he has had his reward. The
Standard battery was the one we found working—it crushes for
the public as well as for the owner, and employs Chinamen. The
other had been idle for some time, but it will probably resume

work soon. So the Standard forms comparatively a busy scene, and the owner intends to make it still more busy with a plantation or maize, and so on, and a residence adjoining it. For Mr. Jansen is a thoroughly practical man, and he sees that while he has to pay £1 a bushel for maize and oats he cannot expect to make a fortune very rapidly out of his horses. Even now he runs a sawmill, and with new buildings he has just replaced the old ones which the ants ate down. Of his two mines, the Eleanor is at present the principal. It is charmingly situated on the side of a high hill, below which in the alluvial over 15,000 ounces of gold has been got. You here obtain a grand view of the romantic-looking broken table-land on the one side, and of the whole of the prettily undulating country for miles round. Comparatively a good deal of work has been done on the mine, but the workings had 200,000 gallons of water in them then. From the surface down for forty feet the ground had been stoped at an angle of about 1 in 3 on the course of a rich shoot. Very good returns have been got from the numerous little leaders, and on the slate and sandstone "floor" of the shoot we saw several nuggetty pieces of gold. The reef has yet to be found, and when that consummation shall have been achieved Mr. Jansen's joy will be complete—conditionally, of course, on the reef being rich. Meanwhile the country opened out is the most peculiar I have ever seen, and the Professor confessed almost as much. I might write a column about it, but the general reader would only skip it. Of the Telegraph Mr. Jansen has great hopes. There is a strong reef cropping up for 250 yards. The "country" is the ordinary sandstone and quartz. The sinking is easy, and payable gold has already been got. The reef is about fifteen inches thick on the average, and when the crushing comes Mr. Jansen expects to be a much richer man. And he deserves to be, for a more hard-working, energetic, practical, liberal gentleman I never met. He gave the fullest information—even showing stones of tin, and saying where he got them; he speaks too of something like galena being found in the neighbourhood. From his books he furnished the following return of the public crushing at his battery during the first two months of this year :—First, 20 tons, 28 oz. ; second, 38 tons, 96 oz. ; third, 50 tons, about 100 oz. The average is satisfactory. The gold is worth £3 5s. an ounce at Pine Creek. Five pounds a week is given to the European miners, and £2 to £2 5s. to Chinamen, in both cases for eight hours' labour. The Celestials feed the battery, and some of them do drill work, and do it well. And this is all that need be said of Pine Creek, the old great centre. To make it so again for reefs and not so much alluvial will be easy. The means, capital properly spent ; but first—the railway.

The visit to Pine Creek was nigh accompanied by a casualty in which, reader, yours obediently was worsted in a struggle against a frantic horse and a furiously running creek. It was a narrow escape, and had he been a non-swimmer he probably would have had to "hand in his checks," and would have been cheated out of a delightful revenge upon confiding readers. As it was, the only loss was that of an antiquated hat and a borrowed riding whip.

CHAPTER V.—THE INTERIOR.

MOUNTS FERGUSSON AND DOUGLAS.—REPORTED TIN COUNTRY.—A FACETIOUS CELESTIAL.—PINE CREEK TO THE TWELVE-MILE.—THE BEGINNING OF THE RETURN JOURNEY.—THE UNION REEFS.—SOME SIGNIFICANT FIGURES—THE CLAIMS PARTICULARISED.—THE EXTENDED UNION. —SEVENTY-FIVE OUNCES TO THE TON.—A MINIATURE PANDEMONIUM—HOW SUNDAY IS SPENT IN A REEF VILLAGE.—TO BAMBOO CREEK—TIN DISCOVERIES, WILL THEY PAY?—BOTANICAL NOMENCLATURE.—DISHEARTENING BOGS.—LATE'S GROTTO.—GREEN ANTS. —DIFFICULTIES OF TRAVEL.—BOTTLED HORSES!—THIRSTY CLIMBERS.—AN UNWONTED LUXURY.—A BEAUTIFUL LANDSCAPE.— SPRING HILL—CHINESE CAMPS.—VALUABLE GOLD DEPOSITS.—THE PRINCIPAL MINES PARTICULARLY, AND THE OTHERS GENERALLY. —MORE SPECIMENS FOR THE PARLIAMENTARY CABINET.—A BANQUET, AND MORE IMPORTUNITY.—TO MOUNT WELLS.—A BEAUTIFUL PANORAMA.—A DISTURBING ELEMENT.—INTREPID MOUNT CLIMBERS.—THE TIN SELECTIONS.—THE PROSPECTS.— NARROW ESCAPE FROM A FATALITY.—PORT DARWIN CAMP.— THE MARGARET.—SOME MINES AND BIG NUGGETS.—A CHASE FOR CORPSES.—BUTTERFLY GULLY.—A ROMANTIC VALE.

THE party were to have gone to the Fergusson River and Mount Douglas—the first fifty miles from Pine Creek and 180 from Southport, and the other twenty-five miles east of the Port Darwin camp; but when we were at Pine Creek news of heavy floods along the southern country came to hand, and to have done the Fergusson would have necessitated a long delay. That settled that proposal. As to Mount Douglas: to get to it boggy land would have had to be crossed, and our experience had been that to go anywhere off the main line of road involved the inconvenience of frequently leading our horses through knee-deep mire. The consideration which suggested the inclusion of the two places in the programme of the route was the fact that both had been taken up as tin selections; but that, most people will agree, was not a sufficient reason why all the paraphernalia— all the little paraphernalia, I should say; for the turnout has been unostentatious enough, in all conscience—should be conveyed over wretched roads, so that the party might by their visit give a fictitious value to these mineral leases; and so it is fortunate that the plan fell through. But, not wishing to be behindhand, I made arrangements for securing a report from the Fergusson from a thoroughly trustworthy source. When my correspondent returned, however, all he could tell me was that only an apology for prospecting had an existence there, but that the country appeared to be stanniferous, and had in a very slight degree been proved to be so. Mount Douglas was taken up at a venture; one of the chief lessees told me that he had not the least idea whether there was tin in his property, or whether there was not; and two men, whom we met on the downward trip—two men who had been specially sent out to prospect—assured us that they could not find favourable indications. Why should the party seek them ?

We left Pine Creek at early morn of March 4, with horses even more jaded and sorry-looking than they had been before, which is almost equal to saying that a skeleton looks less than a skeleton at times. Our humorous Chinese attendant—yclept Ah Sam—has always had the "screws" that some one else had refused to ride any longer; and on this auspicious morn he bestrode an animal with a great sore on its fetlock, through which, to quote Ah Sam, "the stuffin'" came freely out ; with more great ones on its back ; with a hopelessly "gone" leg ; and with all over the aroma of a backslum gutter. Ah Sam was aggrieved and hurt, protesting,—

"If any other but Gove'ment fella ridee this hoss, I think he get him £5 fine Palmerson."

From the rear we could hear him remonstrating with the noble steed thus—

"Lookee *heah !*—you cally me hof way, I cally you udder hof. —*Hay ?* "

And—(witheringly)—

"I say ; when you wantum lay down, you lettee me know. *I* wantum takee my legs out."

But Ah Sam was sarcastic I fear.

We lunched at the Union Mines, being nobly entertained under a canopy of living green by Mr. Bull, who is one of the enterprising prospectors of the Territory. The Union Reefs were once about the richest in the Territory ; but "Ichabod" has long been recorded of them. The buildings at the various mines are tottering to their fall ; the battery which once was heard near the adjacent stream is now playing its tune at the Twelve Mile ; and the other, which has long been silent, is about to be removed to the Extended Union. Meanwhile, such of the few miners as are working who do not pound their quartz in the mortar are stacking the stuff in the hope of getting machinery. The Union is the generic term for a number of claims which extend over a considerable extent of land ; and a good deal of tunnelling and sinking has been done. The best of the claims was the Prospecting Company's, which gave 10 oz. to the ton on one occasion. This is the highest yield ; the lowest—from one of the smaller Companies—was 2½ dwt. per ton. The prospectors alone got over 5,000 oz., and their deepest point was less than 200 feet. No. 1 South Company has returned as high as 10 oz. and as low as 2 oz. The maximum depth is 80 feet on water, which seems to be a spring. From No. 2 South (well known as Westcott's) 1,000 oz. have been taken, several crushings having given 12 oz. per ton. Seventy feet is the lowest depth. No. 3 South, where the deepest point is 40 feet, gave for six or seven months' work more than 600 oz. of gold. The average of the crushings was a little over 3 oz. to the ton; and so with No. 4 South. No. 5 South is the celebrated Ping Quee's, and the deepest on the Union, 260 feet. At that depth no water or mundic has been reached. The average yield was about the same as those of the last-named two. The best crushing from 5A South was 6 oz.; the depth 60 feet. The spare ground between 5 and 6 South gave $3\frac{1}{2}$ oz. to the ton at the last crushing. The gold is of a very superior quality. No. 6 South is yielding $1\frac{1}{4}$ oz. from a very free stone; and from No. 7 South an average of 3 oz. stone has been attained. No. 8 South had been carried down 45 feet; the last crushing from No. 1 North was 15 oz. per ton, and the lowest 8 dwt. No. 2 North is very shallow—it gave 2 oz. to the ton; with No. 3 North 7 oz. and 4 oz. are the highest figures; Mr. McLean, the present owner, has for years made a living pounding the stone in a mortar. No. 4 North gave an average of 6 oz., and from No. 5 North 800 oz. has been taken off a single patch. Nos. 6, 7, and 12 North average a little less, and in no case was there the slighest approach to deep sinking. So rich has been this gold-field—alluvial and quartz—that (I have it on unquestionable authority) Ping Quee alone has bought and sent home half a ton of gold from it and its surroundings. The principal part of the workings now being operated upon is the merged property known as the Lady Alice, which produces a pale-white stone and pale-yellow gold. Eighty tons of stone are ready for the stampers, but the great drawback is the absence of any battery nearer than eight miles. The prospects of a satisfactory yield are, however, good. The other claims are leased by Companies and held by private people; but the place has been locked up for years by the holders. With proper methods for development—and they could be easily applied, as there is every convenience almost, even down to the large dam which the original owners made—this property should be, from all appearances, a very valuable one. Without them it will still manage to maintain its present staff of half a dozen men or so, where half a thousand should find ample incomes.

Going from the Union to the Extended across country we were almost immediately confronted by a large and most curious "blow" of quartz, rising like a huge wall, rock upon rock, fully 10 feet high. The formation of the hills—the Seven Sisters—is the eternal slate and sandstone and quartz, with well-grassed flats between. The Extended Union is on the McKinlay River, and surmounts some worked-out alluvial gullies in which only a few Chinamen now fossick. We saw one squatting on his hams panning off his cradlings, and we asked him what luck he had. The response, with a shake of the head and also of the dish, was the "No savee," which was as good an intimation of success as one could wish from a Chinaman. Messrs. Noltenius and party were at the time of our visit the holders of the Extended, which has since been sold. Started about eight years ago and at sundry intervals allowed to remain idle since, it has given as much as 75 oz. to the ton from nine tons of a shoot sunk down upon from the surface. The country is permeated by most peculiar quartz leaders, some no thicker than a knife-blade, but all rich. The last returns from the top ground averaged 30 dwts. to the ton, the stuff being taken the whole width of 23 feet. In sinking the course of the shoot has been followed, and as it was erratic the workings also are eccentric, beginning in a huge excavation and forking off into a downright and an underlay shaft, continuing in a tortuous direction, and winding up with a downright 170 feet from the surface. The workings are almost full of water now, but they will be drained by an engine to be erected near the main shaft. A ten-head battery will also be furnished to help the five-head one, a little erection which has put through £21,000 worth of gold. That exact information respecting the broad totals might be in possession of my readers I got a statement copied from the battery-books, which show that 4,000 ounces came from the Extended claim, 1,177 from Lorrance's in the neighbourhood (average 6 ounces), 882 ounces from Fiveash's (average about 4 ounces), 150 ounces from Walker's, and 122 ounces from Stuart's— in these cases the averages not given. Besides these other little claims adjacent are being worked. Towards dusk we crossed the banks of the McKinlay, and reaching the Twelve-mile on Saturday night rested on the Sunday. The rest-day is to the people of the Twelve-mile nothing but a time of pleasure, if indeed it is even that. Take, for instance, the way in which it was spent on this occasion. In the morning a rifle match took place, the while a smith shod some horses. Then quoits were thrown, in one or two cases by inebriated men. In the evening many of the residents of the place gathered in a little cottage not far from the quarters of the Ministerial party, and carried on a drunken orgie all through the night and into the early hours of the Monday morning. The language used would put an irate trooper—the *worst* swearer of the worst swearing troopers, if you will—to the blush. Every third word was the sanguinary adjective, and a sentence of ten syllables I heard garnished with six expletives. So superlatively disgusting did one scamp become where all his boon companions were to the last degree objectionable that even a Northern Territory trooper (and he was exceptionally nice, for he had not the free-and-easy notions of some of the confraternity), issued a summons against him, and he had subsequently to travel twenty miles at his own expense and pay a £5 fine. The most curious feature about these goings-on is the fact that there is no public-house within a great many miles, and the storekeeper can sell only a gallon at a time. Whence comes the liquor then, and on a Sunday, too? The storekeeper in an excess of charity gives it away, probably. That being so, you can't blame the men much for drinking it. There is not a white woman in the place, there is no society, there are no amusements, there is no church or any sort of religious service anywhere except at Palmerston; and, in truth, I believe that if the one righteous resident of the Twelve-mile had either to hang or find another the rope would assuredly have to be called into requisition.

On Monday morning, March 6, the party left the Twelve-mile, untrammelled by packhorses, for a visit to the site of the Bamboo Creek tin discoveries. The road thither branches off to the west from that to Pine Creek, and soon becomes a steep blazed track, winding through on the whole fairly good land for agriculture, better for pasturage, and best for minerals. As to the latter, the ruling rocks are the slate and sandstone and the various forms of granite. Our first halt—leaving out of the reckoning the enforced stoppages whilst the horses were being led through the mire—was at the New Year's Day Claim, belonging to Messrs. Walker and Tennant, and situated halfway down a steep hill, to compass the descent of which seemed a sore trial to unaccustomed cliff-climbers amongst us, men and horses alike. The working on the property consisted, at the time of our visit, of little more than a hole about ten feet deep, sunk with doubtful judgment in the very middle of the water-course in the gully. There were several leaders with gold in them, and from the reef some very hard blue-mottled quartz specimens with specks were taken. The "country" is a sort of laminated sandstone, and Mr. Walker, who does the work, has a good chance of success. Wisely he has since begun his development in another place. Our course again lay over soppy, long-grassed plains, with screw pine and the Leichhardt pine, which latter is really not a pine at all, but its timber is useful and almost white-ant proof, and its fruit—a little rough apple about the size of an apricot—makes a capital pleasantly bitter tonic. Then the road wound through maze after maze of tall bamboo-like grass, and bamboo creeks innumerable—some of course with no bamboo at all—and altogether dubbed "bamboo" in fine irony none the less. A flower, magnolia-like, and called so—(it is really a myrtle)—and what the people name the desert rose, but in fact a lemon-scented mallee, and the plentiful and grateful musk-bush lined the track, and made up a queer but pleasant mixture of odours. Boggy crossings many times duplicated, with consequent real hardships, made all the Parliamentary party look lugubrious, as though they repented their enterprise. But we got to Bamboo (or Snadden's) Creeck at last, and on the new scene of the tin discoveries, on the south-west boundary of the 150 square miles radiating from Mount Wells, taken up as stanniferous country. We camped at the latter place, which the Minister decided must henceforth be immortalized as Tate's Grotto, in honour of the Professor. The creek-bed there is formed of indurated slate, with mica and rocky crystals and quartz and bastard granite, very much broken up. Almost all that has been done in the way of prospecting for tin is the sinking of a paddock twenty feet long and five or six feet deep, which was nearly full of water when we saw it. It is sunk on Johnson and Samper's selection, whence the tin ore which caused some sensation down South was taken, and where the wash is two feet thick and rich in tin. We also got some tin—some good tin —from the hole and from the bed of the creek, where the nodules are plentiful enough. Gold also is found in company with them —indeed, it was in washing for the more precious metal that the less was discovered; and a practical opinion is that enough gold might be got to pay the expenses of working. No tin-lode has been unearthed or seen ; but the Professor gave the confident assurance that he could find one in two days, and as to its near presence no doubt he was right. The tin is found higher up the gully than the gold. All the ravines empty into the creek, and the probability is that the fast-rising hills all round contain the lode. So far what is *known ;* what has been conjectured would fill folios, but I leave it out. Downright methodical practical search-work is needed, and I am glad to see that it is since being undertaken, with fair success already. But the full development of the tin, as of the copper, mines depends, though in a less degree, upon the solution of the railway question.

I must not omit a reference in this junction between two points to the green ants that make their habitation in the trees. They were first brought prominently under our notice by an inquisitive young man—a member of the Party—who was eternally poking round odd corners in the hope of finding something new. He saw several green bunches like nests in the trees over our camp, and he reached for one with a bamboo, and then took hold of it with his hand. He did not retain his grasp somehow—*not long.*

" Jee-ee-r-r-u-s-a-lem !"

That was his only remark, but he danced about as though he were insane, or else were trying some burlesque of fancy posturing

—feet describing all sorts of angles; hands emulating a crazy windmill.

" What's the matter ? "

" J-e-e-ee-*ee*-E-E-ru-salem ! "

The only answer at first was that mystic reference to the ancient Jewish capital. By and by the contortions of his features became a little fatigued, and retiring allowed his lips a better chance. Then he shot off as though he were in a great hurry, and with considerable earnestness, the words :—

" Green An————*Hang* it————Ants ! The————*Oh-h-h-h !* Ah-h ! " H'i'm ! "

He had discovered that the leafy bunch was a green ants' nest, and the ants had made with their usual penetration the discovery that plump European is not at all bad diet for a change. He pitched—pitched quite savagely, I grieve to say—the whole nest —some ten inches long by eight wide—into the creek, and soon after the "agglutinated umbrageous tabernacle" (*vide* Knight's Vocabulary !) had dissolved, and the surviving ants, making rafts of the sticky leaves, were floating in hundreds shorewards. And that unforgiving young man fiendishly shoved each leaf-raft under as it came to land !

The return journey was made in a different direction through hard granite country, with some magnificent views from hilltop of undulating land, and experience of plains sticky almost as glue. By the time the party reached the starting-point it was not without warrant that they confessed to exhaustion, whilst the horses looked so utterly melancholy, and so generally unequine, that it was gravely suggested that the Professor should bottle one as a curiosity in natural history. Next day also was a poser. Such scrambling and walking and climbing as the party did on foot, members of Parliament, as such, never undertook before. After an inspection of the Twelve-Mile Battery, which does not by any means save all the gold it ought to save, we started on foot on a visit to the quartz claim. We first came to Lorance's Creek, below Spring Hill, where we caught sight of the little Chinese township and its surrounding alluvial diggings, which have been very rich, but now are only moderately so. They were once crowded with fossickers ; their numbers have diminished. We came simultaneously to Manuel's Gully, and another and a smaller Chinese camp, near which gold once was found plentifully. There is not a man at work there now. Then we reached, after a perilous scramble, the cosy, airy house of Captain Richards, representing the English (Arnheim) Company, and had the un-wonted luxury of a seltzogene, which made cloudy water taste like nectar, and " crisp" limejuice resemble the best-loved draught of the gods. We went subsequently through Morgan's Gully—formerly rich in alluvial gold—to the New Era Company, one of four, part of which Mr. Pitcher, of Adelaide, representing English capitalists, has purchased here. The four have the title of the United Gold-mining Company, the name of the Company itself being "The Arnheim." These mines are situated on the western side of the range. The original owners some time ago amalgamated their interest, and half of it was purchased as indicated. The New Era has been opened along the surface fifty feet, and a shaft forty feet deep has been sunk, underlying north-east and south-west on the course of the reef. This is the direction nearly always here. The principal formation is sandstone, with a reef about two feet thick. Three crushings have been taken from the claims. The yields per ton were—25 tons, 1¼ oz. ; 40 tons, 4 oz. ; 90 tons, a little more than ½ oz. The next claim is the Clifton, in which gold has been traced along the line for between 80 and 90 feet, but only one small crushing, yielding a little over 3½ oz. to the ton, has been taken out. A shaft has been sunk upon the reef 35 feet. There is the usual sandstone formation, but the ground is peculiarly unsettled in character. The geological description would probably be —"a dislocation, and the infiltration of the gold has followed." The reef averages about a foot in thickness, and there is a reasonable probability that the stone, which is not now rich, is absolutely poor compared with that which will be found lower down. There are several undeveloped gold-bearing reefs and leaders yet.

Dry as this subject may be, the reader is not half so dry as the inspectors were when they at infinite pain had succeeded in scrambling to the top of Spring Hill. After they had assuaged their thirst with material hospitably provided, they metaphorically drank in the beauties of scenery like to that which Australians travel to Switzerland to gaze upon—scenery embracing all the prominent landmarks for miles and miles, and every little township, the alluvial diggings, upland and dale, and waving grass in white and green mosaic. Over it the graceful fern-palm, and the many deep-green shrubs, and over them the beautiful white gum, and silver paper bark, the bloodwood, and the anthill ; and throughout the verdant pattern the tributary streams to larger creeks ; and overhead the deep-blue canopy, checkered with sunbeams and light haze.

Our entertainers were Messrs. McGrath and Sanstrom, and the *locale* the North-east Clifton Claim. The work done is the sinking a shaft 28 feet deep and another smaller one. The works have opened out on two reefs, two feet and one foot wide respectively. The

stone shows a little gold—and of course the Parliamentary party had
some. Laurie and Mackenzie hold the next claim. On the hilltop they
have been costeening a paddock, about 10 feet deep, 20 feet long
and 4 feet wide. In two weeks they raised 30 tons of good-looking
stone, besides a heap of washdirt. Two of the most energetic
men in the Territory are Messrs. Laurie and Mackenzie, and they
stand as good a chance as I have seen of being rewarded for their
enterprise. The "Parliamentary" Mine they called their claim,
in honour of the party. Close by, on the same property, they have
another reef which is permeated by a peculiar black gossany
stone, which looks like coal-tar-painted cinders, and which stains
your hands like pitch. The reef is about 2 feet thick, and shows
gold pretty freely. Turning south again—the land north has not
been taken up, but might fairly be—we come to the East Clifton,
the richest-looking mine save Jansen's, at Pine Creek, that we had
yet seen here. It is owned by Messrs. Magrath & Sanstrom, who
have found in it four gold-bearing reefs, one of which they are
exploring with favourable indications. Moreover they have taken from
a mullock leader 12 tons, and netted 72 ounces. Those mullocky
leaders are curious. In most fields they would not yield gold at
all. Mr. Furner—no tin-disher, by-the-way—dug out a pie-tin
full and washed a couple of pennyweights. From his tailings I
got two or three grains. There is no telling how long these
leaders will last, however—not long, probably; but there is
the rich-looking reef to fall back upon. Proceeding, we passed
Driscoll's Claim, which the day before had given only 16 oz. for 20
tons of stone, and caused the unfortunate worker a 50 per cent.
loss. Then we got to the third of the United Company's claims,
suggestively called the Pay-me-Well, which is said to have yielded
more gold than any other in the district. It has paid well for
working from the surface down to about 10 feet from the present
depth. The leaders are not at present payable. The workings so
far have not exceeded 60 feet along the course of the reef. At a
depth of 160 feet from the top of the hill a tunnel has been driven
to that extent. There is a repetition of the mullock, with very
little quartz. The footwall is a splendid black slate with soft
sandstone. Then we came to the fourth of the Company's claims
—the Hongkong. This was one of the few reefs originally taken
up and worked by Chinamen, who have since returned to the
Celestial land. Some grand specimens have been taken from
leaders in the claim, and the returns have been exceedingly satisfactory. If it be possible to make it pay now, Captain Richards is
the man to do it. This closes the list of the claims on Spring
Hill, which is certainly amongst the best auriferous country that
I have ever seen. Through the absurdly large area of land allowed

to each prospector, already the whole Hill is held in eight claims
by sixteen men, who may continue in possession for aye, or so
long as it shall continue to pay them to scratch the surface. As a
matter of fact I believe that they intend to thoroughly develop—
as well as poor men can develop—their properties, but they could
hold them without the development if they chose ; and this should
not be. All these claims are to the north of the battery, and the
ground on which they are, as well as that on which the other
Companies stand, has been taken up for tin-mining by Adelaide
Companies. Going south we first reached Quirk and Williams's
Claim, in which some very rich specimens have been taken from
the surface, or very near to the surface. The adjoining
claim was worked some time but the gold was not sufficient
to pay £4 per ton for carting and crushing alone, and it
was abandoned. It is near the battery now, and is to be worked
again. About a mile off is the Elizabeth Prospecting Claim, on the
banks of the McKinlay. There has been 140 yards opening up
upon the surface on a long run of gold. The returns have varied
from 3 to 4 oz., a crushing three months ago of 72 tons yielded
418 oz., and two more later 29 tons gave 100 oz., save 2 dwts.
Even this did not pay with the heavy charges, and the owners—
Messrs. Clyma and Roberts—intend proceeding with the development of the mine when they shall have erected a battery for
themselves. At present, after twelve months' work, it is suspended. On the other side of the McKinlay is Polson's Claim,
which has yielded as high as 11 oz. to the ton of a small crushing.
The last gave a trifle over 2 oz., but from the stone the " eyes"
had been picked out and crushed in a mortar. Several Chinamen
are employed on the mines. Adjoining is a little claim held by Mr.
S. C. Smith. He has only had one crushing, which yielded 4¼ oz.
to the ton. Then there is the Home Point, belonging to
McIntyre and Delmar, and in the first great throes of the famous
or infamous " rush" giving remarkable returns, but abandoned, as
the gold was supposed to have run out. Work has been recom-
menced, however, and the gold has been met with again. This
exhausts the list of working claims in the district. The whole of
them employ at the most fifty men, and in none of them has any
real trial taken place. Of the wherefore more anon. Meantime
the reader is in a position to judge of the extent, and in a certain
measure of the results of quartz-mining in this the most important
centre in the Northern Territory. I have merely to add that the
average weekly purchase of gold by the European storekeepers is
50 oz. What the Chinese buy there is no means of knowing.

After the arduous labours of the day, the party had, pyjama-
clad, stretched their weary limbs upon their hammocks, and were

fast falling asleep, when at ten o'clock they were aroused and invited to a champagne supper offered by the resident miners as a farewell compliment. The Chairman took the empty soap-case beneath a loose canvas canopy, which from the top let in a view of sections of the sky, and from the sides a fresh breeze and countless mosquitoes and other winged torments. The guests were ranged, in pyjamas still, on one side of the table, on low lounges and benches, whilst the hosts squatted on candle-boxes on the other. In speeches, tasteful enough, and yet sufficiently importunate, several miners brought various wants before the Minister, who promised to do what he could to meet them. And when the formal proceedings closed at twelve o'clock, for a couple of hours afterwards the hills resounded with song. From "Kathleen Mavourneen" to "the Donkey Race at Hampstead Heath," the changes rung, the Minister and his party good-naturedly sitting up half the night to listen to the anything but dulcet strains of some of the songs, and this with the necessity of rising at daydawn to begin the journey to Mount Wells.

Next morning we rose as the sun was beginning the business of the day, and set out for Mount Wells, the famed pioneering point of the tin selections. It is about nine miles distant from the Twelve-Mile, and three miles off the main road to Port Darwin Camp. And *such* three miles! Morass, swamp, bog; horses led a third of the way; constant dismounting, and walking sometimes knee-deep in slush. The Professor almost lost his steed in a soft yam patch, and was himself, with others of the party, utterly exhausted when camp was made at the foot of the celebrated Mount Wells. The Mount is one of the highest in the Northern Territory, and it towers over its immediate neighbours like Goliath over Tom Thumb. Its elevation is more than a thousand feet; and the records show not more than twelve names of Europeans who have scaled it. Our party were not anxious to increase the number, but with the ever-active Chief-director Lindsay, I managed to get on top, though the sun-heat was so excessive as to make the climb the kind of thing you would like an enemy to regale himself upon. But once on the summit the view was worth all the trouble, and fifty times as much. Never, in any of the other colonies, have I seen such a beautiful and far-reaching panorama. Standing on the remains of the trigonometrical station, you see northwards the prominent peak of Mount Douglas, and the ranges skirting the overflow of the River Mary. To the east are caught glimpses of the high table-land of the Alligator Rivers; and south-east you see the Twelve-mile Settlement, with its curling battery smoke; the Union Hill, Pine Creek, and the high land between it and the

Katherine, the sharp-peaked hills tree-clad. Westward lies the table-land forming the watershed of the Daly, and beyond you can trace with the glass the track of the Adelaide, and mark some of its many windings. If Mount Wells never becomes celebrated for its tin it will be a favourite resort for hill-climbers in the distant future—only a patent lift must be placed on its crest for the convenience of travellers. My companion, the better to enjoy the sight, shinned up the old "trig." pole, and was eloquently describing the watershed of the McKinlay and the fifty-miles circle of vision from his place of vantage, when two March flies—there are thousands on the Mount—attached themselves to his person. He seemed at once to lose interest in the view, and slid down the pole as if a sudden thought had struck him, impelling him to an exclamation of intense astonishment. To this day, I am not of my own knowledge aware whether he was overpowered with the many beauties of the exquisite panorama before us, or whether the March flies had imparted a preternatural smartness to his thought. In support of the latter notion it may be said that those same flies are very, very penetrating.

There is nothing especially noteworthy in the formation of the mount as tin country. I candidly confess that I prefer that at Snadden's or Bamboo Creek, though this resembles in general features the country near Stanthorpe and Vegetable Creek, in New South Wales. There is granite not far off, and there are indurated slate and sandstone in the course of the feeble little creek which struggles along at the foot of the mount. But there is not nearly so much of the stream tin as there is at the other place —it is more "dredgy." Not that the fact necessarily tells against the value of the country. At the first blush it does appear ridiculous that 150 miles of land should be taken up for tin because a little of the metal was got from a couple of holes not big enough for graves for a full-sized man. We camped on Quirk, Miller, & Tennant's selection. Mr. Quirk claims to have discovered tin in a creek near the mount, just below a ravine, which it is believed the lode approaches, in October, 1880, whilst prospecting for gold. What followed the public know. The leases allowed on Mount Wells are Quirk, Tennant, & Miller's, 240 acres; Solomon's, 764 acres. These names include several proprietaries. Some of whom since I was there have set to work energetically to develop them. Granted a continuance of this work, under proper management, the results can hardly fail to be satisfactory.

It was afternoon when we left Mount Wells, with fifteen miles of journeying yet to be done, and three of them over hillsides sloping as much as the gable of a steep roof. On one of these our ever-jovial Commissariat Conservator—Mr. Knight, the chief in order—came to grief, and nearly lost his life. His horse went under a low-branched tree, which pushed the rider off the saddle and down shoulder-foremost on the stones with which the hill was besprinkled. Mr. Knight rode fifteen stone, and did not fall a feather-weight, and a staved-in helmet and a scalp wound testified to the providential character of the escape. The only actual injuries inflicted were those to the head, and a severe wrenching of the bones and bruising. It was almost dusk when we passed over the beautiful black loam of McMinn's Creek, and night had long since closed in—a dark, damp, murky night, feebly illuminated by countless fireflies and numberless glow-worms—ere we reached Port Darwin Camp; and there were no deputations that night. That fact was worthy of record. On Thursday morning the party started for the Shackle or Yam Creek or Sandy Creek ; the people call it the first, the Telegraph Department the second, the Local Court folks the other. It is about four miles distant, and on the way Sandy Creek alluvial gold-field, employing only a few Chinamen, is passed. There are beautiful Chinese gardens on either hand, and the scenery altogether is most picturesque. Anxious to inspect the famed Margaret rush and the battery east of Port Darwin Camp, I made a detour of some miles and got to the Shackle by a roundabout. We first visited the old Forbes battery of ten heads, then owned by Mr. Griffiths, and since purchased by a Company. It is the most substantial machinery that I have seen in the Territory, and it is a pity that such valuable plant—it is said to have cost altogether £20,000—should have remained idle long enough for its enclosure and blanket-boxes to go completely to wrack and ruin and itself to rust. The road thence to the rush trends along the banks of the Margaret Creek, where the land is about the best that the Territory boasts in this direction. Applications have been made by the Chinese merchants for selection of this land for plantation purposes—the growth of maize, coffee, cotton, Chinese tobacco, the custard apple, the lichee-nut (I had some, and found them better than French prunes), and such like. Of course there are several Chinese gardens along the road now, and plantains and maize and bananas flourish. I had an interesting interview with a most intelligent Chinese merchant at the Margaret—Quong Wing Chong, second only in wealth and power to the almighty Ping Quee. As soon as we came in sight he hurried his servants with the gin bottle and the tea ; and so soon as we had dismounted he pressed his courtesies upon us. He seems very anxious to start a plantation. He feels assured the soil would grow the articles enumerated, and many more. Last year the Margaret was the great centre of alluvial work. Big nuggets, some as heavy as 25 lb. and more, were got from an average depth of 4 ft. About 2,000 Chinamen were at work, and fights between the two camps were of common occurence. Now the number of Chinamen has dwindled down to eighty, and the average purchases of gold by Quong Wing Chong are only 25 oz. a week. There are two reefs at work—Ping Quce's, where the three Chinamen engaged got £500 worth from one bucket of stone a few days before we visited them. It has always been a marked feature of the Margaret that the gold occurs there in patches. The other claim is the Grove Hill, which is being worked by tributers, who are doing well. Recently they crushed out 365 oz. in a mortar. Then they had to do some dead work, as the shaft fell in, but the week before we saw them they had got 28 oz. After lunching off damper and tea at a diggers' camp we threaded our way at infinite trouble and some danger through the abandoned grass-grown holes of the Margaret. This country—which has been pretty thoroughly turned over— was once the scene of races between the troopers and the Chinamen. The former would find a corpse lying neglected on the diggings, and would chase the reputed relatives and compel them to take charge of the body of the deceased. But if they got hold of the wrong man, and could not quit their unsavoury find, they would take it up and place it in the centre of the gambling house. The right party to move the "trouble" would soon be found. Just out of the Margaret the path loses itself in excavations and holes, and Chinese gardens and grass. Consequently we had frequently to pull up our horses on the bank of a great chasm and zigzag the place in delineation of a crosscut saw. Thus came we over frowning crags to Butterfly Gully, where wave the biggest of fan palms, and grows other tropical vegetation more profusely than in any other part of our journeying. Under a bold, jagged, superin-cumbent mass of cliffs are two little caves, and in the creek which they overlook—another Bamboo Creek, of course!—there seem to be indications of tin. Then through stretches of grass fully sixteen feet high, each separate plant short, stiff almost as a rapier's point, and the seeds sharp as needles, our horses flew at a gallop, and *such* a thwacking as our faces got with the rebounding grass. It lashed us as whips lash, and our cloth-ing was stuck as thick as a working pincushion with the barblike seeds. On the banks of another part of this creek we caught sight of the broken tableland, and the huge white and granite bluffs beyond the Shackle, and on the creek bank too vast granite rocks were piled upon each other in fantastic confusion. At one point there was a miniature Logan-stone, and looking at it you would think that the slightest touch of the lightest hand would capsize it. And so to the Shackle, where the rest of the party had arrived long before, and where for once they rested, because there was little to be seen. Towards evening Professor Tate went to the Bluff—a prominent upshoot of the broken table-land—and was much interested in the peculiar formation of the upland, where sandstone and other ridges rise above each other like tiers of huge walls.

CHAPTER VI.—IN THE INTERIOR.

THE SHACKLE OR YAM CREEK.—PERPLEXING NOMENCLATURE.—A DECAY-
ING PLACE.—THE ONLY YOUNG LADY.—A CIGAR "SMOKERESS."—
LEWIS'S CAMP.—NO COAL.—A BOILING SPRING.—EXPLORERS.—
THE FOUNTAIN HEAD.—SOME FOOLISH BIRDS AND THEIR ECCEN-
TRICITIES.—SOME HOTEL-KEEPERS AND THEIRS.—THE JOHN BULL
MINE.—A BUSH DINNER.—THE GOAT EATERS.—ANOTHER
DEPUTATION.—MORE ABOUT THE HOWLEY.—THE OLD HOWLEY.—
BEETSON'S BATTERY.—A CHINESE CAMP.—BRIDGE CREEK DIG-
GINGS.—A LONELY GRAVE.—" WORM PICNICS."—AN ENTERTAIN-
ING FUNERAL.—THE EVERLASTING "SQUARE."—CHINESE HOSPI-
TALITY.—ANOTHER COPPER MINE.—BRIDGE CREEK.—A CELESTIAL
BANQUET.—SOME LINGUISTIC DIFFICULTIES.—A LUDICROUS SITUA-
TION.—A WORD OR TWO ABOUT BRIDGE CREEK.—NO. 1 DEPOT.—
THE ADELAIDE RIVER.—THE STAPLETON AND THE OLD VIRGINIA
MINE.—POIETT & MACKINNON'S COFFEE PLANTATION.—A MAG-
NIFICENT ESTATE.—AN EXTRAORDINARY SPRING.—CINCHONA
PLANTING.—CHEAP LABOUR WITH A VENGEANCE.—AN IMPORTANT
INDUSTRY.—FURTHER INFORMATION ABOUT THE FINNISS.—THE
END OF THE MINING INSPECTION.—NO TRIAL ! NO TRIAL ! NO
TRIAL !—THE SWINDLES.—CONCLUSIONS.

THE Shackle is not a lively place. The gold leads seem to
have marched past and left it on the flank. Whether it
became disheartened at that, or by reason of the strange
mixture of nomenclature concocted over it, let some profound reasoner discuss. The fact is that the place is apparently on its last legs, and feeble, tottering shanks they be. I
spoke of its nomenclature, and I ask you whether you ever saw the
like. Before a Telegraph Office was built upon it it had a "shackle"—
a break in the line where travelling operators could speak the different offices with a hand instrument, and so it got to be popularly known
as " The Shackle." When the Government established a postal and
telegraph business they called their place " The Yam Creek Office ;"
and when to it they added a Police Court, they christened it
"Sandy Creek." And the little hamlet has had to jog along ever
since, burdened with three names, to the endless confusion of
travellers. There are worse-looking places than the Shackle, but
that there are duller I beg to dispute. It is one of the stations on
the overland telegraph line, and some time ago was important enough
to be made an " official " centre. The Deputy-Warden (Mr. Nash)
was quartered there, following Mr. Knight, to act also as Resident
Magistrate, and several etceteras. The police sub-office was there
fixed, and Corporal Montague—and a right good corporal, too—
placed and continued in charge. There was a miners' hospital,
where good, kind-hearted Mr. Knight, formerly a well-known archi-
tect in Melbourne, and the present Chief Warden, then stationed
there, healed the sick and helped the poor at great personal sacri-

fice, and with small encouragement— if the encouragement of hearing thanks from saved patients in all quarters be small. Mr.
Knight was called upon to desert the settlement when it began to
sink, and soon most of the buildings went gradually to the white
ants : all save the hospital—that died an easy death off-hand, and
ever since the very sick diggers have had to die as comfortably as
might be, either on the road to Palmerston or in their huts. One
hundred and fifty miles of mineral country and no hospital !
Pleasant and satisfactory, eh ? You can't blame the Government,
however ; this Northern Territory has been a perfect *terra incognita*
to it and its predecessors, and that fact may account for a looseness
and mismanagement shown in other matters more than this—

> " But now
> There is clearly no use in considering how
> Or whence came the mischief—the mischief is here.
> Broken shins are not mended by crying—that's clear."

Yam Creek will probably soon be altogether deserted. Port
Darwin Camp—four miles east—has taken its place in importance.
The Telegraph Office has decayed so much that a new one will
have to be built, and as the present one is quite out of the way of
business, and the camp is right in the way of it—and as moreover, any railway to be made should miss Yam Creek and go
through Port Darwin Camp ; and particularly as the Minister has
been importuned on the subject—it is probable that the new
building will be put up at the latter place and the line diverted ;
and if so, then the Police Court and Warden's Office will know the
Shackle no more. At present it has the only Court in the Territory out of
Palmerston ; and when the Magistrate gets a sitting he well up-
holds the severe dignity of the law—as witness the case of one of
the Twelve-mile disorderly topers, who had to lose two days to
travel to the Court, and then to pay £5. About the best country
hotel in the Territory is that at Yam Creek, and it is well and
widely known as the place where resides an actual, real, live young
lady ; for white ladies are scarce. We met only four since we left
Southport, and now that I am so far from them I may say that
three-fourths of them were not so young as they used to be.
One excited my admiration by the foppish fashion in which she
smoked a manila. Few ladies could have done it half so well.

The only diggings round the Shackle besides Sandy Creek are
the places known as Lewis's Camp and Drummer's Gully, where
a few Chinamen fossick. There are of course in the district,
including the Port Darwin Camp, a few Europeans engaged in
alluvial ; but only those who think the getting machinery for
quartz-reefing hopeless. Altogether, with those working in the
famous Stuart's Gully, there are about 200 Chinamen. For all

the district Port Darwin Camp is the centre. On the way to the Territory I was met with great talk of coal discoveries in this region. I found that only one of the six inhabitants of the Shackle had heard the rumour, and he didn't believe it; and for the life of me I couldn't find any existence of a coal series, though I zigzagged a lot of country to try to see it. Warden Knight has prospected over and over again in diffirent parts of the mining districts, and he never saw it; and more, he never saw anybody else who saw it. But if the people haven't coal, they have a boiling spring about twelve miles south-west. They are duly proud of it; they have little else beyond personal merits to be proud of. On Thursday, Messrs. Mair and Harriss, who left Port Darwin three months before to explore the country around the Elsie River and Limmen's Bight, with a view to stocking on behalf of a Sydney firm, dined with the Minister and his party. They travelled altogether 1,200 miles. They are two hardy and reticent fellows —reticent because they consider their information is first their employers'. They ran a slight danger from flood, but in every case they had no trouble with the blacks, who cleared away directly they saw them coming. About the only thing new in Messrs. Harriss and Mair's information, so far as they imparted it, was that the country generally is not very good. We left the Shackle early on Friday, March 10, and passed through a tiny stretch of alluvial workings, crossing Yam Creek, where the bridge had been burnt down just before. The morning was a bright one, for the sun was on his good behaviour, and kept the elements likewise. Gaudy butterflies—the brightest creatures there—flitted cheerily about; and Mounts Osborne and Shoobridge gay in their deckings of green— looked positively resplendent with the glittering dew-spangles which gave each leaf of every tree a silver sheen. For all that, the land is not much suited for cultivation; for pasturage it would do. Just beyond is the Fountain Head, opened by Radford, who was drowned in the Gothenburg. He and his party did some reefing, and crushed somewhat less than an ounce to the ton. Then Manning and others took the property and worked it for a while, but they gave it up, and it is idle now. The alluvial, however, even now employs more Chinamen than any other part of the Northern Terri- tory. There are between 300 and 400 of them all getting gold. Some have made big "rises." The gold is the finest and most powdery I have seen here. Years ago there were more than a thousand Chinamen digging it out. Why the place was called Fountain Head is a legitimate question for the future Debating Societies of the Territory to struggle with. On the rule of contraries, I suppose; for this flat low-lying land no more suggests a fountain head than a blacking-brush suggests a snow-flake. That aside, however, I think the land is well worth a trial—for reef gold particularly. There are some well-defined leads. Just beyond the diggings is the Glencoe Cattle Station. Coming back again Port Darwin campwards you approach the Princess Louise Mine and the old " Westcott's Western Bonus Lease." Most readers will know something about the Louise, which was one of the claims taken up and worked upon in 1872. It was kept going till 1875, there being in the meantime got out of one shoot 1,000 ounces of gold. Afterwards a fairly large four-ounce crushing was obtained. Then the depth made working disproportionately expensive ; and a new shaft is the desideratum which the employment of capital must supply. The general formation of the country is the ordinary slate and sandstone. The last crushing from Westcott's was at the rate of six ounces, but the water in the mine was too strong. (Arrangements have since been made to work these properties with the Grove Hill Battery.) Other mines which were abandoned, with a good record, are the Pioneer and No. 5 North, and there are several besides—never tried, of course. The recommencement of work on them will possibly be synchronous with the starting of the battery, but the first really energetic work probably with the passing of the Bill for the construction of the first section of the intercolonial railway.

As we branched off from the Shackle-road, which we had not traversed previously, on to the Howley track, which we had gone over, and which has been already described, we had leisure for a short study of the different ornithological specimens which flew by. There are not many that are rare or specially beautiful. Parrots of gaudy plumage there be, but there are others quite as pretty, and with the same lively chatter, in all the southern parts of the colonies. The cockatoos are little different from their family below—a trifle more intelligent and talkative, maybe. The emu, the bustard, and the pelican are just as ungainly, but more plentiful, and the quail are no less impudent because they are a little more bulky. The kingfishers, so far as I can judge, are larger than the South Australian ; the pigeons are really beautiful. One kind is a very impertinent bird, by-the-way, fond of strutting about on the road till your horse is close upon him, and flying away with a peculiar whirr, which makes you think the bird is extending its claws from its nose, and contemning you. It has red eyes, and a bronze back, with matchless setting. The bower bird, a beautiful glossy black, and about the size of a pigeon, is passionately fond of fun. Its nest of twigs has connected with it a little promenade or bowling alley, about 5 feet long, in one corner of which is placed a heap of coloured shells, and beans, and leaves. The never-monotonous amusement of the bird is to shift the positions of these gauds—at least so says a reliable gentleman who has watched the play. The jungle bird, about the size of an ordinary fowl, foolishly rears for itself huge hillocks of earth, some of them 10 feet high, and 12 feet in diameter, very trimly shaped. One in the gardens near Palmerston has been used as the foundation of a summer-house, and it gives a good elevation, from which to gain a view of the Gardens. There is no pretension to architectural effect amongst these feathered builders, and the main thing you wonder at in looking at the mound is why any sensible bird should spend so much down-right hard work in making it, when it might have lived just as comfortably in a couple of empty wicker dead marine envelopes. Then the pheasant gives itself a world of trouble to make an elaborate nest of grass as big as a haycock—a nest which is burnt every year—when it might accommodate itself and all its callers in some snug niche in the hillside, without danger of being burnt out.

We camped at Brock Creek, and soaked through by a heavy rain, regaled ourselves on fibrous india-rubbery sandwiches and soapy bread, jammed together promiscuously in an old thickly-inked newspaper. That was the sort of thing all through. Sandwiches and white paper with no squeezing out of shape are incompatible. The hotel-keepers have patent methods of bungling in the Territory. I am fearsome that they laid a foundation for a superstructure of dyspepsia which shall convert most of the party into counterparts of the sage of Chelsea—in *one* particular at least. A whole chapter might be devoted to a discussion on the question whether an hotel-keeper's conscience goes out call-making whilst its owner is drafting his guests' bills, but I refrain. Eventually we got to the John Bull Mine, which began to yield up its treasures about ten years ago. The stone had then to be carted five and a-half miles for crush-ing, and the average of two ounces to the ton was hardly equal to paying for that. The proprietors abandoned their claim, and re-moved the Howley battery to the Extended Union, which they worked. The present nominal owners by-and-by resumed work at the John Bull, and bought the ten head of stampers now on the ground, involving themselves with their bankers. They never quite recovered their position, though they tried pluckily to do so. A slight derangement of the pumping gear early in December last preceded a heavy flood, which wellnigh filled the shaft and stopped work, which has never been resumed. The property is in trust for the benefit of the creditors. The machinery is fairly good, though the gold-saving appliance is imperfect. The reef—an enormous saddle, followed from the surface 145 feet down on an underlay—contains at the lowest depth a good deal of mundic. The ground is easy for working, and the reef varies in thickness from 2 feet to 3½ feet, carrying gold at the rate of from one to three ounces to the ton. More work has been done on this claim than on any other in the Territory; and though financial considerations compelled the workers to do a little "eye-picking," they have been fairly systematic in their operations. The mine paid its way for fully six years, but the terrible handicaps killed it. The reef has a hopeful look of permanency about it, which augurs well for future operations. The John Bull is notable as the one place where the explaining host presented specimens without producing the omnipresent bottle of square; and we felt so thankful for the deliverance, that the drenching flood, which increased each saddleweight full half a stone, was accepted without a murmur as we plodded patiently on to the Howley Crossing. Host Nott's dinner was a surprise—roast pig and ditto fowls, of course (the poultry and pig death-rate must have swelled terribly the last four weeks); but, moreover, the native companion, with its flavour of stewed mackintosh and tough mutton; and goat—delicious and toothsome. The fastidious ate it as mutton, and looked pale when they knew that they each formed a disgusted envelope for a section of disgusting goat. The experience was an apprenticeship to a dose of boiled water-snake, or something closely akin to it, subsequently dished up at another stopping-place.

At night there was a deputation—a deputation of deputations, who let their memorial explain itself, and didn't drown its meaning in a deluge of words. The Minister gave a graceful reply, somewhat marred, however, by the gasping snores of a sleeper in the next room. In closing he gracefully acknowledged the universal kindness the party had met with, and the auditory showed appreciation of the compliment by making the old airy room resound with the noise of cheering. And then peace reigned again till the frogs in the billabongs took up their chorus at the point where they had dropped it before the rainstorm burst. The horse bells chimed in, dogs assisted, and sleep was impossible.

The first quartz claim to get payable crushings in the Howley District was that known as the Britannia Prospecting, seven miles to the east of our hotel. It was taken up by W. McMinn towards the end of 1873. The first crushing yielded eight ounces to the ton, and two others six and five respectfully; but the mine was never systematically worked, and has been idle for some years. It has one whole shaft upon it; the depth is fifty feet and that is about all that need be said concerning that side of the Howley District. The same old story—good indications and no trial. We started early on Saturday, March 4, on a long circuit through the surrounding diggings, sending the packhorse direct to Bridge Creek, only about four miles off by the main road. For the first six miles of the track we followed—a varying track of knee-deep water, mud, and grass—there is nothing of much interest to be seen. The soil is mostly brownish, deep, and good for agriculture, and the anthills rise loftily and plentifully above the flats—so much alike that if ants were only human and banquetted occasionally, they would often have to sit down and pick their teeth in the late hours while they mentally debated which of a score was their own habitation. Out of the more level land you reach the steep hill, where mined the Agrigulha Company some years ago. They got a tunnel in 150 feet through the hill, and then stopped work, when another fifty feet of driving would have brought them to the reef they sought. Consequently they got nothing worth writing about, unless it were a copper vein. But then there is more or less of copper through a large area here, and even if the lodes are developed and prove to be very valuable the railway alone can make the claims pay for working. Near by is Cruikshank's Gully, where a few Chinamen are at work, making fair returns. The Europeans kept it for a while to themselves, and when they'd had the meat they let the Celestials take the pickings. I would not like to speculate upon which got the most nutriment. A great deal of work has been done there, as well as in Lorance's Gully, which shoulders it, and of which the same generally may be said. As we ascended the hill the sound of stampers met us, and we followed it to the top, and descending again came upon Beetson Brothers' battery, which is midway down. The battery has ten heads, and the Messrs. Beetson brought it last year from Westcott's claim near Port Darwin Camp. The Beetsons are two plucky brothers, who have manfully stuck to their ground about six years, and who are reaping a rich reward. "We are perfectly satisfied," they told me, and indeed they may be, for they have crushed as much as ten ounces to the ton. The battery is almost the only one at which the amalgamator is used. It has been grinding away all the season, but is never cleaned up. They want some effective means of saving what might easily be saved if they had these means. The deepest point reached in the sinking is 75 feet. Pyrites were met first with in quantity at 60 feet, and the deeper they go the richer is the stone. The average width of the reef is about eighteen inches. Some years ago Mr. Scott, working on one part of the property, got some splendid stone and subsequently lost the lead. Just before we visited them the Beetsons had got it again, and now they are in the heyday of their prosperity, and yet with only half a dozen men at work. Their crushings from the reef proper have averaged $3\frac{1}{2}$ oz. at least ; on one notable occasion 27 tons yielded 200 oz. They are now putting through the mill—making the plates look rich in amalgam

—10 or 12 tons of mixed stuff a week. They have peculiar mullocky leaders—more flinty than those at Spring Hill. Some
of the specimens have a strong alumy taste—they look like
alum schist—and rapidly clear muddy water into which they are
put. The Messrs. Beetson come of a pioneer family well known
in Adelaide in the early days. The prosperity which is coming to
them is well deserved. They are two of the few who have stuck
to the Territory through good fortune and through bad, and
perhaps no men have unaided done more to give a fair trial to its
minerals than they. Leaving them we went through Long Gully,
where rich finds in the alluvial were made by Europeans years
ago, and where now a few Chinamen make scant returns by
fossicking. This on a flat, and in the saddle between two ridges.
On the rising ground are more mullock leaders. The fact is—it
is wearying to repeat it—the ground has never been fairly tried.
It looks as promising as any I have seen, having regard in forming judgment to the rich alluvial finds all round.
It is here that you see the shaft of the Palmerston Company,
which was formed in Adelaide in the mining mania days. The
claim was abandoned, and the battery was shifted to the Extended
Union ground. Gold was got in the leaders, but I am told a
payable quartz reef has since been found there. I cannot verify
the information, however.

Under the scant shade of a spiral tree rises a little grass-grown
mound, beneath which lie the bones of poor young Fisher, brother
of the deceased doctor of that name who lived and died in
Wallaroo. The horses and the natives walk over it, and not im-
probably camp fires of stranger travellers have been lit upon
it, for no fence or mark of any kind protects it from intrusion.
In a country which periodically is for months without a clergyman, and never has a doctor, the burial ceremony is hurried
through anyhow. There is usually no sacredness or solemnity
about death. A funeral is called a "worm picnic." The carcasses
are buried anywhere, and often anyhow. The Police Inspector
takes on his country trips a prayer-book, and if a man dies near
where he is, he reads the "Service for the Dead;" but often
they are buried off-hand, particularly in the remote parts. A
friend of mine was visiting one of these one day when a funeral
took place. The grave had been dug overnight, and when the
mourners came, sorrow and coffin burdened, they at once began to
lower the tangible part of their load into the hole. Then they
saw a wild cat in it. Solemnly spake the chief mourner—
"Hist, boys. 'Tisn't often we get such a chance of fun.
S'posin' we turn the dogs on?"

When they had got through with the cat-worrying, they

"planted"—that is the word they use—the "worm's food." We came next to a Chinese camp, which boasts an assayer and several storekeepers. One of them—Quong Hing Shing—entertained us nobly with fragrant cigars and gin and porter and delicious tea, made as Chinamen alone can make it; and, as the staple, the inevitable "square." Quong &c. estimates the Chinese population of the Howley and old Howley at 350; and that is about correct I think. The yield of gold is very small, he says: he prophesies abandonment. Well, that may be; but he admits that last year a party of Chinamen found some leaders about 30 feet deep in decomposed quartz and that now they are enjoying a festive season in Hongkong. The worked gold country extends three miles beyond here, following a line from the Old Howley diggings to Mount Paqualin (beyond Bridge Creek) about thirteen miles. All the way good returns have been got for surface-scratching in both the alluvial and the quartz. The alluvial gold, indeed, is generally mixed with quartz, and it has the rough, jagged appearance which indicates to the practical miner that it cannot long have left the parent reef. On the way to Bridge Creek, along the line of gold, we inspected the Howley Copper Mine, about two miles from Beetson's. Though the lode is strong and good so far as the few days' work upon it have exposed it to the view, I would not care to spend money upon it yet. It is practically worthless without a railway, I fear. There are several lodes of copper on the ground. The stone in general character resembles that at Copperfield. Thence over slate outcrops and steeply-slanting hills we came to one more gully, yclept Sanders —where 200 Chinamen were at work, surfacing mostly last year. Now there is not one. Through McKenzie's Gully, where the track is mined away, we came to well-grassed country; we passed Douglas's Hill, with the remains of the sturdy old captain's camp still standing; we hurriedly inspected Cement Gully, where the only Europeans on the diggings—a dozen merely—work on the quartz, and get a little gold proportioned to their little work; we crossed Nelson's Hill taken up by a Company during the rage of the mania, and never worked; we took entertainment at several Chinese townships and reluctantly refused proffered hospitalities at others; the Minister acknowledged the obsequious bowing and scraping of the Celestials, and thus returned we to the pestilential Bridge Creek. At night the Chinese dinner took place in the local hotel. It was not an elaborate affair at all—just an ordinary public-house dinner, with no special features. Five Chinese merchants dined with the party—the principal, Ah Foo, an aldermanic man with a fat puffed face beaming like a stage sun, and withal thoroughly good-tempered. The attempts they, unaccustomed, made to eat with knife and fork were not brilliantly successful, and such a fumbling, such a tinkling, such a clatter as they made was something to be witnessed. By-and-by the wine came on, and Ah Foo rose to his legs to make a speech, introducing it by a comprehensive flourish of his glass above his head—

"Missa Gennelmen—We welly glad a see him you coma heah. We want um nish one. Spose livee in Queenslan', Wictolea, Sydney, him Chinamen get him plenty gold; sposin' no gold, him all yite, him plantation—savee—all ce same money—welly good —*hay?* We wantum allee same."

The Minister pondered deeply at the end of this oration. It was affecting, but it required study. All thought so. To gain time Mr. Parsons proposed the health of the Queen, and all honoured it. Then I prevailed upon Ah Foo to rise, and shake his glass about, and say,

"Missa Palsons."

The Chinese cannot pronounce the "r," you remember. Before Ah Foo committed himself, however, he whispered me, interrogatively,

"Him welly good fella?"

Childlike and bland as ever, you observe! Then there was an awkward pause, but the Minister adroitly proposed the health of Ah Foo and the other hosts; and the honoured rose with those who honoured them, and flourished glasses, and hip-hip-hurrahed to their own glory just as heartily as their European glorifiers. Then we sat down again, and, to save awkwardness, Ah Foo was asked politely by a friend,

"Now, *what* DO you mean?"

But meantime the Minister had risen, and commanded the profound attention of the Celestials—who, by-the-by, were carefully got up in European costume, ill-assorted and ill-fitting, it must be confessed. They stared at the honourable gentleman as though he combined the sageness—apocryphal and other— attributed to Confucius and half a dozen Chinese Emperors.

Quoth Mr. Parsons—"I am very much obliged to you, indeed, Ah Foo and gentlemen, for inviting us to dine with you this evening. I feel that it is an act of great courtesy on your part, and it has afforded me and my friends the greatest pleasure to accept your hospitality——

"Yah, yah; all yite." [It was Ah Foo's interjection.]

——"You are here for the time being in this land and under the law of this country. You are contributing towards the cost of its government, and in your several positions we wish you every prosperity. When we came to Bridge Creek the other day you were good enough to meet us with a very marked expression of your welcome. We never heard such a firing-off of crackers in our lives before. [Here Ah Foo's mouth began to expand alarmingly.] We were glad to see it. We therefore beg to thank you for that act, which I accept as meaning that you are glad to see someone connected with the Government, and that you wish to keep the laws of the country in which you live."

Here Ah Foo's benignity became intolerable. I uneasily shifted a few inches away, till the first paroxysm of his appreciative demonstration had subsided, and his mouth had contracted somewhat. Then he turned to me and asked,

"I spose him talkee welly good jush now? What him mean? You savee him?"

Well, this was not encouraging. I told him that the burden of the address was—"You welly good fellow; me likum you"—and he said in effect that that was perfectly correct. Then he was called on to make a speech, and with prodigious gestures and flourishing of glass—that glass was never at rest—he began—

"My countleeman likee fahm (farm) nish countlee allee same Englishman; takee up lan', glow lice (rice, of course!) savee fahm, *hey*? Nish one new countlee. Chince notting do. Must findum somethin' do. Him wantum Gov'nment givee land glow lice allee same Englishman. How muchee money, Missee Palsons, Sir, you chahgee Chinee piecee lan'?"

The Minister reserved his defence, as he hadn't—not being accustomed to pigeon English—the slightest idea what Ah Foo meant, or what the allegation was. Then Ah Sam, our Chinese boy, was called to interpret. He explained the first oration which amounted to—"If a Chinaman wants to take up land for plantations can he do so (he needs employment during the dry season, when he cannot wash for gold), and if he does 'do so' what will we have to pay per acre?" Not "the Chinamen want an Englishman to prospect for them," as our host said was the matter with them when we came down. Then Mr. Parsons explained the 7s. 6d. an acre clauses, and the Chinamen grinned with satisfaction; and Ah Foo, chuckling said to me—

"Allee yight. Me tlink ten tousan' Chinee long a Tellitoly two t'lee year." And others, by-the-way, have said the same. "We make nish place allee same Singapo'," one observed. Significant that. They're all going to start plantations.

On went the amusing dialogue. The Chinese wanted a hospital at Palmerston, and the Minister suggested that they should subscribe half its cost. They said they would. They wanted the gold duty off, and Mr. Parsons made no promise, but cleverly introduced the subject of the miners' rights, and told them they would have to pay for them. They promised to do so when it was suggested that they could pay the fee quarterly. They told me afterwards that the reason why they had not paid hitherto to any extent was that some of them coming in November had taken up the rights, and then more money was demanded from them in December, and they thought they were being imposed on. Yearly rights dating from day of issue are the only remedies for the wrong.

And so ended our Chinese banquet, of the stately ceremonious ludicrousness of which I can give but a very slight notion. The English language is not capable of conveying to a reader a full idea of the guttural intonations of the Celestial throat. But was ever Colonial Minister banqueted by Chinamen before?

Beyond saying that Bridge Creek extends to Mount Paqualin, along the reef we had followed the day before, and that you may reckon within it the now deserted—deserted because of the water —diggings of No. 1 Depot, I need add little more than that there are 250 Chinese on the field, if their gold buyers may be trusted. There is a dispute as to who discovered the field, and a good deal of heartburning exists between rival claimants for the honour. The place is mostly given over to alluvial work, and consequently Chinamen. Three men were working on a reef, but one took fever and went down to Hospital, and the others are resting awhile in other fields. The water is the main difficulty this wet season. We journeyed to the Adelaide River on Sunday—the object being to cross the barrier ere the heavy rains made it so in reality—and we succeeded so well that by luncheon-time on Monday we were inspecting the Old Virginia Mine, at the Stapleton, the first mine passed on the way from Palmerston to the gold-fields. It has previously been mentioned that this mine has been purchased through Mr. Pitcher, of Adelaide, for the (English) Arnheim Gold-mining Company, and the work of development has gone on energetically since October last, when it was restarted. In that time 62 feet has been sunk, the shaft being now 152 feet deep ; and the week before the day of our visit a 2-feet reef was struck. Mr. James Devin is the manager, and he has twelve workmen, including two Chinese. The Europeans get £3 a week and board and lodging. The first crushing will have been put through by now. The stone is nearly all mundic, and the workings are so wet that the men working on the bottom of the shaft are continually exposed to a 40-feet spout-like fall of water. The average yield under the old Company was 1¼ oz. to the ton, but probably half the gold went away in the tailings and pyrites. The battery—a 12-head—is situated on the other side of the hill. Communication between the two was established by a tramway some years ago, but the rails were never really used. The battery is sub-

stantially built, more substantially than most of those in the
Territory ; but it is slightly out of repair now. The ripples and
blanket-boxes are designed differently from the ordinary ones, to
the end that the peculiar obstructiveness of the stone might be
overcome, I suppose. For the same purpose Atwood's revolvers
were used, but were not considered effective. Though certain
alterations are to be made in the battery, the Company will have
to be very discreetly managed if it is to pay dividends. The
mundic is as difficult to deal with as excessive iron in copper ore.
The average outlay per month since the Company has had the
mine has been about £250, and there is a good deal of work in
the way of buildings and explorations to show for the expenditure.
In one of the buildings the party, invited by Mr. Devin, drank
success to the Company. The only other mines in the neighbourhood are Dean's and the Terrible—called so because of the terrible
climb you have to do to get to it ; and that is about all that is
known with certainty respecting either.

There was a thunderstorm with a heavy fall of rain in the afternoon, but we pushed through it to the Rum Jungle, about midway
branching off to the west to see Poiett, Mackinnon, & Co.'s coffee
plantation. They have altogether 3,500 acres, and from the time
we entered its western boundary till we left its northern we were
riding through a grandly fertile plain of red-and-chocolate soil,
generally only damp, despite a rainfall, and not boggy. There
was but one exception to this rule. That bog resembled an
agglomeration of wet blacking, and our horses sank in it as
though it had been a quicksand. In every part the land is covered
with long grass, it has thick patches of jungle, and altogether has
more of a tropical appearance about it than any other piece of
scenery we have passed here yet.

At the clearing, which has been made at a most picturesque
spot, we met Mr. Mackinnon, who is acting as manager in the
absence of Mr. Poiett. Work was begun on the 11th of last
December, and already a patch of about four acres of jungle has
been cleared. On it the framework for a capital bungalow
has been erected, several huts and offices have been built,
and two acres have been trenched and closely fenced for
use as a nursery. In this, one bed has been planted for
cinchona, which was just peeping above ground. The seed
was not good, Mr. Mackinnon says, and he expects only 4,000
or 5,000 plants instead of twice as many. The beds have
all been prepared for the reception of Liberian coffee—they
fear the Arabian will not succeed. Mr. Poiett was in Ceylon
arranging for a supply of Tamil labourers, who get 8d. a day
there, and would, he believes, go to the Northern Territory for 2s.

a week more. Mr. Mackinnon assured me that he would have no
difficulty in getting 500 or 1,000 men at that rate ; and he speaks
in the highest terms of the Tamils as workmen. At present six
Chinese, at £1 a week and the privilege of free cartage of rations, are
employed on the plantation, and the manager characterizes them as
lazy and impertinent. The Chinese carpenter gets £3 10s. a week.
The intention is to put 500 acres under coffee next year if possible :
and also to plant cocoa. the indiarubber-tree, and maize, amongst
other things. Three years hence (Mr. Mackinnon thinks) there
will be 500 men employed on the plantation.

After partaking of Mr. Mackinnon's hospitality, and drinking
success to his Company's venture, we went over the clearing, and
saw one of the prettiest sights the Territory has to show. Near the
office, in the middle of the creek, is a dense jungle, made up of
trees unusually tall and stout, with intertwining laces of wiry
creepers making an impassable network between their trunks. At
one point a matted roof is formed in this way, leaving a clear space
of a dozen feet from the ground. Below there lies a cool and limpid
spring like a sheet of glass—so beautifully smooth and transparent.
Looking some feet to its bed you see a slight displacement of its
white sand crust in about a dozen places. Through these the water
bubbles brightly up, and the spring is never less or more than it
was when we saw it. It is a truly beautiful place, and the estate
is a magnificent one. Ere we arrived at the Rum Jungle our
horses were so jaded that they needed a great deal of urging, for the
last week's journey had been particularly hard on them and on their
riders. Nevertheless, the start next day was made at daybreak,
and the sun was only properly showing himself as we passed
through the Finniss country, which we penetrated on the downward
journey whilst a heavy rain fell. It is thickly covered with
granite in various forms, and does not look so inviting for agriculture as it did towards dusk, when the waters partly covered it.
It is more promising for minerals—some of its rocks are really remarkable. The ground closely skirting the bed of the river is
rich enough. About twelve miles from Southport the party
were met by the mail-coach—sent to convey them to the port
should they wish to be relieved from the inconveniences of further
horseback travel. All save the Minister accepted the
pleasant alternative ; but he thought it would be cavalier
treatment of his steed—the long-since historical Gaylad—if he
deserted it, and so he stuck to his saddle the whole journey through,
and came in at the head of the little troop. The arrival at Southport marked the close of 300 miles travel on horses—and
such horses. It is only justice to the party to say that—
from the time when Mr. Bright returned—they all went through

the inconveniences, the slight dangers, and the many discomforts
of the trip with more energy than one would expect, opposing to
obstacles a cheerful good-nature which won the ready assistance
of the residents wherever they went. Especially is this the case
with regard to the Minister, who was ever to the fore, and, in
season and out of season, interviewed sundry bores and far more
numerous intelligent imparters of information. Deputations
were received at all hours almost, and trouble undertaken early
and continued late. The warm welcomings of the people everywhere must not pass unacknowledged. The fact that all the important mining districts have been traversed, and that
information has been collected respecting every point of interest
within them, is greatly due to the willing assistance of the residents. It seemed as though the wet season had been partially
suspended to facilitate the progress of the party, for such fine
weather at such a time was never known there before, it seems.
And so it is not too much to say that the trip through the mining
districts thoroughly accomplished what it was intended to do.
Whether the Professor had opportunities of getting sufficient information for an exhaustive geological report is a question
which admits of no discussion. No scientist in the world, were
he strong as Hercules, and had he all the eyes of Argus,
could do impossibilities. Necessarily, therefore, the Professor's
investigations were comparatively limited ; but it is only due to
him to say that he made the most of the time at his disposal.
Both in botanical and natural history and geological researches he
was indefatigable, even when suffering severely from the fatigue of
a wearisome journey. Personally I had exceptional facilities
for collecting information ; and, that it might be perfectly trustworthy, I took some pains to check from different quarters any
relation of reported facts respecting which there was any possibility of doubt. I have indeed erred by intent rather on the side
of under-tinting than over-colouring ; and in closing this part
of the narrative of the trip, I can only repeat generally that
the country abounds in minerals, the extent of which has to be
proved by trial which has never yet been applied, or where
slightly used, with results perfectly satisfactory ; that a comparatively small proportion only is fit for cultivation ; and that
almost all of it is good for grazing. There are many
suggestions which will be made when this record shall
have concluded. In the meantime, I may give, as the result of
very careful enquiries, the opinion that in the whole of the mining
districts including storekeepers and Government officers, there are
scarcely 250 Europeans. The Chinese I estimate at 2,200. There
is great difficulty in arriving at an absolutely exact computation of

their numerical strength, because they are scattered over so large an area, but I interviewed the leading Chinese merchants and gold-buyers in every place I came to, and they gave me as approximately accurate the total I have given—a total verified by my own observation. I cannot too strongly impress upon the reader that there has, as a matter of fact, been positively no sustained systematic attempt to develop any part of the mineral country. There are all over the Territory only nine batteries, and all are more or less defective. I have seen all of them, and at the time of my visit only three were working, or had been for some time. It is not too much to say that eight-ninths of these crushers lose at least one-third of the gold, and that fact should be remembered in the computation of the yield the stone they treat returns. The main drawbacks to the prosperity of the mining industry will have a reference hereafter. At present I will only incidentally refer to the operation of the swindles—that is their name up here—of some years ago. To them primarily is traceable the ill-savour of mining enterprise here ever since. In several cases Companies were formed with fluctuating share-lists which did no work at all. Land was pegged out anywhere, leases were applied for, and the ventures sold when not a single prospect had been taken. A well known and "straight" mining manager in one of the principal centres here assures me that years ago he received no fewer than four telegrams in one day from brokers in Adelaide to this effect :— " Peg out claim anywhere. We'll float it." What but a crash could come of this? A crash did come, and I direct attention to the facts now, that a repetition of anything so disgraceful and so utterly inimical to the best interests of our grand northern estate may be avoided. I can see—any enquiring visitor can see—that the dulness and the apathy in the Territory, and the disgust outside respecting the Territory, were all born of this floating and bursting of bubbles in the days gone by. For legitimate enterprises, and for well-directed speculation, there is no better field than the Northern Territory presents, and, granted a railway, I warrant that our reviving white elephant will soon develop into one of the most useful animals any colony could wish to be blessed with.

With a grateful acknowledgement of the courteous assistance of the Minister, I resume my narrative, merely adding, in justice to Inspector Foelsche, Mr. Lindsay, and Mr. Knight, that the arrangements for the trip were better than they could under the circum stances have been expected to be, and for their effective carrying out a word of thanks is due to Messrs. McDonald and Poelnitz, the police officers in charge of the assistants.

CHAPTER VII.—AROUND PALMERSTON.

TO the three hundred miles of horseback riding which the trip
through the mining districts involved should be added fifty-
two miles of sea travel to and fro between Southport and
Palmerston. When we arrived at Palmerston we found that
the weather outside had been very rough, and that then
the harbour, perfectly sheltered as it is, was agitated by some
respectable rollers. The Agnes, a cable steamer of about 1,000
tons, lay in the harbour, unable to proceed with her work, and the
idea of putting out to sea on the morrow—at such a season—in
even the largest available steamer in Port Darwin was ridiculed.
The next day broke stormily, with an inch of rain between daybreak and breakfast time, with an atmosphere really cold, and
with wind constantly chopping about, and a sea vexatiously shifty.
We were to have started on our trip to the Daly at 11 in the
morning, but under the circumstances it would have been folly to
have carried out that intention. So 10 a.m. next day was fixed
upon. At that hour on the morning of Thursday, March 15,
therefore, we found ourselves on board the 29-ton steamer Maggie,
about as suitable for a 300-miles sea-trip as a popgun would be
for shooting an alligator. There were ten passengers besides the
crew, and there was no room for a single one below deck. Above,
the only seeming protection from the weather was a canvas roof,
but the event proved that it served but to keep off a little sun and
to direct the water it collected down the backs of those it
hypocritically seemed to shelter. The deck, moreover, was
hampered with packages; the aft cabin—that in polite parlance,
in *fact* the hole near the rudder—exhaled a frightful smell of bilge-
water, the hold amidships emulated it, and the fore-cabin beat
easily the both together. The funnel sent with diabolical
ingenuity the sooty smoke full in the passengers' faces, and it had
a valuable ally in the cook's galley near the fo'c's'l. Captain
Marsh, the Harbour Master, was in charge of this delectable
steamship, and we crept off with a prodigious fuss and little speed,
the while the flag was dipped from the Government Residence,

and handkerchiefs in bewildering confusion were waved from all the windows within sight. The sun shone in double-power splendour, the sky had put off its wet-season apparel, the wind murmured never so lowly, and the sea had no mischief written on its face. In an hour, however, all was changed. A wind came up first, and every hon. member was soon after enduring the agonies of sea-sickness. Even Mr. Bright, who did not succumb to the *mal-de-mer* all the way from Adelaide hither—even he had to give in. Then the rain came on, and as we reached in four hours the northernmost part (Point Charles), a stiff westerly gale blew dead against us, whilst a mist hung over the water. Thunder rolled and lightning flashed, and slight sea-sickness became severe. The wind then chopped around and round impartially from every quarter, and the little steamer, which nevertheless shipped no water, was three hours making half a mile of headway. The decks were all awash with rain, and there was scarcely a man on board who was not completely through. As the gale freshened by the time we had reached our fourteenth mile—five hours after starting—even Captain Marsh's cheery face became overcast, and he counselled a return. The Minister alone of all his party objected, but he would not accept the responsibility of continuing the journey against nautical advice, and so the expedition ingloriously failed. Personally I do not think a catastrophe to the ship would have happened had she gone on, but it was certainly not unwise in Captain Marsh to remember that discretion is the better part of valour. We arrived at port again at 8 o'clock, and shortly afterwards, though then the habour looked calm enough, a high wind rose, so cold became the atmosphere that sleepers were fain to wrap themselves in blankets, even though the wind raged violently. Had the party been out in such weather and escaped a fatal accident each would hereafter have been able to boast of a doleful experience on the 15th of March, this year of grace, in our northern seas.

The same evening a council was held to determine upon future movements. The consideration that the weather outside would be unsettled at this season for some weeks, and that there was in the whole place no better or safer craft than that in which they had tempted Providence that day, produced the determination not to do the Daly at all. The programme drawn up included one day's official business in the departments by the Minister; a couple of days of general visits to institutions, and of enquiries; a visit to Delissaville and the other plantations on Cox's Peninsula; a Chinese banquet; an European ditto; and then return by the Menmuir. On Friday—a very unpleasant day—the Gardens were visited, and in the evening a mild sort of party was given in the

Minister's honour at the Residence ; and on Saturday—another
miserably wet day—nothing of importance was done, if I except a
visit to the Chinese quarter of the town.   At half-past 6 on Monday morning a start was made in the little steamer for Delissaville.
This well-known plantation is on Cox's or Douglas's Peninsula,
about eleven miles north-west of Port Darwin, and is approached
through Wood's Inlet, narrowing in places to less than a chain in
width, with the tide rushing past like a whirlpool, and a big one at
that.   The scenery by the way is mostly uninteresting.   Ere the
inlet is entered there are some pretty stretches of beach and reaches
formed within the grand harbour of Port Darwin, and the most
prominent landmark Talc Head, called so because of the abundance
of talc upon it.   In the inlet itself mangroves, with barnacles and
small oysters clinging to their roots, rise out of the water on either
side, and completely shut out the land beyond.   The steamer
stopped within a mile of our destination, because the master, with
a pardonable exaggeration of the size of his noble vessel, was
afraid the lying aground after the tide had run out would injure
her ; and we had to " boat " the rest of the distance against the
strong current.   The rowing was through a mile of sinuous windings, every foot of the cleared mangroves having been cut down by
Mr. De Lissa and his assistants to secure a passage way to his jetty,
which is 300 feet long, and at the end of which even a moderately
large vessel, watching the tides, could lie.   When we reached this
structure on Monday morning Mr. De Lissa had put everything in
trim for a grand reception ; and after it had been given and
acknowledged right heartily, the Minister, in a buggy drawn by hand-
some Timors, and the rest of the party on horses, were conveyed to
the homestead, two miles further inland, between the two largest
patches of cane, and laid out with an eye to picturesqueness.   The
reception here was in cordiality a duplicate of the first, and feasting
followed fasting very gratefully.   Soon after the fortifying
of the inner man had been completed, the party began their
exploration of the estate, which comprises 10,000 acres — a
grant from the Government of South Australia to the De Lissa
Sugar Plantation Company, of Adelaide.   A detailed description
of the country would be wearying ; be it sufficient to say that the
part of the selection we inspected contained some capital
patches of deep black soil, and some indifferent ones.   The latter
are due to the presence of strong runs of ironstone, the planter's
objection to which is that it will not decompose like most other
stones.   Mr. Owston, the Daly planter, viewed this ground before
Mr. De Lissa inspected it, and he condemned it for sugar-growing
principally on that account.   The land is intersected by two
deep, ever-running streams of crystal-clear and pure water ; one

of them rushes by about a hundred yards from the houses, and
there on a clear night you can hear the pleasant plashing of one
of the most beautiful cascades we have seen in the Northern
Territory. Here grows a splendid piece of jungle, with paper
bark as the staple. There are several sturdy varieties of the ficus
jostling the "lawyer's cane"—so denominated because of a habit it
has of fastening its thorns in all passers. *Why* so denominated I cannot say. Then there is the native india-rubber or milk-
tree, which in its season is clouded with flowers and redolent of
sweet scents. The endless screw-pine raises its head pretty high
here, and in some cases the trunks are covered with green
moss. The leaves of a similar tree are used in the Mauritius for
making into sugarbags, and Mr. De Lissa intends to utilize
them similarly here. About half a mile beyond this gully is
another beautiful one between two high ironstone ridges. Fern-
clad it is, but its chief glory is a grand native banyan-tree, with a
perfect maze of roots laid bare against a huge perpendicular shelf
of rock. In the interstices grow clinging plants and ferns, and
the effect, with the dripping of the water, is very pretty. So
much from the ornamental point of view. Coming to the cane
plantations, the mill, and the different quarters for the men,
which surround the house occupied by Mr. De Lissa, his assistant,
Mr. Levi, the overseer, and the sugar-boiler and engineer, we note
with surprise the vast work done in the very short time
—about eighteen months—since operations were begun on the
new land. It needed great determination, and strong hands and
willing ones, to accomplish what has been effected. Altogether
there are 200 acres of cane (obtained from the Government
Gardens at Fannie Bay), and there are 50 acres of maize. Last
year the white ants wrought great damage to the sugary reeds,
but now they have apparently been almost overcome. The
remedy used was lime, burnt from shells brought from the
adjacent harbour-sides, and the canes were each passed through
a solution of carbolic acid before they were planted. Mr.
De Lissa contends that the carbolic treatment retards the
growth of the plant. However that may be in practice, the
remedial measures seem to have been effectual, for excepting in
one place we could not detect the presence of the omnivorous
ants. That floods may not injure the canes each is planted in a
little knoll, over which the water passes, and drains off as soon as
the rain has fallen. This in a place where a week before seven
inches fell in five days is a great consideration. The canes
throughout are not big or tall, but they look healthy. There is no
comparison between their appearance and that of those in the
Government Gardens, but it as well to remember that the latter

sprang from rattoons, and the former were only cancheads, and unsatisfactory besides, Mr. De Lissa says. He is hopeful that the canes will spring up rapidly now towards the end of the wet season, and he is so sanguine of success at last that he is going to fight against disheartenment even if he have not a big or average crop this year. The different plantations are separated by roads; in fact, roads are laid down on a definite plan, and the ironstone in places is so level-topped that the track goes over it without the least preparation.

We did not go beyond the limits of the three miles of fencing on the estate ; but we saw all that has been done in the way of development and improvement, and the verdict unanimously was that the improvements are as perfect as is compatible with other considerations. The fifteen Chinamen working on the estate at £1 a week have their own galvanized iron quarters, and the blacks —the Port Essington tribes—who do the weeding and such like, have theirs on the opposite side of the creek. These blacks, who have their lubras with them, are fed and housed, but do not receive a stated wage. They look and speak like intelligent fellows, and work as such in various parts of the estate. Mr. De Lissa will allow no communication between them and the tribes round Palmerston. Some of them essayed to break through the ban a few months ago, but Mr. De Lissa gave them such a fright, by means of rockets and such like, while not injuring them, that they have not tried to do so since. So now, whenever he goes to Palmerston, he distributes a bag of flour and some trifles amongst them ; and if they hint at going over to their old ground, frowns upon them unutterably, frightening them effectually. Mr. De Lissa puts it that health is the first consideration in the Northern Territory climate, and so he has made provision for the bathing of every man under his charge. Then—though the sparkling creek is so near—every house has its well, in which the water is beautifully cool and fresh. Forethought is evidenced in the stacking instead of burning the wood cut down in clearing. The mill has many months' supply already. Another saving is effected by the mowing and chaffing of the native grasses for hay, and wherever the long grass has been removed, a soft, succulent, and shorter has sprung up in its place. The working cost is £60 a week, and the expense so far nearly £16,000. At noon the mill whistle sounded, and the party were invited to witness experiments with the machinery and to inspect the building. In one of the vats there were a few gallons of a strange-looking, dirty, treacly liquid. After watching the operations of the other machinery, therefore, they witnessed the placing of this disagreeable-looking mixture into the "self-balancing centrifugal" which is used for the drying of the sugar. This centrifugal revolved at the rate of 2,000 a minute, and in five minutes a good, wholesome, well-granulated white table sugar was taken out, under the direction of Mr. Sachsie, who will henceforth be known as the first manufacturer of sugar in South Australia. Mr. Sachsie, by-the-way, has obtained a patent for an ingenious arrangement in connection with the machinery, and Mr. De Lissa has his own patents for other parts.

By the machinery the old blood process and animal charcoal are dispensed with as necessary adjuncts in the manufacture of sugar. Magnesia takes their place, and as the De Lissa Mill is only the precursor of scores in the Territory, particularly as it is the first and only one ever erected in the colony, I had better describe the whole mill and its immediate surroundings. Advantage has been taken of a good position on the hill, where stands on the one hand the homestead, and on the other the beautiful ever-running creek before described, to excavate a deep cutting, so that the sugar sap might be forced from one part of the building to the other by gravitation instead of by pumping. The buildings are of paperbark wood, grown on the estate, the roof and sides being of galvanized iron. The main structure is 100 feet by 64 feet, and the other 70 feet by 30 feet, and there are besides boiler-sheds and a sugar store. Entering the building you find yourself in a large smithy and workshop, containing a bewildering array of appliances of all kinds adapted for all sorts of work. Leaving that you approach the machinery proper, which may best be described as it was in operation the day we visited it. The canes are first passed through a powerful mill composed of three horizontal rollers geared up to give great pressure. These rollers, driven by a 16-horsepower engine, are warranted to crush at the least 60 tons of canes a day, and at the most 90; and a smaller duplicate opposite (provided for use in case of accident to the larger one) is equal to 40 tons in the same time. As the canes pass through the mill they give out their juice into a receiver below, while the crushed fibrous mass is expelled on the opposite side, whence it is carted away. It is valuable for manure and fuel, and it can be manufactured into paper fibre. From the receiver an inclined canal takes the juice to plate-iron clarifiers, of which there are four, each containing copper coils, through which steam passes, and it boils the surrounding juice with ordinary aids. The processes conducted here are usually a series of experiments or tests in chemistry. The juice, as it goes through the mill, is of course charged with all kinds of dross—waxy and albuminous particularly, and others generally. This has to be got rid of, and to Mr. A. Sachsie is entrusted the task of quitting them. To effect clarification he uses calcined magnesia (to seperate the drossy admixtures) and sul-

phurous acid—both processes the invention and patents of Mr.
De Lissa. From the clarifiers the juice is conducted by a lead
conduit to the first of a series of separate compartment-pans,
technically known as the battery. These are wrought iron, and all
together look not unlike a huge cooking-range. Under each a fierce
heat is brought to bear by means of an arrangement of flues and a
large oven with an independent chimney of sixty feet high. Here
a thorough cleaning is given to the juice, and it is concentrated to
a density of about sixteen. It is then let off into two large
receivers, also provided with copper coils. It is here boiled again
by steam until it is absolutely rid of dirt and all other extraneous
matter. This is the last cleaning it gets. It is now lifted by a
rotary pump, driven by shafting from the main engine, through
the roof and into the adjacent building, known as the crystallizing-
room or drying-room, and deposited in four large receivers, where
it remains until it is drawn off to be finished—" cooked," they say
technically.

In this operation two large copper finishing-pans are brought
into use. A noticeable feature in these pans is that they boil by the
mechanical action of compressed air, supplied by two rotary blowers
worked by independent engines. The air is turned on below the
surface of liquor in the pan, rushing through longitudinal tubes
perforated especially. The moment the air is turned on a
mechanical ebullition is produced the while the liquor boils, and
the temperature can be regulated by means of cocks and piping
placed, as well as the steam coils, in the pan. These pans are the
patent of J. W. Sutton & Co., of Brisbane, to whom the specifi-
cation was sold by its creator (Mr. De Lissa). Mr. Sachsie is an
inventor as well as Mr. De Lissa, and what theoretically ought to
be a great saving should be effected in this department when it is
in full work by the use of Sachsie's Patent Steam Economist, by
means of which all exhaust steam from the engines is collected
into a large cast-iron receiver, and used over again. Any overplus
which may accumulate in the chamber above a certain pressure,
regulated according to requirements, escapes of its own accord.
But we left the cooking sugar-juice in the pans. As soon as it is
granulated it is drawn thence by slide valves and a wooden conduit
into the coolers, which supply space for 30,000 gallons. Let us
hope it will all be needed. In these coolers of course it undergoes
a more perfect granulation as its temperature decreases. It
generally remains here about two days, but sometimes only an hour
or two. In any case it is dug out by spades and conveyed in tubs
(looking the while like a mixture of dirty sand and dirtier treacle)
into two large, over-driven self-balancing centrifugals. These are
really metal baskets hanging on spindles which revolve at the rate

of 2,000 a minute. The baskets are of finely-perforated copper, and the sugar when placed in them is by centrifugal force separated from its liquorous body. Two or three minutes' revolution leaves neatly packed over the perforations, in a perfectly dry state, the sugar as we set it on our tea-tables. I should have mentioned that outside of the baskets are large cast-iron bombproof cases, which, besides acting as protectors to the basket, receive the syrup which is forced from the sugar by the centrifugal action. This syrup runs off into a small wooden conduit, which conducts it to plate-iron tanks. Thence a small rotary pump conveys it once more to the finishing pans where it is reboiled and tested as before. The product is "seconds" sugar. Then the syrup it leaves goes through the same ordeal until no more crystals can be got. Then, the crushing complete, the sugar is put in wooden bins to air, and in due time sent off to market. The syrup or molasses is generally turned into rum, but it will not be here, as there is no machinery for the work and no wish to have it. So it is regarded as the waste product of the factory, and will be used as a fodder for cattle—it fattens very rapidly—mixed with a slight proportion of cracked corn. Or it will be once more boiled, and filtrated and refined, going to market as " Golden Syrup," or less esteemed treacle.

It should be mentioned that there is in connection with the mill a large multitubular boiler with a 50-feet chimney (Mr. De Lissa has a weakness for imposing chimneys.) The masonwork—it is very, very solid—is composed of anthill, mixed with the ironstone found far too plentifully, I fear, about the place. The resultant mass dried is as compact as the United Kingdom and as hard as the heart of an ordinary Northern Territory digger. (Pharaoh has dropped out of the running up here.) All the machinery has foundations of this mixture seven feet thick, and also of heavy bed-logs of paper-bark, some two feet square and 18 feet long in the straight—about the biggest timber in the Territory. The whole of the structure cost, in round numbers, £10,000, and it has been erected in advance of the crop in the hope that through it the Company may be able to secure the £5,000 bonus offered by the Government for the manufacture of the first 500 tons of sugar grown in the Northern Territory. As to the little bag of sugar manu-factured in our presence, it should be explained that it came from ten tons of cane from Government Gardens, crushed in the mill towards the end of last year, but giving so little juice that there was not sufficient to cover the coils of the pans. Some of it, how-ever, splashed over them, and became a little more concentrated than the rest. This was set in a cooling-place till the day of the Parliamentary visit. The rest your readers know, and I should like to emphasize my opinion that, whether Mr. De Lissa has good

ground or whether he has not, his methods of work are very praise-
worthy. In a short time he has performed a task almost Herculean,
and every well-wisher of the Northern Territory will join me in
the hope that he may soon realize his expectation of three tons of
sugar an acre—of sugar worth £30 per ton in the southern
markets. In the evening our kindly and genial host provided
quite a banquet, and the only want which he had to bring forward
was a request that the time for the payment of the bonus for the
first sugar might be extended. That will probably be granted.
Then the evening was spent in a semi-formal, half-informal style.
There were speeches and toasting; the health of the host was
drunk with warmth, and many appreciative things were said of
him, and properly replied to. And so passed the best of the night.
The party steamed back again to Palmerston early on Tuesday
morning, March 21, and devoted the rest of the day and night to
formal enjoyment, including a Chinese and an English banquet—
the latter discreditable to some festive spirits amongst the atten-
dants. At 10 o'clock on Wednesday they started by the Mennmir
amidst the cheers of the assembled residents.

I remained some weeks after the party left, and thus had
another opportunity of visiting the Peninsula. To make the description as connected as possible I finish off the record of the
journeying thither in this chapter. About two and a half miles
away from Delissaville is Mr. G. T. Bean's Adelaide Plantation
Company's 5,000 acres of ground. Mr. Bean returned to Adelaide
about a month ago ; whilst he was here he managed by assistance
from Mr. De Lissa to get twenty acres planted with caneheads from
the Government Gardens, besides erecting quarters and outhouses.
There are the plantation overseer and his assistants and six Chinamen now on the plantation, which should succeed if good and well-
watered soil could ensure success. This is the only one of the
70,000 acres of land, to which the special Act applies, which has
begun to follow the example of Delissaville. The rest has never
been touched. Of the land under cultivation on the Peninsula
the most developed is that of Messrs. Ericson & Cloppenborg, who
are the pioneer planters, and whose place is on West Point. I
thought it well to accept their invitation to go to see what they
had done. · I went. The visitors included Mr. J. G. Knight, S.M.,
and Mr. Harrison, J.P. It may be mentioned, as showing the
uncertainty of the weather here, that though West Point is only
seven miles at the furthest from Palmerston, it took us five hours
of sailing to get there, for wind and tide were opposed to us, and
we had to struggle against sudden squalls, which knock the water
in bumpy heaps in five minutes. There are no jetties at West
Point yet, and so we had to run aground and mount blackfellows'

shoulders in order to get dryshod to land. The estate fronts one
of the very rare stretches of beautiful beach which set off the
mangrove edges of the harbour—of beach hard, dry, and pebbly,
running down to the sea from a slanting solid wall of curious
natural masonry. The proprietors have quite a little mansion
facing the entrance to the outer harbour, in a situation less
picturesque than comfortable, and not so much elevated as
healthful—a place with actual gables and arched windows,
and other of the fripperies of fashionable architecture. The
inside is gorgeous with imitation rainbows; and there are
most curious devices in furniture and fittings, some of the
latter from the wreck of the Brisbane—a wreck which was
quite a godsend to the folk thereabout. You meet with " Brisbane" relics everywhere. I need not repeat the information I
have already given about the plantation itself, which extends over
320 acres. The 56 acres of maize look remarkably satisfactory.
The cobs filled well in all cases, though unfortunately too many of
them had the fair seeming without much to back it. Their
hearts had gone to caterpillars, that seem to have had so much
fondness for maize that they contemned any other thing growing
on the plantation. To their efforts was due the fact that
the crop would probably not give more than about 15 bushels per
acre. The five acres of sugarcane do not look particularly well.
The plants are healthy enough, but they are stunted, and
they have not made so much cane as they ought to have made.
They were, however, when we saw them, better-looking than those
at Delissaville when we saw *them*—but there was a fortnight
between. In both cases there was an undue proportion of misses,
put down to the delays in the transfer of the cane-heads from the
Government Garden, to the lateness of planting, to the unusual
dryness of the wet season, and in Messrs. Ericson and Cloppenborg's case, to inattention to the plant whilst it was growing
up to lately. The canes looked so badly, they thought attentions
would be thrown away upon them. The outlook for this year's
sugarcane crop is not bright, to put it negatively. There is just
a chance that the season may be later than usual, and more
propitious towards its latter end. If so, there need be little
to complain of under the circumstances. For any land to yield
sugar properly it must be treated as land in established sugar
countries is. That in the Northern Territory will never have had
a fair trial till the planters use cane-heads from their own nurse-
ries, and eventually, may be, grow from the rattoons. No qualification is needed in writing of the West Point rice crop. The
cultivator threw in anyhow a few handfuls of rice and seemingly
never gave it another thought. When we visited him he had a

grand area—the heads big, healthy, and bursting with plump grain ; the stalks and leaves a hardy, cheerful green. The soil on which it grew had not any special points about it ; it was a fairly deep mixture of beach sand and black mould. Wherever we saw rice growing in the Territory we saw it flourishing ; and one leading gentleman in Palmerston was so impressed with the important industry the cultivation of this useful cereal would become ; impressed also with the fact that the rice planter would work with a protective duty on his side, and that the cost of production is a mere bagatelle, that he next day arranged for the planting at the proper time of a hundred acres or so bordering another part of the harbour as an experiment. Ericson & Coppenborg were trying pigs too. They had had some hundreds, and their first attempts at bacon curing, though made in the hottest weather, had been successful. One of the firmly held beliefs was that bacon could not be cured in such a climate. Their numerous poultry were plump as regulation cherubs, and found ready sale at high prices amongst the China- men on the other side, besides keeping the land practically free from white ants. Peanuts and sorghum flourished, and of melons and pumpkins they produced 200 tons a year. They professed to have good building stone and brick-clay on their land—and that, under the cir- cumstances of Palmerston, is a valuable consideration ; and, climax of good fortune, the partners are going to have a sugar mill erected for them at the point. Altogether they have what in commercial circles is known as "a very soft thing." But they have bought it dearly by pioneering midst discouragements and muscle-wrench and sweat. Whether there should be, as nautical men suggest, an efficient beacon or light on West Point, which marks-in the entrance to the outer harbour, to guide mariners, the Marine Board may profitably consider when the Reefs Railway Bill shall have been passed.

Not far from Ericson & Coppenborg's, Messrs. Harriss & Head have another half-mile block. Maize is their staple, but they are trying cotton this year. Near to them is Mr. Vangemann, with another half-mile, who is growing two acres of tobacco, but is greatly troubled with caterpillars, as indeed are nearly all the settlers here. They get into the maize-cobs and work mischief. Alto- gether some good experimental work is being done on this side the harbour.

Subsequently, kindly piloted by Mr. Surveyor Lindsay, I rode through country to Lee Point—the headland which helps Point Fright to enclose Shoal Bay—and back some distance along the coast, availing myself of the opportunity to examine the Casuarinas, which Palmerstonians lay great store by as their principal watering-place when they shall become citizens in truth as well as by courtesy. Speculators meanwhile have bought up the land. There is nothing especially noteworthy in the ride thither from Palmerston. For the first three and a half miles you follow what must be the course of the railway—along the telegraph line almost. The ground is fairly high and very firm, sprinkled with ironstone. Railway sleepers would be as stable on it as the rails usually are on them. You branch off the line, and go two and a half miles through good agricultural country pretty heavily timbered, but almost free from undergrowth; and then you come to Rapid Creek, which rushes swiftly along its bed during the wet season, but at other times is dry. Its waters are clear as crystal. Thence to the Casuarinas the bridle track winds through more good agricultural country, some hundreds of acres of which was fenced and settled upon as a plantation years ago, but abandoned before any trial was made of it. It is really disheartening to think that a vigorous plantation will not spring up spontaneously, as Topsy believed she did. Such of the fences of this estate as are not burnt are rotten; and the charred uprights of the plantation-house help them in their monumental chronicling of folly.

The Casuarinas is a romantic place. It was named after the Casuarina-tree—averaging about fifty feet in height, and graceful-looking, with a leaf like a pine drooping weeping-willow fashion, a seed or cone like a small sheoak apple, and wood like the sheoak itself. Before you get to the Casuarinas you have to pass the Diphthong Caves, which are hardly worth the name of cave at all. Their principal characteristic geologically is the soft beautifully-mottled soapstone, or such like, of which their little arches are composed, and otherwise the multitude of shellfish which doth inhabit them. Amongst these fish are some very pretty and rather rare kinds, which have aforetime been well described by an old former Palmerstonian and conchologist—Mr. W. T. Bednall—of whom it is currently reported here that he was so enthusiastic in his hobby that he has been known to lie hatless at full length on the scorching sand for hours at a stretch, examining the points of some new discovery in his favourite science.

The tale goes that a friend went out with him one day for a walk. Mr. Bednall abruptly fell full-length on the beach behaving in a most mysterious fashion. The friend strolled away by himself and coming back two hours afterwards found the conchologist in precisely the same position gazing intently at a shell.

"What *is* the matter?" was the query.

"*Don't* interrupt me!" pleaded Mr. Bednall. "I—I—really believe this is a new kind of shell, I—I'll see!" The friend went home at once.

There are marketable sponges here, there is beautiful mushroom-shaped coral not far off, and there are full-powered mosquitos, too. Here run horses—born and bred in the country from Sir T. Elder's stock—reared promiscuously, and yet upstanding, shapely, active, and spirited, with proudly arching necks, and all the rest of the Arab "points." They furnish satisfactory negatives to the assertion that horses bred north of the 13th degree of latitude are of no account.

The land is very similar to that at West Point near to the beach. I suppose it will never be tried for agriculture of any kind. Beyond, in the jungle, it may fairly be, for it is moderately good generally, with patches as to which the qualification is not needed. In one of these there is an enormous native banyan tree, 80 feet high in places, and covering with its numerous twisted ramifying roots 2,000 square yards. A sight well worth seeing, this tree. All round in the jungle the natives had been tapping various trunks for honey, which here is pretty plentiful. Of trees none were seen uncommon to the other jungles, excepting, maybe, the sensitive plants which close up their leaves immediately they are touched. With one kind you need only to stamp upon the surrounding ground to make them retire within themselves. Facetious people call them members of Parliament. I don't know why. The only animals of any note that roam the jungle are kangaroos—stunted and unhappy-looking. The biggest of them is not larger than the average farther south.

Excepting the Government Gardens, I have given descriptions of all the plantations in the Northern Territory. This is a fitting time for a note or two about plantation prospects. First of all let me say that though there has been, and palpably is still, shep-herding of plantation grounds for other than plantation purposes, there has been a set-off of honest work and enterprise in promoting this important industry. And though not more than £25,000 has been spent upon it, all through the country there are evidences of that sum being considerably increased. On the Adelaide River alone 70,800 acres are protected by special survey applications (under the 7s. 6d. purchase clause) for sugar-growing and similar work, and if all this is devoted to its legitimate purposes, thousands of men must be employed upon it. Messrs. Fisher and Lyons have applied for survey of 21,000 acres in the Hundred of Bagot, north of Palmerston. On Douglas Peninsula, besides the 75,000 acres occupied under the Sugar Grant Act, 1,500 acres have been chosen as subjects for survey applications, so that nearly all the good land on the Peninsula has virtually gone from the Government. In the Hundred of Ayers 3,000 acres are held for plantation purposes; and near the coffee plantation at Rum

Jungle, over a wide radius, to all the land the same remark applies, as it does also to a great deal of that surrounding the harbour, particularly near Southport, so that the recent decision of the Government to stop awhile all sales of land will not affect the progress of the plantation industry. Within nine miles of Palmerston a block of 1,100 acres is to be broken up and planted with sugarcanes forthwith, and within a year a mill is to be erected on it. Coffee and spices, indigo, cinchona, opium (by Chinese), and many other tropical products are to be tried—fairly, let us hope—and if these ventures are economically managed by experienced men with capital to back them, there cannot be on the part of any one who has closely examined the country and witnessed its wonderful productiveness the slightest misgiving as to the result. The purely experimental work has been already done with indifferent soil in the Government Gardens. The planters now can avail themselves of certain knowledge where two years ago all was uncertainty. It has been proved not only that the canes will grow, but that they yield a sugar which would show to advantage placed side by side with samples from the principal sugar-manufacturing countries in the world. Outside the Gardens there has been as yet absolutely no fair trial of sugar-growing. The only trial, then, has been thoroughly successful. The logical conclusion is that the success will be general as experiments multiply. If our own capitalists do not accept to their own advantage the commercial suggestiveness of that conclusion, they will find in distant places other men who will ; they will discover that foreign money will do what they might much more easily have done. The Northern Territory will not for long be the *terra incognita* it has been. The newspapers are spreading its fame throughout the world, and consular authorities and Government officials at Palmerston are frequently addressed from America, China, Mauritius, and other distant parts by men of capital and practical experience in plantation work, and asked for precise information about a place they have seen referred to in papers in the various countries where they live. These enquiries have been answered and in some cases responses have come— generally to the effect that the questioners were satisfied with the prospects, and prepared, when cheaper labour should be obtainable, to invest their money here. That labour steps are being taken to supply, the Indian Coolie Immigration Act having already passed the Assembly. But if it should not become law even now, if the Government do not obtain labour from India, intelligent and shrewd Chinese capitalists will get it from China. They are closely watching the Government now. They have told me so on all sides, and some of them have gone to work already. There is a recognised Chinese labour agent in Palmerston, and

European planters have transactions with him. Already Chinese have invested in plantation land, for several European names upon the land list stand for Chinamen, and the latter have themselves avowed (as I before have noted) to the Minister their intention of establishing plantations. By way of killing two birds with one stone—to give an idea of what the greatly misunderstood position of the Java planters really is, and to show that their thoughts are turned towards our land—I copied a letter which Mr. V. L. Solomon, the Dutch Consul, has received from a planter at Banjoemaas, on that island, and which he courteously placed at my disposal. The writer began by saying that his attention had been directed to the Territory by an article in the local paper on its capabilities. He says, then, in effect, that if the article be true he will better himself by changing places, and he explains his position thus :— " The cultivation of the sugarcane has always been through the intermedium of the Government. The planters pay them a certain amount per year per acre of the ground on which cane is grown, and the natives are ordered to do all that is needful for the prosperous growing of the cane under the supervision of the planters. The natives are paid by the Government certain moneys for the lease of their land and their labour in the cultivation of the cane. The result of the whole operation was a net surplus of some £600,000 for the Treasury. In the year 1870, however, a law was passed to the effect that, to begin in 1878, the Government would gradually diminish the acreage to be cultivated through its intermedium at the rate of one thirteenth of the whole, with the object of terminating all Government assistance by the year 1890. The action of the Government is undoubtedly a right one, but the consequence for all sugar making concerns will be higher rates to pay for getting land and labour and consequently smaller profits, while some planters may be obliged to liquidate altogether." Incidentally he gives a few particulars about the yield of sugar in the Java plantations. It will be sufficient to reproduce the information that last year the 700 acres he holds produced from 1,940 to 2,420 tons of good sugar. Last season the total was 2,540. Striking a safe average, this is three tons an acre. Allowing the same conditions in the Northern Territory, but a ton less to the yield, and valuing sugar at £20 in southern markets, and leaving out of the question treacle and rum, and the many articles of which it forms the base, a 5,000-acre plantation will give its owner £300,000 a year to pay expenses and to fill the profit-treasury with. And surely a two-ton average is low enough to build the calculation on ? A 5,000-acre farm, with wheat at 5s. a bushel and ten bushels to the acre—a high average in South Australia, at least— gives less than £13,000. Now let the reader cogitate.

CHAPTER VIII.—GOVERNMENT PLANTATIONS AND THE RIVER COUNTRY.

THE GOVERNMENT GARDENS.—A TRANSFORMED WILDERNESS.—THE LABOUR AND ITS RESULTS.—CHINESE VERSUS EUROPEANS.—A GOOD WORD FOR THE YELLOW-SKINS.—THE SUGARCANE.—DEFIANCE TO WHITE ANTS.—THEIR DESTROYER.—VALUABLE SUGGESTIONS FROM A PRACTICAL SCIENTIFIC GARDENER.—FORTUNES FOR FUTURE PLANTERS.— A GREAT RICE, INDIGO, AND TOBACCO GROWING COUNTRY.—THE RESIDENT'S LITTLE JOKE.—THE UNVISITED DALY.—ITS SOIL.—THE PALMERSTON PLANTATION COMPANY'S HOLDING.—AN ADVENTURE.— ANOTHER.—DIFFICULTIES OF NAVIGATION.—A RUM RIVER : A NASTY RIVER.—THE ADELAIDE RIVER.—SOUTH VERNON ISLANDS.— A WONDERFUL MIRAGE.—THE LAST OF THE PARLIAMENTARY SHIP.— BLACKFELLOWS AND THEIR SONGS.—NO ARTISTIC PERCEPTION—A DUSKY INTERVIEWER.—ESCAPE CLIFFS.—EASY NAVIGATION OF THE RIVER.—ITS WINDINGS.—PIONEERING DIFFICULTIES.—AN ALLIGATOR TALE. — THE OMNIPRESENT, OMNIVOROUS MOSQUITO. — A PARADISE FOR A NATURALIST.—CONCLUSIONS.

WHATEVER else the reader may have skipped, I would ask him not to fail to make the acquaintance, through this medium, of the Director of the Palmerston Gardens (Mr. Holtze), and to post himself up in the miracle which that gentleman and the soil he cultivates have jointly wrought. The garden is about four miles from Palmerston, verging on Fannie Bay, and it was established by the Government for " the express purpose of raising plants of commercial value and distributing them over the country." There was another garden once nearer Palmerston. The old enclosure is used as the police paddock now. Eight acres of it were cleared, and it subserved principally the highly important purpose of growing vegetables for the officials. Mr. Holtze succeeded its former Director about four and a half years ago, and audaciously hinted that to cultivate cabbage heads was not the greatest ambition of the true gardener, or the most important operation for the country. So he cut down the supplies and put in various tropical trees and other plants, and then suggested that a fairer trial would be given to the average of the Northern Territory soil if a different plantation were obtained. He was allowed to get another, and he selected the present garden—then thick jungle mostly, in the position indicated. He has been blamed for doing so; the land is indifferent, the blame-givers say. And he says so too, but significantly he pleads that his selection is the best for experiments, and that he is now able to tell intending planters—

"You see, gentlemen, I have grown canes so many feet high on this indifferent ground ; on good land you ought to have 25 per cent. more of measurable success."

And he has repeatedly urged that there should be another Govern-

ment garden up-country—at Yam Creek for instance—where there
is good soil. What one failed in might be the other's strong
ground of success. The area of the garden is thirty-two acres, and
it was chosen at a time when crowds of Chinamen came in from
the gold-fields, half-starving, to demand rations from the Government. They were engaged (as on a relief work) at 1s. a day to
clear the selection, and they did it—did it "most horribly," Mr.
Holtze assured me. By the 1st of November, 1879, it was fenced
ready for planting and then trenched twenty inches deep. The
plants from the old garden had to be conveyed to the new; and as a
most rigid economy was enforced, Mr. Holtze, in the early morning
and late night, before and after superintending the operations of the
day, carted them himself, and got nothing more tangible than
thanks for doing so. And now the reader knows the history of
the place, and it is important that he should to appreciate the
sequel, as I describe it as I saw it two years and four months
after its establishment. I ask him to bear particularly in mind
the fact that only so short a time ago the land was thickly covered
with jungle, and that the soil is merely second-rate. To
reach the gardens you branch off from the telegraph line on the
road to Southport, and continue to ride for a mile through high
grass and patches of thick jungle. The position of the place is
picturesque in itself, and it commands a grand view of sea and
sea-beach, backed by distant, hazy, slightly-rising land. The residence of the Director is built upon what are known as the
"Northern Territory Government architectural lines," and the
artistic effect is not wholly bad, whilst the comfort of the person
residing in the erection is fairly promoted. There are huts for
the Chinese gardeners, and there is a place in which a little of the
produce can be stowed, but a seed-house and a few other
structures are badly wanted. Mr. Holtze's salary is only £250
per annum, with quarters. Seventeen Chinamen are employed.
Two of them get 25s. a week each; two more, 20s.; and the rest
only 15s., without rations in each case. Mr. Holtze gives them
an excellent character. He prefers them to Europeans for garden-
work; and he has had both working, and ought to be capable of
forming judgment. He remembers, of course, that men slaving
nine hours a day, wet or shine, for 15s. a week, cannot be expected to be over-energetic, unless they are pretty thoroughly
overseered. Granted that reservation, he says that, whilst they
certainly are "slow," they work well and get through more than
any Europeans he has had ever got through whilst they
were with him. I got this information from Mr. Holtze ere
we had gone into the gardens. When we had done that I had an
opportunity of seeing the men at work, and they put in a great

many strokes to the minute whilst we were looking on. When their master's back is turned towards them, however, they are not, I have since found, too eager to injure themselves by over-exertion, and you really cannot expect them to be, with such pay, when they know Europeans would get £3 at least. The examination of the gardens was the greatest surprise I have had in the Territory. A wilderness a little more than two years ago is now an umbrageous paradise. Acclimatized trees shoot aloft and tower above the native ones outside full twenty times their age; they bear most luscious fruit, in quantity unstinted. Creepers indigenous to a foreign soil planted here have run at once over the place and now grow everywhere in wild profusion; and many herbs well known and grown down South after a year of cultivation here attain an immense size and spread weed-like through the adjacent land. Each area of the garden is only another greater wonder than the last, and if I but cared to wax rhapsodical I certainly could not be justly charged with wanting warrant for it. But I do not choose to go into rhapsody, and so I will condescend to the practical, with some little detail as to the most prominent experiments and their results. First, as to sugar-cane, of which there are eight varieties, spreading over sixteen acres, in the gardens. Mr. Holtze affirms that it is bad this year, because he could not cut the last year's crop till the end of December, having orders to have some sent to Delissaville for crushing—the crushing which proved, through certain blunders, so disastrous. Through this the canes lost six weeks' growth, and Mr. Holtze feels very much annoyed at the result. Yet everybody outside agrees that the canes are grand successes, though they are a trifle less satisfactory in appearance than were those of last year. When I visited the gardens some of them had made six or seven feet of "cane," and that is almost twice as much as any else I have seen here have done. Of course it should be remembered that these grew from the rattoons. Speaking of the growth of sugarcane in the Territory Mr. Holtze says—and it will be of interest to give the result of his experiments—that it should be in by the commencement of October. Mr. De Lissa and others planted in December, and he predicts that their crops will not be one-half so good as they might have been. In sugar-cultivation generally he thinks it would be better for the first year or two to plant only cane-heads, and take the old roots up, and also to observe some rotation of crops, alternating the cane with something else. An idea of the important work the gardens have done for the promotion of the sugar-growing industry of the country may be gained from the fact that 140 tons of cane have gone this season alone from them to the various private plantations and a little to Chinese gardeners. The latter further took, including a few to Europeans, 8,000 banana trees and 13,000 pineapple plants. This year the numbers already were respectively 2,000 and 5,000. All these are given away. The cane is even cut at the expense of the Government, and thus the garden gives no return whatever, except a very intangible one in the shape of fruit for Government officers and fodder for their horses. Mr. Holtze suggests, and I believe the planters do not object to the suggestion —that a small charge should be levied for the cane at least—say a couple of pounds a ton. Then the persons getting it would enjoy a great advantage, which they would not have had they to ship the plants from Queensland, and in the latter case they would not get them in nearly so fresh a state. Besides the planters, many diggers and settlers up country are getting seeds from the gardens. Mr. Holtze gives the carters those of the foreign grasses he has proved to be best adapted to the soil, and gets them to scatter them all over the country in the neighbourhood of their camps. The pine-apples and bananas thrive even better than the sugarcane. I tasted all three—I tasted so many tropical fruits and vegetables on this trip that I believe I could name them each by flavour ten years hence—and I found them all that could be desired. The sugarcane particularly, with its soft, sweet, soppy juice, keenly appeals to one's susceptibilities. It reminds him of the days when he, like the pulpy cane, was in his infancy.

Going through the sugar acreage one naturally wants to know where the white ants have been that the crop should be so healthy. I closely examined each plot, and only in a few cases were there any signs of the ants. Mr. Holtze has a wholesale contempt for them; and when you ask him whether he thinks the little pests will be a considerable factor in the planters' losses you see an indignant man. He opposes to the ants arsenic and potash, and the common so-called remedy of carbolic acid he impeaches with Teutonic warmth as—

"Nonsense. It is all very well for the first time, so long as the smell is there, but when it leaves the ants are coolly walking over the powder and taking it to whitewash their cells with. Now I dilute my arsenic and potash in hot water, and take sugar and flour and make a paste. Whenever I see white ants I make a hole and fill it with a spoonful of the mixture. I never have the least trouble with them. Arsenic is a never-ending poison. The father ant takes it and dies. His sons affectionately eat him, and they die; their mother and sisters devour them, and all give up the ghost, and so destruction goes on for ever."

If this be the true solution of the ant difficulty, it certainly is a very inexpensive one. Four years ago, in the old gardens, he bought a half cwt. of arsenic; half of that he has still. With what has gone he has conquered the ants. Maize is the next principal crop in the garden, and it is looking as well as it can look anywhere, notwithstanding that it is the third crop in a year. Rice simply flourishes, strengthening the evidence I have had throughout, that the Northern Territory will be a great rice-growing country. Only the hill kinds are tried in the gardens, because the ground is too high for the swamp varieties. Cinchona has not been successful. The seeds did not even come up, and Mr. Holtze maintains that the climate is too hot for it—

"It is all very well to say that it thrives in Ceylon, but there are high mountains there. We haven't got those mountains."

On Messrs. Poiett & Mackinnon's plantation at Rum Jungle, however, the seeds have germinated, and the little plants look healthy enough. But then the climate is different and the soil is better. Dr. Schomburgk wrote years ago that cinchona should be successful there. Coffee does not do well in the gardens. The prime cause is said to be the fact of its being planted so near the sea. The Arabica is not unhealthy-looking above ground, but it has no root. The Liberian looks sturdy, and Mr. Holtze is confident that it will succeed on the plantations. It needs great care and attention, however. Tea and several spices have failed. They have been tried fairly, and though they make plenty of leaves they have no root. Cocoa is moderately successful. Tobacco has not been so satisfactory as it was believed it would be. The plants I saw were very young, and I could not judge of them, but my conductor said that he has grown leaves 27 inches long by 18 inches wide, and that, I should think, is satisfactory enough. But he fears otherwise—says the soil is not fit for tobacco. He suggests, however, that in the more favoured parts of the country 100 acres in a crop of tobacco alternating with rice every year would pay well. One of the best things in the gardens is the arrowroot, which actually overruns the place, growing in grand perfection weedlike. Mr. Holtze ground some of the roots with a nutmeg grater, and carried a few pounds of the powder he got in this way to the storekeepers for an opinion as to its quality, without letting them know whence he got it. They told him it was superior to any they had in stock. He took the roots from a fair average area of the crop, so that he might make a calculation as to the probable yield if all were ground. He is satisfied, as a result of that calculation, that even the indifferently good soil in the gardens will yield at least 25 cwt. of the finest arrowroot per acre. Though cotton grows well there was a question in my guide's mind as to whether it will pay while labour is so dear. He submits, however, a proposition which he conceives to be perfectly reasonable : that though he would not advise any one under present conditions to start cotton-growing, yet if the Government want a cotton plantation, and will give him the use of 10,000 acres of land, he will try for five years to establish one. If he be successful then he will pay 7s. 6d. an acre ; if not, he will yield possession again to the Government. There are two sides to that proposal, however. Among the grand successes in the garden is the cultivation of indigo, information concerning which Major Fergusson received special instructions to obtain whilst he was visiting India. The plant has run from the gardens into the surrounding scrub and jungle, and you see the bright blue flower and the pretty dappered leaves on all hands. It overruns the gardens too, and indeed it seems as though it never enjoyed its most congenial climatic influences till it got them here. In India its average height, if one may believe the books, is not much more than two feet ; here it is over five feet.

"There'll be many fortunes made in the Northern Territory in indigo," said my conductor.

And I quite believed him. Those who have travelled lately through India say that the necessities of its immense and ever-increasing population in the shape of food supply are always becoming greater and more pressing, and as a consequence the cultivators of indigo have to make food production their prime business. So the acreage under the dye-plant is gradually decreasing, though, as a matter of course, the demand is in an inverse ratio. Hence, and for other reasons, it is safe to back the prediction given above. I should have mentioned, when I wrote of tobacco, that Mr. Holtze gave me some cigars which he had made roughly—for he confesses to not understanding the work—from leaves grown in the gardens. Although new, they smoked as well as the best Manilla, and they were milder, or at least they seemed to be—smoked as a variation of the exercises of sugar-cane and maize and peanut and chili chewing—for I had scrupulously to sample everything that grew, and I felt like an Indian salad dish. And, by the way, there appertains to these cigars a little joke. The Government Resident had a box of them, and he valiantly championed their virtues whilst, as usual, men who ought to be the first to support "local industries" decried them. They were colonial ; that was enough to damn them. He determined to give them a fair test. Shortly afterwards he gave a whist party, and placed these cigars before the company without remark. Unasked for came exclamations of surprise at and comments upon their

excellence. And then the murder was out! I can understand the commendations, for I have paid sixpence for a much
worse cigar in the southern capitals. The first energetic and
competent tobacco-planter and curer in the Northern Territory will
doubtless make a fortune rapidly. When I tell the reader that
there are nearly a thousand kinds of plants in the gardens he will
thank me not to detail all the experiments. And so I pass over a
great many, which meant months of careful watching and study in
their consummation, and most of which were successful, notwithstanding that there is not the slightest forcing to gain success.
Not so much as a shovelful of manure has been used in the whole
garden, and not a single plant has been watered except by dew or
rain; for the Director contends that if a thing will not grow
without watering, then it is no good for the Northern Territory;
and to the end that the conditions necessary to general success
may be tabulated as far as possible, Mr. Holtze studiously takes
every day thermometrical readings, and by a gauge registers the
rainfall. The new planters can, having registered the rainfall
whilst they were clearing, come to the gardener and say—

"My register is so-and-so. Temperature so many degrees.
Here's a sample of my soil. Shall it be sugarcane or cotton,
indigo or maize?"

Easy as most theories, you observe. But, continuing my
summary, I may add that, much to my astonishment, I was introduced to the grand old Scotch kale, healthy and hale as its kin in
the old country; to its warm friends pepper and cloves, and capsi-
cums and cinnamon, all either flourishing or looking like to
flourish; to healthy lycheenuts, mangoes, and bread-fruit, guava,
jack-fruit, yams, melons, beans, and sweet potatoes. Peanuts
particularly thrive. Last year one-fifteenth of an acre gave 4 cwt.
Eight hundred pounds to the acre is considered a good crop in
California. The Manilla almond looks better here than on its
native heath, and English apples, grapes, and peaches grow, but
the first and last, I thought, seemed pining. Some Spanish and
navel orange-trees were in fair health, but the ironstone-sprinkled
ground is not the fittest for their tribe to live on. The mandarin
oranges, however, as I proved by sight and taste, had not
depreciated one whit by transplantation, nor had the limes,
lemons, citrons, and pomegranates, nor the many-formed
hibiscus, nor Cape gooseberries, chilis, custard apples, carob-beans,
figs, almonds, plantains, earthnuts, sorghum, sesamoil, cassava,
castor oil, sweet sob and sour sob, rhea or Chinese grass plant, and
others whose names are semi-legion. The cocoanut was tried, but
not successfully. The nuts were planted on the beach, and one
can hardly affirm that the experiment was a fair one. To Baron

von Mueller the Director expressed his obligations generally, and particularly for recommending trial of the India-rubber tree. Four months before I visited the gardens its seeds were sown, and I was introduced to a flourishing tree eight feet in height. The expressed and conjealed juice of this indiarubber plant will unquestionably be one of the important minor articles of export from the Territory. So will palm oil from its tree, which grows luxuriantly. A big shade-bamboo nursery in the centre of the gardens is filled with many rare and choice young plants. Here, as with respect to some parts at least in the open, scores of acclimatized and native grasses grow. The best to succeed is the common Phillips's. The English lawn grass grows well under shade, but does not seem to stand the heat, and yet I have seen a capital lawn in Palmerston, where, exposed and not artifically watered, its growth is satisfactory enough. The Alizana Indica thrives in the gardens ; but Mr. Holtze's opinion is that the native grasses are just as good as the imported are in their own home, and better than they will be here. He has been experimenting with the tall rank kinds I have described in my notes on the down-country travel, and he discovered that by cutting them down frequently he got at last a thick, soft, fast-spreading, somewhat dwarfed buffalo grass, which surpasses the best couch for lawn and feeding purposes. English lucerne grows well, and the reana, a luxuriant fodder-plant about fifteen feet high, springs up with surprising rapidity. Jute, has failed this season, owing to the unusally dry weather. The plants got sickly, and were attacked by a maggot like a gentle. The so-called broom-corn, from which American brooms are made, grows splendidly. I saw a thick plot, averaging fifteen feet in height. All the Chinese oil-plants grow well. The " teal" has spread— self-sown after the first year—all over the garden. Its juice is a capital lubricating oil ; 1,200,000 acres are planted with " teal" every year in India. The six odd figures would give us a grand export for the Territory. Many different sorts of millets yield a heavy crop, and a row of mulberries are strong and healthy. The Director is importing some silkworms to live in them, and thus he will nurture two industries in one. Of Chinese bamboo-silk I took with me some good samples which I combed out from various thriving trees eight feet high. There is no doubt as to the success of this plant, and as the fibre is valuable in cloth manufacture, its cultivation would be an important subsidiary aid to the planter. An African fibre-plant is equally successful, and so is the Indian physic-nut, used medicinally. The papoya—papa—papaw—papia (for it has locally as many names as a Chinese sharper has tricks) is amongst the most healthy fruit producers. It is a peculiar plant. (*Carica Papa-ya*) Papaw—and natural order Papayaceæ. There are male and female. The male tree yields only flowers ; the others add the fruit. The males are the hardier, and on one plantation I visited there were no females, and hence there was no fruit. The males have to be inoculated by bees, it is said, and where the bees neglect their duty the tree is of no account except for ornament. The fruit itself is to some tastes delicious, though others don't like it. Its flavour is a cross between rockmelon, banana, and pineapple. And now, having served my purpose, I think I may finally close my notes on this important subject. I cannot do better than confirm from my own observation during several visits what the gardener says—that " everything imported that grows in this country thrives." At first plants which are most notably successful now pined. The proper season for planting them was not found till experiments had been made. When it was discovered there was no further trouble, and it is only a reasonable surmise that the same thing will repeat itself till, when the purely experimental work shall have been completed, we shall have thousands of vigorous acclimatized plants where now there are only hundreds. That the trial may be perfect Mr. Holtze is getting from all quarters every variety of each plant, and of course he gives exchanges. The garden, be it understood, is not a place for floral beauties or the kickshaws of cultivation. Its strong point is its strictly commercial character, and in that point it is simply Herculean.

And now come we to the Daly River, which the party made an unsuccessful attempt to reach that stormy Thursday. On the return after that failure I tried to arrange for a trip to that comparatively unexplored region, but I was confronted by difficulties which practically were insuperable, and I feared that I should not be able to give an authentic description of the country. But just at this juncture there arrived from the river a small boat containing two well-known authorities on soil and soil products—Mr. A. Edwards, planter, late of Fiji and Natal, who came to the Territory to inspect and report upon the Melbourne Palmerston Plantation Company's land on the Daly ; and Mr. Reece, a cotton and sugar planter in one of the Fijian Isles, who came to look at the land with a view to taking a large area up if he found he would be justified in doing so. I interviewed them in conjunction with nearly every man—and there are not many in the Territory— who had visited the Daly or any part of it. From them, as to the soil itself and the appearance of the country, I obtained the substance of what follows, and I think, judging by the position of the parties—Government officers are included --that it may be accepted as perfectly authentic. Messrs. Edwards and Reece left Port Darwin for the Daly in the steamer Maggie. and were three days getting up the river. The scenery for the first 30 or 35 miles

is not inspiriting. On either side are low-lying plains, stretching
as far as the eye can reach, and submerged at high water. The
soil is mostly a stiff bluish clay, which, sodden in winter, in
summer cracks into big cakes. At present it is worthless. In
course of time, if drained and treated as such land has been in
the West Indies—by a system of irrigation, dykes, and embank-
ments—it may be made fit for cane growing. Beyond the point
indicated, the land gradually improves. The washing away of the
ground on the bank reveals a fine, light, sandy soil, which further
on changes into a deep loam, varying from chocolate to black, and
higher than the highest water-level in the river. The Palmerston
Plantation Company's ground is forty-five miles up the river.
This estate was a grant of 20,000 acres from the South Australian
Government to Messrs. Owston (who now manages it), Peterson,
and Spence ; and before he finally chose it Mr. Owston put the
authorities at Port Darwin to a great deal of expense in conveying
him from place to place in their boats. The block is an irregularly
shaped one, with about fifteen miles frontage to the river. It is
something less than twelve months ago since Mr. Owston, on
behalf of the Company (which represents only Melbourne
capitalists), began work on the land. He then had the assistance
of the steamer Ellangowan, which they bought, but which was
wrecked in the river. Since then he has had to hire the little
steamers at Port Darwin when he has had cargo to send up ; but
it is the intention of his Company, when Mr. Edwards shall take
his place as manager, to bring into use another little steamer,
which they are now obtaining. At present, as is only reasonable,
little has been done on the plantation. Twenty acres have been
planted with canes from the Government Gardens—canes which
placed in soil cross-ploughed five inches deep in November, are
flourishing. (This applies to the end of March). They have made
between two feet and four feet of strong wood, much
more, it must be confessed, than those at Delissaville can
show. This applies to the Meera (Queensland) cane, which every
one who ought to know avers is best suited to the Territory. The
other has only just begun to perform the operation technically
known as "making cane." Be it remembered by the reader,
moreover, that the cane-heads were not planted as soon as they
were taken from the gardens, but there was an interval of six
weeks, consequent upon difficulties and drawbacks of transit.
Hence the manager, fearing to perpetuate indifferent cane on his
estate, will not plant till he can get fresh cane-heads ; and to get
them he is rearing his nursery first. From that he will obtain
supplies for the great area, and he will not crush till 1884. The
machinery will, however, be ordered as soon as the good character

of the soil for the growth of sugar shall have been made manifest. The Natal maize is having a trial over a small acreage ; the crop looks exceedingly well. The station at present is a small place. It consists of a few galvanized iron erections merely. There are about seventeen employés—fifteen Chinamen at £1 a week; a white labourer at 30s., with rations ; and a European ploughman with 10s. more. There are no white ants on the land, which is heavily grassed—a flat plain, lightly timbered, and that timber for the most part gums. The altitude is 38 feet above the common level of the river, and there is no danger of inundation. There are no creeks of any size in the selection, and no hills properly so called. The grass almost everywhere is so high and thick that it is very difficult for a pedestrian to make his way through it. Messrs. Edwards, Reece, and Owston had in consequence an adventure, which looked somewhat serious at one time. In a small boat they were continuing their exploration of the river beyond the plantation. They left the boat moored to the bank while they went inland, forcing their way through the high walls of grass. After they had gone on a while, examining the black soil, rich almost to rottenness, they tried to make back to the river, but, after several ineffectual attempts to do so, discovered that they had lost themselves. They cooeyed again and again to attract the attention of the men they had left in charge of the boat, but the only response was an answering cooey from some armed natives, who approached within a few yards; their heads and spears just showing through the high grass. As time passed their numbers gradually increased. Mr. Edwards's party were without arms, and to keep the natives back they shouldered long bamboos to make the menacing savages believe they carried guns. The *ruse* succeeded for a while, but the duped ones were just awaking to the facts of the case—for as they grew stronger numerically they became bolder—when the boatmen came on the scene, and the natives then dispersed.

" We thought it was all up with us," remarked Mr. Edwards to me.

On the station itself the blackfellows give very little trouble now. They did at first—they stole all the stores, but they were punished for it. They have not forgotten the lesson taught them. They are fine athletic fellows—fiercer than most of their degraded kinsmen in the Territory. They have not yet been brought into immediate contact with the whites long enough to share to the full that degradation. The climate is warm ; the glass varies from 90° to 110° in a thatched hut on the river bank in the wet seasons ; the mosquitoes are five times as big as the average southern latitudinarian, and fifty-fold more mischievous.

The alligators are numerous, large, and playful.   Mr. Reece does not share his comrade's opinion that the land is almost perfect for the growth of sugar.   He fears that it is not strong enough.   It is just the thing for cotton, he says ; and he has offered to take up 20,000 acres, and plant and put machinery upon it at once, if the Government will give proportionately the same bonus for cotton that they offer for sugar.   The twain had another adventure coming down from the river to Port Darwin.   They hastily did the trip in a little open boat not one-tenth so large as that the Parliamentary party essayed to do it in ; and they performed it, too, in very rough weather.   For four days were they exposed to that weather—to heavy drenching rain ; to high-mounting seas which swept over the little craft, threatening, at times to quite engulf it.   They gave up all hope of getting to their destination, and from the outset almost they had scarcely anything to eat. Part of their provisions was washed away, and they arrived at last almost famished.   They would not attempt the trip again for a thousand pounds, they say.

Just mentioning that it is the intention of the Company to farm out some of their land to a small planter—just as it is the intention of the Delissa Company to do to Chinese—I will proceed to enlighten your nautical readers with what can be gathered from the best authorities respecting the river itself.   It has never been surveyed really ; but Mr. Howard (who next to Captain Marsh is the officer in charge of the Government vessels here) has been oftener and further up the river than any one else.   He has taken observations and soundings during his various trips, and he had summed up a rough chart, which unfortunately was lost in the Ellangowan.   He informs me that eighty miles was the greatest distance he could compass up the river in a small steam-launch. The mouth of the river is divided by a long island, which, of course, turns it into two channels.   The eastern is the deeper.   Inside there is about three fathoms at dead low water.   Fairly inside, the stream widens out into a reach of about two miles, but the fairway is broken up with sandbanks and channels here and there.   The eastern side is usually kept all the way along, and it is singular that the water is deeper close to the banks than it is in the middle. The country is all flat, and the water in a heavy " fresh " deposits the shifting *débris* in the centre.   The widest part of the river is about three-quarters of a mile, and it narrows down to as little as eighty yards.   The current is very strong   About thirty miles up the river there is an eight-hours' ebb, and in spring tides the water rises fully 18 inches, lifting a boat " clean up."

"You can hear the advancing wall roaring half a mile off," says Mr. Howard ; " a sort of tidal wave rushes along on each bank ;

you suddenly swing-to and see the tide rushing by like anything. It is not safe to go on the river at night. Some of the reaches are full of 'bores' and snags, and you have to turn your craft sheer round in some places."

He was on the Ellangowan (not in command) when she struck, and, though he says she used to get aground every day, he thinks the accident might have been avoided. He believes the survey of the river will be a difficult task ; he sees, indeed, no alternative but to have a fresh survey after every wet season, the conformation of the river bed is changed so by the constant floods. Through these the positions of even the sandbanks are frequently altered, so that a chart which would be correct to-day might not be next week. It is, as Mr. Howard expressively puts it, " a shallow-water river, a rum river, and a nasty river," and he closes his " interviewed " confession by confirming what Mr. Edwards had said about the physical features of the country, adding—

" When you get high up, the ranges dip steeply to the river, which has here little else but a succession of rocky bars and sandspits. The scenery is beautiful ; water clear as crystal, and the land beyond the banks is capital." One thousand square miles of this land is held under pastoral lease by Lyons & Fisher. The inevitable conclusion in a comparison of the Adelaide and the Daly Rivers is that each has a retarding fault and a compensating virtue. The generality of the land along the former is indifferent, but it is easily navigable— has no difficulties whatever ; the latter has good land, but itself is perplexingly complicated and even dangerous. On the point whether it will ever be properly navigable for fairly large vessels there is among experts a difference of opinion. The solution lies in the trial.

On March 22 (the day on which the Parliamentary party began their homeward journey) I started at early morn for the Adelaide River—a point to which a good deal of attention is now directed —in the steam-launch Maggie, in company with Mr. H. W. H. Stevens, the Manager for Messrs. C. B. Fisher & H. Lyons, who have an immense pastoral area in the Territory. The invitation was courteously given by Mr. Stevens, and it extended also to Mr. Cuthbertson, of the Land Office, and other gentlemen. The trip along the harbour out past the varied points of interest was one of the most enjoyable things I have experienced here. The coast has nothing of the ruggedly romantic about it. It is low-lying and flat, though adorned with vegetation besides the ever-present mangroves. By noon we had anchored (to wait the turn of the tide, which rushed between the islands at a terrific rate) in the South Vernon Passage. The South Vernon at ebb-tide looks as

interesting as an unbroken vista of blank wall. At high tide the
greater part of it which the mangroves do not affect is covered
with twenty-five feet of water—now it was nothing but a big
barren table of coral strewn over with loose rocks of the same,
looking at which you found yourself debating whether the more
difficult problem was how on earth those stones got there, or why
on earth the island was made at all. The Meumuir, with the
Ministerial party on board, passed us some miles off later on, and
honoured us with a flag salute, which we responded to as best we
could by hoisting a triplet of silk handkerchiefs and a pair of
sailor's highly-coloured blue breeches. The launch aspired not to
the dignity of bunting. Long after the vessel left us we could see
her standing out against the horizon as a beautiful mirage. This
is the home of aristocratic mirages—we saw several subsequently,
each as the day advanced more wonderful than its predecessor.
We ran the gauntlet of scenic attractions, and even overhead were
some. The clouds got up a special panorama in a place where
cloud effects are ever beautiful; and it seemed as though the combination had inspired the erratic Maggie to a better mood, for she
spanked along, breeze-helped and tide-assisted, fully seven knots
an hour. But then the perplexingly changeful tide turned—
turned upon us so savagely that it was all we could do to maintain
our positions fairly and make a little headway.

We had four blackfellows on aboard—Wilwongas, whose *habitat*
is on the banks of the Adelaide. They are intellectually far in
advance of the wretched Larrakeeyahs, but it is after all as the
intelligence of a mule to that of a donkey. Our "Billie," a noted
member of the tribe, has a head like Linnæus's, he is thin-lipped
as a European, and the contour of his face many a perfumed
dandy might envy. The old man with us—Billie's guardian or
foster-father—possesses a cranium as elegantly shaped as a
baboon's, and not unlike it ; that of the old man's twenty-year son
was a compromise between his father's and a sheep's ; but the
little boy, ten years old perhaps, had a grand head and a beautiful
tenor voice. I drew a bust-picture of one of these, our sable
helps, and I showed it to him.

"No savee," was his remark.

I asked him what it was, and he said he was adjectived if he
knew—a burnt stump, he presumed. I told him that it was his
portrait. He studied it awhile, puzzled-looking, I fear, and,
handing it back, he enquired—

"What fellow make him ?"

I asked him wherefore his curiosity, and he remarked—

" 'Cause I tink him too muchee big fellow fool."

I am afraid that the blackfellow's mind is not as yet educated up to a perception of the beauties of amateur face-sketching, though he has a wonderful conception of music. The dress of the natives who were with us was various, mostly hand-palm size, covering their nakedness as a fig-leaf covers a Venus. But yet they were proud of the little apology for clothing they had—more *as* clothing than as covering, may be. They would wash it often, and hang it out to dry, and they were innocent, Adam-like, barring arm-circlets of plaited grass, in the intervals between wetting and drying. They have all wretchedly sore eyes—the eyeball knobby, like the yellow-tinged beaten white of an egg, and the sight itself obscured by heavy excrescences. Their constant sitting in smoke to be out of the way of mosquitos may partly account for this. They are very inquisitive and unconsciously humorous. I showed one the workings of a watch, and made him listen to its ticking. It pleased him. He asked what it was, and I told him; and I added—for fear he might be tempted to lay unrighteous hands upon it whilst it lay about—that it was a little " debbil debbil." And then he innocently queried—

" Him you friend ? "

We stipulated for a mixed native corroboree and all the tribal songs. We got them, and they were wondrously well given : the fierce wail of the Woggite, beginning on one side of the musical hill, ascending to its top, then sliding down at a tremendous rate, and skidding out over the plain and splashing into the lagoon with the peculiar whir-r-r-r, which winds up all their performances. They sang the peculiar death-wail—a repetition mainly of

" Waw-n-e-ee !   Waw-n-e-e-ee ! "

long drawn out, and itself drawing from the boy a tenor strain as pure, though untrained, as I have heard in any concert-room. They mimicked, too, the ducks and geese and the Port Essington blacks—mimicked them in a song sounding like a reminiscence of that relating to the marching proclivities of the corporal remnants of Old John Brown. The basso was something to be heard ; his voice would, I believe, recall to some of my readers the ominous creaking of a prison door. They accompanied their vocal efforts by the beating of slender pine sticks, and the time they kept was perfect. All the natives I have met, of all the tribes, have a wonderfully good ear for music, and capital voices as a rule.

But whilst the concert was proceeding we had sighted the Escape Cliffs, where in 1864 the Hon. B. T. Finniss established a settlement for the South Australian Government—a settlement which soon collapsed. All that is left of it now is an old well, if I except the crumbling foundations of the place. There are

hundreds of buffaloes, and off the coast and especially near
Port Essington the bêche-de-mer attracts the Malay proas,
and probably, ere long will be interviewed by Queensland fishermen. A local firm sent out a boat this season,
but though they caught plenty of fish mismanagement killed the
venture. On the other side is Charles Point, in the vicinity of
which grow many sturdy cypress-pines. Lots of them were taken
thence for use in the erection of Government offices. The white
ants rigidly draw the line at these pines. The waters were alive
with minute marine forms. There are sperm whales, too, people
say, but we did not see any. We noticed, however, several
dugongs—a sort of porpoise-cum-walrus—sporting about, and
kangaroo-fish leaping, and turtle clumsily turning in all directions;
and in-shore the curious little flat-nosed fish which climb the
mangroves over the oysters that cling thereto.

We entered the Adelaide River, the mouth of which is fifty
miles from Palmerston, on a flood tide which sent us up fully eight
knots an hour. The coast-line all round here is close-bordered by
two kinds of mangroves, which matted together look like a mottled
green wall, with lattice-work about it. At the mouth the stream
is about a mile wide, and has two branches, the lesser known as
the Saltwater Arm, and the other of course the main river, which
runs south. The other is west of south. We did not follow it,
but those who have done so—the Government marine surveyors—
say that it takes a general south-by-west direction for three miles
from the entrance. It then divides into two branches—one
trending about six miles to the south-east and the other about the
same distance to the south-west, when, after carrying two or three
fathoms for some distance, they terminate in what at low water is
a mere flat overgrown by mangroves, amidst which alligators and
wild fowl are very plentiful. We followed the main stream, and
as we went a little beyond the point in the river which the nautical
surveyor (Captain Wickham) reached many years ago, it may be
well to give first his summary as ours, with some little difference :—

" I traced the river for eighty miles following the windings of
the stream, but in a direct line south about 43 miles, the river
varying from 80 to 250 yards in breadth, with an average of five
fathoms of water. It is navigable for vessels of 400 and 500 tons
about 45 and 50 miles, where the water is only slightly brackish
at high tide. For about fifteen miles above the entrance the
banks are fringed with mangroves. . . . At somewhat less
than 40 miles there are bamboos and some jungle. The water
here is always fresh, and the bamboos rise to a height of 60 or 80
feet. Between 20 and 70 miles from the mouth the soil is a good
mould. Further on the aspect of the country changes from that of

low plains to that of slightly-wooded and undulating. Higher up the river at a narrow point divides into two branches, the one running southerly and the other easterly. The former was blocked up by fallen trees, and the other was too narrow for a boat's oar to work in. The main river at the furthest point examined was subject to about three feet change of tidal level, it being there high water six hours later than on the coast at the mouth ; but there was no perceptible stream, and the water, which for thirty miles had been muddy, was here clear. Small driftwood was observed in the branches of the trees at eight feet above the water, showing the height to which the water attains at certain seasons, and the probability that the lowland is periodically inundated."

That probability we on our trip reduced to a fact. But now more fully for detail. As we entered the river, where the average depth at low water is 25 feet, we were borne on the breast of the incoming tide, which met the ebb of the stream. The two opposing bodies contended for the mastery, and caused rapid circular revolutions of the muddy water—little whirlpools innumerable. Near a break in the bank, whence you gain a fine view over mud flats of slightly elevated open country, is the only point at all dangerous to the unwary navigator of the river. The place is called the Narrows, where rocks and sandbanks in the centre and extending towards the eastern bank divert vessels to the western ; but there is even then room enough for the largest ships to pass. Then the river widens out into grand reaches and averages about 150 yards in width. There is just a little patch of ground a couple of feet above high tides. The water has exposed the strata, which are those of a deep, rich, brown mould. The corkscrew palm and paper bark grow here, and the old hands delight to point out as the most prominent landmark an iron tank which Mr. Finniss's party left on the river bank, and which they say still holds water. For two hours we saw nothing but mangroves and swampy heavily grass-grown land, which, judging by what I saw of the soil, I should say would never do for sugarcane—close to the river at any rate. There is a thin surface of black soil, and a substratum of blue clay, which, however, might cause swamp rice to flourish. But as dusk came on, after we had followed the windings of the river for some thirty miles, the country began slightly to improve. On the left bank we could see beyond the swampy ground, somewhat elevated rich, green, fertile, timbered land, which the maps and charts show not, but which the natives on board, who claimed it as their country, call Minissee. The banks here are about a foot above high-water mark. It was here that at night the tide began to ebb, and we anchored till it should flow again, as it would have been folly for our little craft to have been forced to fight against so strong a rush. It was here, too, that at early morning we met the first alligator—a huge monster about twenty feet long, floating by log-like. It was here, moreover, where a well-known speculator, to whom truth-telling is said to come only by accident, fixed the scene for a wild yarn told once to a public company. He thought they all were ignorant of alligators' nests, and.so he spun his threads thusly—

"You see, it was this way. I was chasing along the bank an alligator that had taken my silk handkerchief as it hung over the boat's gunwale, and I had near come up to him, when flop he goes into a big pyramid-looking place in the mangroves. It was a pretty place, with walks all round it and a long stretch of green running from one part into the river. I put my head in, and found the handkerchief hanging on a bush, and pocketed it. But the place *was* the queerest. It was a hundred yards round, and a beautiful shelving basin of clear water, cut into two parts. In one part were 200 eggs as big round as this," and he stretched out his arms to their full extent. "In the other the old alligator was teaching the young ones to swim, and a great fuss she *did* make of it. The stretch of green running down to the river was a tunnel, through which the youngsters went in and out."

The tale-teller received a prompt reward. There is a mystery respecting his whereabouts now. But we got a real alligator's nest higher up—the well-known local traveller, Mr. W. D'Arcy Uhr, disturbed an alligator sitting on it; it had no fewer than 400 eggs. These are deposited in layers in a sand mound from eighteen inches to two feet high and six feet round. The last layer for the time being is covered with wet sand, which is scraped off when the alligator wants to add another. You would think such an awkward, ponderous beast would smash the eggs; but it does not; of our nest only three were cracked. The eggs, which are hatched by sun heat, are about the size of a duck's, but they are longer and whiter, more hard-shelled, and pimpled and blotchy. They have a strong flavour—somewhat musty, too; but the blackfellows eat them readily if raw, and with great relish if cooked in the hot ashes.

Early next morning, with the tide in our favour, we were passing along the big Horse-shoe Bend, just beyond which the bamboos grow to an extraordinary height. From the leafy groves we heard the cooeying of blackfellows, and thousands of ducks and geese and shags and cranes flew overhead from the offshooting creeks and marshes. All along the river, indeed, birds positively swarm. The perky white cockatoos are particularly numerous. We shot some gold-bronzed yellow cranes, which generally are very scarce, but here they rose pretty plentifully from the grass cane, as it is called. It is almost as much like sugar-cane as grass in taste. At about noon we passed off Beatrice Hill, with its "trig." station. It is a prominent, though low bald elevation, split up into several heaps well grown with succulent grass, and at its foot there is a very extensive fresh water lagoon—the overflow of the Litchfield Creek, which flows from the west. The water here is always fresh, and the banks for a short distance are overflowed at high tide. The tidal change in the river—which is about 200 feet wide—is about nine feet. At the back of the hill porphyritic rocks crop up occasionally. There are some patches of good soil near the range, and inshore the bamboos grow in great profusion, and with their lacework of ivy-like creepers look exceedingly pretty. Indeed, in the most luxuriant tropical growth in any part of the world it would be difficult to find a place more really beautiful. About six miles below the river supplies a little creek, shooting off from the eastern bank, and continuing for six miles in a south-westerly direction beyond the first hills of any magni-tude near the river on that side. The creek has about seven fathoms of water in it half the distance, but it gradually shallows and narrows till it becomes unworthy the name. We anchored at the junction, and pulled down to the half-way mark between very high overhanging bamboos. We landed opposite the point where Mr. D'Arcy Uhr is establishing under Mr. Stevens's direction a sheep and cattle station for Messrs. Lyons & Fisher, who hold all the land along the eastern bank of the Adelaide with the exception of about 30,000 acres special survey, as well as 20,000 miles upon the western. The prospect of good grazing country looks from the creek dull enough, but after you bury your feet in the soft, slippery mud, covering a few feet of the bank, and after you penetrate the thick growth of bamboos, you come to some really good land, heavily grassed and well watered. There are no cattle on this magnificent run at present. Work had been proceeding less than a month, and in that time a great deal had been done by two Europeans and two Chinamen. They live now in a wretched hut, but are building on the first of the little ranges (called the Clump Hills, because of a peculiar clump of bamboos growing on the top of the otherwise bald head of one of them), a very good framework of a homestead station, which will command an extensive view of all the country round for some few miles. Here, of course, where the land is so flat it is impossible to see so much of it at once as can be seen where there are high points of observation. So far as we tested it the good land is patchy. Where these patches occur, however, it is rich almost to rottenness. One of the post-holes on the hill showed 3 feet 6 inches of perfectly black mould,

and the next only about as many inches.   Beyond that a soft slate
intruded.   All the material to be used in the building has been
carried on men's shoulders, some of it for miles, and Mr. Uhr has
had to cut timber twenty miles down the river, there being none
nearer home.   These facts give one a good idea of what
some of the least of a pioneer squatter's difficulties are.   Add
to them the risks of driving cattle and sheep hundreds of miles
over almost impassable country, and one has a better.   Going back
to the launch we saw several hundreds of flying foxes hanging by
their curious claws head downwards on the trees.   Flying,
they look not much unlike a crow, though they are really
greatly different.   We shot several, but could only secure for stuff-
ing one large specimen and a very small one ; the others hung
after they were dead on the top branches, and we could not get at
them   They are a most peculiar semi-bird, half other animal,
with the head of a fox in miniature, and wide-jointed, hooked,
black indiarubber-like webbed wings.   When skinned the skeleton
bears a closer resemblance to the human in miniature.   The foxes fly
very steadily, and on their perches make a disagreeable clucking
noise.

But every other live thing in this region must cry a very long
second to the mosquitos.   We went back to the station at night
to take some observations as to latitude by shooting stars
with sundry scientific instruments.   We walked for that purpose
to the hill where the station is being erected—about a mile from
the river, and (one would have thought) free from mosquitos.
But the little pests followed us up ; and we commenced operations with our heads and hands tied up in handkerchiefs, and our
eyes dimmed with the smoke from fires placed at various points in
the fallacious hope that they would keep the mosquitos off.
The man taking the observations had to attempt his work
while four men waved handkerchiefs all round him, and another
puffed cigar smoke in his face ; but even then the mosquitos bit him so severely that he found it impossible, as did his
successors, to perform the task, though all ordinary conditions to
success were present.   The lively little wretches got into the
quicksilver even, and by the time we had reached the launch
again every exposed part of our bodies was smarting intolerably
from their bites.   The natives were sent ashore to the station
that night, and next morning they returned very severely
bitten.   They were almost naked when they got ashore,
but they soon laid hands on all the "unattached" clothing
to be found, and donned it.   I beg the sceptical reader to
accept my statements as quite within the mark when I assure him
that at night the air is absolutely thick with mosquitos that make

incessantly a most monotonous buzzing noise. There are three kinds of the insect. The most important is the black, three-quarters of an inch long, with a couple of feelers, forceps-shaped, in front of its head. Through these they draw the blood, standing on their noses, and swinging their legs to give them the greatest possible momentum. Lying under my cheese-cloth mosquito-net in the early morning, I have seen dozens of them bore right through it, and effect an entrance, and they frequently drew the blood through fairly thick tweed trousers. Then there are the light pink or brown kinds, about half as big as the others, and more pretty. They are most vicious biters, and my hands for days were covered with little blisters which they raised. The third sort is the ordinary small one, and which, though so annoying down south, is scarce accounted here at all. Before I visited the Adelaide I scouted as wholly incredible this little anecdote, which was told by a reliable man, but I half believe it now. He had lost a white horse some miles away, he says ; and looking for it with a friend they passed one a few yards distant— a peculiar dark-coloured steed.

"Oh, that can't be ours," they both agreed, and went on.

But thinking it strange that a second horse should be at large in these solitudes they turned back, and found that the horse was their own, but that the mosquitos that swarmed all over him had caused the mistake. When they can, the horses, like the natives, roll themselves in mud, so that they may avoid the maddening pain which the bites produce. I need not say that we did not remain in this delectable place longer than we could help doing. We pushed on up-stream, rounding some of its corkscrew windings. (There is no more irregularly-shaped river anywhere. To navigate it you have to sail to all points of the compass.) There was a heavy "fresh" on, and it brought down large floating islands of bamboos, joined together with creepers, and some little driftwood, of which, by the way, there is a remarkable scarcity here. As we advance the bamboos gradually become less thickly grouped, but enough so to suggest the idea that they would form a valuable article of export. There is material for many hundreds of bungalows and chairs, and the thousand-and-one other uses to which the bamboo is applied in China. We proceeded on past Beatrice Creek, which is nearly dry at low water, to somewhat less, I believe, than the eightieth mile, but past the farthest point reached by the surveying schooner Beatrice. The land some little distance below this begins to rise, and well-grassed plains, flooded from creeks, stretch away to the foot of the first of the long series of Daly Ranges. These are on the western side, and on the east the only noticeable elevation is Onetree Hill, which is almost perfectly innocent of trees or shrubs, but which has on all its sides some fertile land. We examined it after a wearying walk of half a mile through grass and mud and water, in places waist deep, and we confirmed the verdict which we had previously arrived at—that almost all the way along the river inundates one or other of its banks during the wet season. We went up a little further where we had a better view of the Daly Range with its thick covering of trees; and of Manton's and Fred's Passes, in the latter named of which poor Bennett, whose grave now forms such a prominent feature in the scenery of Palmerston, was fatally speared by the blacks some years ago. Beneath this pass there is a large lagoon. From this point the river gradually becomes narrower and shallower till navigation is impeded by Pearson's Bar, about ten miles farther on. One of the party who went by land right through to the Adelaide Crossing by the telegraph line, where the Parliamentary party camped, says there is beyond Pearson's a succession of rocky bars which a boat might cross for about twelve miles, but which a ship could not. There are also several cliffs, and at one point, where the stream is not much more than 30 feet wide and two feet deep, the banks on the east side rise to a height of 20 or 30 feet, and are lightly timbered with paper bark, bamboos also being present. Then there are chains of lagoons and undulating country, fit for the cultivation of sugar, but more particularly for that of rice. Before this point is reached the tidal influence has ceased, and the river is unworthy of being so called. Near Mount Gun a branch of the Adelaide trends away west, and throws off shoots due south. Then the main river degenerates into a thin rivulet, and loses half its volume in extensive back waters, lagoons, and billabongs, full of fish. According to the surveyors the river takes its rise in open flats and undulating rises, all well grassed, and the valleys containing good soil.

On Friday night we were borne swiftly homeward on the ebb-tide, past numerous alligators that we disturbed basking on the banks in the sunlight. We fired at some, but the unwieldly monsters, being mud-coloured, do not present a good mark, and if they did and were hit, their thick hides would render them impervious to the ball, unless they were struck on the head. One of them was nearly making a dinner of Mr. Cuthbertson, who had shot a duck, and was putting his hand on it to lift it into the boat as it floated on the water, when there bobbed up within a couple of inches of his fingers the ugly snout of an alligator. Both hand and bird disappeared in a very short time—the one above and the other under the water. Some ibises (the sacred "Ibis" of Japan) and "jabberoos" (a peculiar long-necked, long-shanked, white and red and black bird, with a plaid striped neck beautifully marked) subsequently bore company with the duck in the investigation of the internal economy of alligatordom. We reached Palmerston when Saturday night had far advanced; and in closing the record of this trip it may be said that so far as navigation is concerned there is no better river than the Adelaide; but it seems generally speaking more fit for pastoral than agricultural purposes. There are patches of exceedingly good land, but so far as we could judge by a somewhat cursory examination, and so far as one may form an opinion from the reports of Mr. Lindsay and other surveyors, as to the west bank, at any rate, the average quality is not so good as it might be. I believe, and others more technically informed than I aver, that rice will flourish upon it, but that the sugarcane will not be spread over a very wide area. Special surveys have, however, been made and applied for for sugar blocks, which I will more particularly refer to at the proper time. There is now no regular means of communication between the river and Palmerston, except that which is given indirectly by way of the goldfields road, the nearest point of which is fifty miles distant from Pearson's Bar. Mr. Stevens intends, however, to frequently run a little sailing vessel—which is now on the way up —between the Station and the Port, and also to the farthest navigable point, to facilitate the conveyance of goods to the Adelaide as well as to the Glencoe Station—of which, and stations generally, more anon. Let it be sufficient to say in closing that three chains of the river banks is reserved for travelling stock; and, parenthetically, that for the natural history collector there are few better places than the Adelaide River.

CHAPTER IX.—PALMERSTON.

To Palmerston at last.—The Harbour.—"One of the Best in the World:" the Common Verdict.—The Various Apologies for Wharf Accommodation.—The Government Fleet.—The Customs and the Customs Officials.—The Free Port no Benefit to the Working Men.—The Storekeepers gain every way.— Curious Duty of the Landing-Waiter.—The Inception of the Beche-de-Mer Trade.—The Gold Duty; how to make up for it.—Some Statistics and Deductions therefrom.—South Australia least Benefited of all the Colonies by the Northern Territory. — The one Practicable Remedy; a Railway.— China our Chief Competitor. — Another Singapore. — The District Council and their Palatial Hall.—The Population and an Unique Way of Estimating it.—The Assessment.—A Dispute with the Government.—The Curse of Absenteeism.— The Ever-useful Chinese and the Occasionally Ditto Blacks. —The Government Residence and its Terraces. The Offices. —The Hospital.—The Cemetery.—The Overland Telegraph Officers and Offices.—The Eastern Extension and China Ditto.—The Ravages of the White Ants again.—Chaff and Hay from the Native Grasses.—The State of the Overland Line.—Extension of Mail Service.—The Police Quarters and the Officers —The Courthouse.—An Extraordinary Gaol.— Its Miserable Condition —A Peculiar Chinese Disease.—The Institute.—Immigration and Emigration.

IF Palmerston has one thing which it is entitled to boast about more than another, that thing is its harbour. I should have described it at first, to make the descriptions follow their natural sequence; but that with the Ministerial journey programme was not possible, and the event proved that it was just as well, because I had more frequent opportunities of seeing it and hearing discussed the "burning questions" it is the subject of. Port Darwin is really a harbour within a harbour, so that vessels lying in it are doubly protected. The outer sheltering headlands are East and West Point (Douglas Peninsula). The inner are Point Emery and Talc Head, each rocky rises of about twenty feet high, and both showing exactly the same strata. It looks, indeed, as though they had dissolved a close partnership, and put a couple of miles of ocean between them, for the entrance is nearly two miles wide. Within the only prominent landmarks are King's Table, Blackmore and Haycock Hills on the south, and Fort and Stokes Hills, near to Palmerston, on the north-east. Within Emery Point (I am somewhat indebted to official information) Port Darwin increases to seven miles in breadth, and then stretches into three arms. The East Arm is about two miles broad at the entrance, whence it is navigable by a boat for ten miles, and for larger vessels a much less distance. The banks are thickly lined with mangroves, and in the stream there are some rocks above water. The Elizabeth River, and Mitchell's, Browning's, and other creeks empty themselves into it. The next is the Middle or South Arm, on which Southport is built, and the eastern branch of which I have already described. The western has been traced six miles, and the depth of water varies from six to thirteen fathoms, but within the dividing islet the channels are mostly occupied by shoals until they become locked up by masses of granite farther inland. The West Arm is the most tortuous of all. It is a narrow creek, winding nine miles from its entrance, which is barred by a shoal extending some distance from Talc Head. Within the bar there is between two and three fathoms for three miles up the channel. Everywhere almost there are thick mangroves, with very little sandy beaches, bounding the view from a vessel, except there be (which there in very few places is) some elevated country. High up the arms of the harbour there are plenty of alligators, but the brutes do not come so often near the jetties as they did. The tides are very irregular. It is high water, fall and change, 5 hours 30 min. Springs rise as much as 24 feet, and neaps occasionally only 2 feet. Thus much in detail for nautical readers at a distance. To the general observer the harbour is merely a grand expanse of almost perfectly landlocked water, taking the shape of an irregular square—its surface enlivened ever and again by silver-flashes, marking the spot where jumping and flying fish of various kinds carry on their gambols. Prawns and other edible fish are caught and retailed by the Chinese. The passage from the Vernons to the mouth is somewhat intricate, and vessels arriving off them in the late evening generally wait for daylight to go in; but that fact does not in any way reflect upon the safety of the harbour itself. It is, however, subject to sudden squalls, and is, of course, affected by the strong monsoons which blow during certain seasons of the year. But a fatal accident, even with the smallest sailing boat, has never been known to happen in it, unless the craft were in bad hands. The unanimous verdict of the masters of all the steamers trading there whom I have interviewed is—"It's one of the safest and best harbours in the world. The largest fleet afloat could lie at anchor in it."

Palmerston is situated exactly north from the centre of the harbour, and Point Emery is part of the township, which looks very picturesque from the deck of an incoming vessel. After passing East Point the first sign of civilization you see is the Government Garden, and the next the Hospital; and these, backed by the somewhat irregular lines of snow-white offices and other buildings, with a beautiful variegated carpet, principally of rich green vegetation stretching in a gentle slope down to the

water's edge, from their high elevation, cannot fail to impress
a stranger favourably. It is well that it should be so, for he has
hardly time to record his impressions before he catches sight, if he
arrive at high tide, of the top of a long pole surmounted by an
empty nail-can, on the northern side of Fort Hill; and he
scarcely gives mouth to his surprise, ere he sees at the other side
of the Point another pole similarly capped. These mark the
termini of the two apologies for jetties, and they are placed there
to warn vessels not to run into them. If he come at low water,
they will appear as beacons at the edge of a sea of high-flavoured
mud. Where there is such an enormous rise of tide, jetty-
making becomes a serious business ; not that the ground at
the bottom of the harbour is unsuitable for it—on the contrary,
it is a compact mass of decomposed micaceous slate, in which
iron piles, when screwed, would be as firm and rigid as possible—
but because a jetty which would be available for vessels at high
water would be far above them at low, and *vice versa.* You
cannot see a single inch of any of the present jetties at
high tides, and small craft go completely over them. Neither is
used by any of the steamers ; all their cargo is lightered, and the
transhipment from the ship to the shore—a distance of 300
yards—costs fifteen shillings a ton. The goods are landed short of
high-water mark sometimes, and what with scarcity of drays, and
tide, and rain, considerable loss is incurred each year by im-
porters. Accommodation was first sought to be given to ship-
pers by the construction of a causeway to the north of Fort
Hill in an exposed position. That is Cook's Jetty, the one denoted
by the first of the nailcans. It is never used, and is less
likely to be now than ever it was. The baths separate it from the
stump end of a semi-jetty, quarter-breakwater, which, of solid
rocks, was run a foot or two into the sea from the centre line of
Fort Hill, and then discontinued. The position of this structure
is said to be worse than **that** of the other, as the fullest
rush of the currents passes it, and it would be difficult for a vessel
to lie alongside of it. If it were continued a hundred yards or so
as a breakwater it would shelter the third of the apologies—
the Gulnare Jetty, so called because a former Government schooner
of that name staved in her sides across it, and now forms
part of it, with her ribs in the middle of it. This is the jetty
which is used by the smaller craft. Its top, of loose slimy stones,
and the side beams which keep them together, are slippery as a
greased eel, and it is quite an exhausting exercise of ingenuity and
agility to step from it to a boat, or from a boat to it. When a distinguished stranger essays that feat the Government Resident courteously
drags him jettywards, while the boatmen prop up that portion of

his corporeality which last leaves the boat under these circumstances. And the walk along the top of the oily mass is quite as
amusing—a walk full of surprises, and varied, if the pedestrian be
not mighty in carefulness, by occasional full-length tumbles.
These in a shark and alligator and swift-current harbour would be
sensational were it not for the fact that the danger is lessened by
some stakes which have been run along outside and close to the
jetty to keep from jumping it at high water the reckless craft who
ignore the warning conveyed by that nailcan! Seriously, I think I
will command all the "Ayes" when I say that the wharfage
accommodation at Port Darwin is about as bad as it could be—so
bad that for any real use it is there might almost as well be none
at all.

Bad as the accommodation is, I believe, and the general opinion
even of the residents is, that it will be quite sufficient for many
years at least, unless a railway be made. If the Parliament puts
its veto on that railway scheme, then the reader who shall not
have read this before need go no further. But if they sanction it,
the most common-sense thing for the Government to do will be to
take practical steps in the matter of wharf accommodation before
they turn a shovelful of sod on the track.

The Harbour Master is Captain Marsh, and he has charge of the
Government fleet, sailing occasionally in command of its principal
ship—the Flying Cloud—which he brought up from Adelaide nine
years ago, and which seems to have been so profoundly affected by
that exploit as to be content to rest on its laurels and not risk
foolish experiments again. The Cloud really is a little cutter
wholly unfit for the work in which nominally she is engaged. It
takes her so long to get about that if she started to the relief of a
shipwrecked crew with the wind and tide against her it is probable
that she would be found, after beating about a day or two, to have
achieved only an Irishman's progression—backwards. The cast-
aways would have made the acquaintance of David Jones long ere
she could atone for her bad behaviour. This matter is especially
important where tides so strong and winds so fierce prevail, and
safety and economy equally demand that the Cloud shall be
replaced by a craft with some suitability for the work she under-
takes.

Captain Marsh's deputy and the Government boatman is Mr. W.
H. Howard, who has charge of the rest of the fleet—the cutters
Larrakeeyah and Woolnah, and a resplendent Governor's gig (in
which distinguished visitors are conveyed from ship to shore), and
a dingey. The fleet is used principally for the carriage of cypress
pine and other wood from the islands for the erection of Government buildings. The crews number altogether a dozen Malays,

and excellent boatmen the merry fellows are. The police officers work their own boat. Since August 16, 1880, when Port Darwin ceased to be a free port, the Customs Department has been one of its chief institutions. Its head was Mr. J. A. G. Little, superintending officer of the Overland Telegraph, but he and Mr. Cate, his second, have been displaced on their resignation by Mr. Searcey, who combines the duties of both offices. There is a staff of assistant officers. The head office is in connection with the Telegraph Department, and there is besides a galvanized iron store and office on the beach at the end of the Gulnare Jetty, in which all the outdoor business is transacted. Since the reimposi tion of the duties the Customs business has been steadily on the increase, though the present is a dull time ; and speaking of the abolition of the duties, I may mention that all through the gold-fields I found the utmost indifference amongst the diggers and miners as to whether duties were on or off.

"When the port was free it didn't make the slightest difference to us, except in spirits and tobacco. The storekeepers' prices for other things were just the same as they had been before, and when the duty was reimposed they stuck on an extra percentage. No ; *we* don't want the port to be free."

I have not heard the country storekeepers make answer to that. Of course, in so young a place the work of the department fluctuates greatly. About twice a year, for four or five weeks, there is not a steamer in; the week after the arrival of the first four, others occasionally follow. The usual Customs hours are observed, but the officers at some of the southern seaports would be nonplussed if they were asked to do off-hand the work to be done at Port Darwin. It partakes a good deal of the detective's profession, for to some of the Chinese smuggling is as the breath of life. Mr. Cate informs me that he has frequently found an astute Celestial hiding at night in the bow-chains of the vessels, and a boat with another Chinaman lying-to at the oars some little distance off. The game is to get one of the Chinese crew to pass some article over the bow, whence it speedily goes to Chinamen in the town. They have another game also, and the bones of their deceased countrymen play an important part in it. Since the gold duty had been enforced—some two or three months after—Mr. Cate heard that the bones which left by some of the steamers had had gold dust stowed away in them—in the skull and little passages. Ever since that time he has made each Chinaman seeking to pass the bones through to the ship bring them into the office for examination ; and a gruesome task that scrutiny is, especially when the skeleton happens to be green. He has never been rewarded, moreover, by the discovery of any treasure, and it is just possible that the rumour was another libel upon childlike and industrious John Comprador. I must not omit to mention, for it is important as marking perhaps the small beginning of a big ending, that this year the Government have appointed a temporary officer at Port Essington in the person of Mr. W. O. Robinson, the only white man over a very large area, who is in charge of the Coburg Cattle Company's Station at that place, and who leads a very lonely life. This action has been taken on account of the large number of proas which come across from the adjacent islands—Macassar, amongst others—for bêche-de-mer, &c., bringing with them for the purpose of barter with the natives a large quantity of raw spirits, arrack, and tobacco. These until lately have entered this part of the Territory without paying duty. The result of the application of the Port Darwin tariff to them has yet to be ascertained ; but it will at least have the effect of securing a record of the imports and exports at Port Essington, and it costs only £20 a year. The necessity for having officers at the Daly and Roper Rivers as settlement increases is kept in mind by the Sub-Collector.

Before proceeding to give a synopsis of the Customs statistics for the last year it will be well for the sake of distant readers for me to enumerate the few articles upon which import duty has to be paid in the Northern Territory. The list is :—Beer, ales, &c., 9d. per gallon ; rice, ½d. per lb. ; fish, dried and salted, 1d. per lb. ; spirits, 10s. per gallon ; tobacco, snuff, &c., 2s. per lb. ; cigars, 5s. per lb. ; opium, 20s. per lb. ; wine, 4s. per gallon. The only export duty is on gold, 2s. 6d. per oz., and the Minister has almost promised that it shall be reduced to a nominal figure for purposes of registration only and not as a tax. As will be seen from the figures which follow, the receipt from the gold export is a considerable factor in the revenue returns, and if it be removed the deficiency (say practical politicians) must be made up somehow. "As a duty on exports is subversive of the principles of political economy, and in this case inflicts a positive hardship upon the working man, and him alone, it no doubt should be removed." I shall deal more particularly with its effects in my mining summary, but meanwhile I would point out that substitutes might easily be found for the duty. Primarily the best means I have heard suggested is the levying of £2 or £3 from each Chinaman entering the port to settle, in payment for four or six years' miners' rights, at 10s. a year. I have it on the highest authority on the gold-fields that only sixty of these rights have been issued to them this year, and this shows that not more than three or four Chinese in every hundred obey the law in this particular. So that if they were compelled to pay when they arrived, the levy would be a very

different thing from a poll tax. It would be perfectly just, for
if Chinamen will not voluntarily contribute the paltry sum
demanded from them for the protection afforded to them by
the Government, they should be compelled to do so. At
the same time, be it remembered, the staples of their diet are
heavily taxed, while the Europeans' food comes in free. If
the deficiency were not made up in this way the balance
to debit could be met by small duties on articles such as
tea, soap, kerosine, &c., or by an extra ½d. upon rice. This
latter would also fall principally upon Chinese, but I question
whether there will be any rice import two years hence. The
Celestials are begining to grow it. In the meantime the impost
would act as a protective duty to the cultivators. Another plan has
been proposed by a Chinese gentleman to whom I was introduced
on the downward steamer—Mr. Hoo Chun, a member of the great
Yan Woo Company, of Hongkong, who have the monopoly of the
opium-farming from the Colonial Government there. He is now
travelling through the colonies subsequently to visiting England,
the Continent, and America ; and he very strongly urges the ex-
pediency of the opium tariff for the Territory and South Australia
generally and the other colonies being revised. Whilst he would
retain the 20s. per lb. on the manufactured article, he would place
only 5s. on the raw material. If that were done, he says that his
Company are prepared to establish opium factories in most of the
colonies, and forthwith at Port Darwin. As, with the small population of that place, 1,323½ lb. of opium, valued at £3,105, were
imported last year, such a factory would, no doubt, pay when the
expected brightening of prospects is realized, the more especially
as the long-headed Chinese threaten to combine poppy-growing with
sugar and rice cultivation. But there are who would object to an
opium factory in South Australia, and others to making what is
virtually a protective duty to support one. All this is written in
explanation of the suggestions made to meet a deficiency from the
repeal of the gold duty. Whether it is absolutely necessary to
meet that deficiency by fresh taxation I leave for discussion.

And now come we to the Customs records for the last year,
which are most interesting and suggestive. They show conclusively
what, from its position, might naturally be expected : that, whilst
South Australia has lost so much on the Northern Territory during
the time it was unable to pay its expenses, all the while, as well as
now that the corner is turned, she has reaped and is reaping
infinitely less of the advantage than the other colonies. The
details of these statistics have been, I presume, buried in due form
in the *Government Gazette*, and I will not disentomb them, though
they would be an interesting study. Suffice it for me to say that

during last year the value of duty-paid goods imported into Port Darwin was £31,578 14s., and that the proportion for each importing country was nearly as follows:—Hongkong, £23,500; Sydney, 5,050; Melbourne, £2,570; Java, £172; Singapore, £150; Adelaide £150; Queensland, £64. Of free goods the value was £70,147 4s., proportioned as follows:—Sydney, £39,706 11s. (or more than half); Hongkong, £10,993 6s.; Melbourne, £10,946 10s.; Adelaide, £4,949 17s.; Queensland, £2,692; Java, £274; Straits Settlements and Timor, £585. The total value of imports was £101,725 18s., and the amount of duty received £14,759 13s. 4d. The proportion of the whole was:—New South Wales, £44,745 15s.; Hongkong, £34,382 6s.; Victoria, £13,516; South Australia, £5,099 17s.; Queensland, £2,801; Java, £446; Timor, £375; Singapore, £360. The total exports were valued at £112,682 1s., and of this gold contributed £111,945 1s. Only 2 oz. (£7) went to South Australia. The other figures are:—Hongkong, £39,352 1s.; Melbourne, £37,339 10s.; New South Wales, £32,770 5s.; Queensland, £2,476 5s. The duty from this export was £3,938 13s. 9d. and that is of course the sum which will be deficient if the impost be removed—a little more than a quarter of the whole receipts.

Do these significant figures furnish, from South Australians' point of view, an argument for a through railway? In what other way is she to get her share of the trade of her now little but promising and sturdy community on her northern coast? It is but natural that, whilst she is practically further from it than any of her neighbours, they will monopolize the business; and she cannot well put on at Port Darwin a protective tax on all goods imported by any but herself. Let her people ruminate over this. There is another point, too. She is by steamer five days further, and Sydney is one day more distant from the Northern Territory than the commercial heart of China is; and when Hongkong (which includes other Chinese ports as well) comes forward in these statistics with £34,382 worth of imports against Adelaide's £5,099 17s., the fact is sufficiently suggestive to need no laboured comment from me in these sketchy articles. As despite the teeming millions of China, she can afford to have a food export; and as all her sons, sail whither they may, are sure to draw their supplies thence; as, moreover, our Northern Territory is next door to that great country; and as we do not yet produce the articles the Chinamen most do use, we may expect in the first place a very rapid influx of Chinese, and in the next to furnish an increasingly important market for their country's productions. It is within my knowledge that from Port Darwin have gone several educated influential Chinamen to bruit abroad in

their own land the fame of the Territory ; and I have again and
again, interviewing the best and wealthiest of the race now
residing there, been assured that it will become a second Singapore if they can make it so—a greater Singapore, because it has
its rich gold-fields.

"You see," said Yee Kee, the Chinese labour agent, and a plan-
tation-owner near Hongkong, "this country close by China. It got
grand land for garden and plantation; and I going home next
month to speak of it to rich men in Hongkong and start Company,
to grow rice and sugar and Chinese fruits." [This was after the
Minister announced his advocacy of the railway.] "We will send
out thousands of Chinese workmen to make your railway for you,
and then China do big trade with this place. By-and-by gardens
and plantations ready, grow things employ lot men when cannot
work gold-fields—no water. Suppose railway made right Adelaide,
get all through country. *Welly* good."

So some colonists doubtless will see two sides even to the railway question! But this shows that the Chinese are thoroughly alive
to the importance of these colonies ; and it, with many other things
I have seen and heard while amongst the Chinese population in the
Northern Territory, convinces me that our poll-taxes have not by
any means disposed of the "yellow agony." The old conservatism
of the Imperial Government of China is fast breaking up. The
presence of telegraphs ; the prospective reticulation of the streets
by water-pipes, and bridging of interior space by the railways ; the
building and manning of gunboats, and the adoption of many of
the ways of modern civilization—all these are having their effect
upon the former marked jealousies of the Chinese, and the effect is
greatly increased by the return of every man of influence who has
been successful in Australia. Remember that one of every three
men in the world is a Chinaman. Is it likely that they will *always*
be cooped up in such narrow bounds? The national increase,
if nothing else, renders that impossible. As surely will hundreds
of thousands of the labouring population attempt to migrate to
these colonies, their nearest point, as the Northern Territory will
be the place—the only place where they have not to pay a poll-
tax—whither they will first tend. The climate is the same as
theirs. California is played out, and we are nearer to them ; and
Chinese man even the steamers which give communication between
us. Now, let the thoughtful reader accept or reject my conclusions, and frame his own, while I conclude my sketch with the
record of the fact that last year there called at Port Darwin 56
vessels, representing 504,804 tons, and 2,544 men in crews, and
that very nearly the same left. The immigration was 336 males

and 18 females, and the emigration 1,105 males and 30 females—a considerable loss, it will be observed.

Having explained all that needed explanation in connection with the port of Palmerston, we will, if you please, interview Mr. J. Skelton, the Acting Chairman, and Mr. J. G. Kelsey, the Clerk of the District Council, in the official hall, which is about the size of three small piano-cases, and ventilated in much the same way. Our hosts apologetically explain that £500 has been voted for a Town Hall and Institute combined, but that they cannot purchase a suitable piece of land to build one ; and that the block they ought to have they have not. After Palmerston had been surveyed by Mr. Goyder, the Governor in June, 1874, nominated a District Council to administer its affairs. Palmerston is well laid out. When it becomes a city its street lines will be those of a model city. It is at a high elevation above the sea, and provision for its perfect drainage has been made by Mr. Knight (the father, brother, uncle, aunt, and numerous other watchful relatives of the place) with the aid of prison labour and a long civil engineering practice. The ground plan is saddle-shaped, with a bordering of park reserves. The town land is divided into 1,019 blocks of half an acre each ; 800 are sold, but only forty are occupied. The assessment is £490 per annum, and there is a balance of over £700 to the Council's credit. Several streets—straight as the straightest line—intersect each other at right-angles—streets about a chain wide and nearly two miles long—streets fit for accommodating busy traffic if it were only forthcoming—streets better than those of many a city. Though no metal is used the soil is so admirably drained and so free from mud that none or very little is needed. Some years ago, when the Government were beset by unsuccessful Chinese diggers returning from the goldfields and throwing themselves upon them for relief, the Resident wisely set them to work to earn the food they needs must have. The rate fixed was a shilling a day, which just enabled them to find themselves in rice and some simple vegetables enough to keep them from starving. They were organised in gangs, and set to work under European supervision in clearing the streets (which up to that time were only such on paper) and forming them with footpaths and watertables. Now they are periodically stripped of weeds and an acclimatized herb, similar to horehound, which has completely overrun the place. The blacks do this work, and do it well, for food and tobacco. Besides the wharf frontages the Government have, amongst other reserves, Point Emery, Point Elliott, and the old Gardens. There are squares and " places," and esplanades, and indeed all that is necessary to accommodate a population of 30,000 people. I asked Mr. Kelsey whether there were any means of ascertaining exactly how many persons live there now. He said—

" Wait a minute ; I'll think."

And he checked off on his fingers the various houses and their occupants. His total was 170 Europeans, and approximately 300 Chinese. Eight years ago there were seven public houses and seven English stores, and a population in proportion. Now the figures are two and three respectively. The Chinese, by the way, have a town to themselves. I will describe it by-and-by. The Europeans are almost entirely dependent upon them. There are a Chinese bootmaker, tailor, baker, and hairdresser, several dobies or washerwomen, and gardeners unlimited, and a Chinese Company is being formed to bring cattle from Queensland, and compete with European butchers. Altogether there are ten stores in this quarter. There is no place at Palmerston in which public enter-tainments can be held. There was an old store used for the purpose till recently, but it, like several other buildings, has been blown down by the strong winds which prevail. The obvious need here, and that also for the accommodation of the Council, spurred them on to bring before the Ministers their stock grievance—that the Government Residence and the Overland and the Batavia Telegraph buildings, occupying some nine acres in all, are erected on a public esplanade, which the original plans show the Council alone have control of. They contend also that the land on which the workshops and offices are built, near the beach, does not belong to the Government, and they want the esplanade at least handed over. The buildings certainly spoil the architectural uniformity of the place and the sea view. I have seen all the plans on which the Council base their claim, but, of course, can say no more than that. The Supreme Court will possibly have to give a decision on the matter. The Council particularly want that part of the land (twelve acres) known as the B.A.T. paddocks, in the heart of the town, to build on it the hall and institute for which the £500 was voted. The curse of absenteeism was never more prejudicially felt than it is in Palmerston. Though there are 1,019 half acres in the town area, only forty of them are occupied, and of these four alone are owned by those who reside on them. The others are mostly held from English owners under building leases. For one of these leases, having ten years' currency, a storekeeper pays no less than £75 a year, and at the expiry of the term he will have to give up his buildings to the owner of the ground. The lessee cannot help himself. He finds it practically impossible to buy land in the township, for these absentees have a huge monopoly. Years ago

the Government threw in one of the town allotments to the
buyers (or recipients might be the better word) of 320 acres of
land beyond. They did not cost more than about £5 each.
Now, for each of the blank half-acres on either side of the store I
have just referred to the price asked is £2,500. And nearly all
the owners expect so great a future for the place that they avow
they will not sell at all. I believe I am perfectly right in saying
that half-a-dozen allotments in good positions in Palmerston
could not be purchased now, or, if purchased, for less per foot
than the market value of land closely suburban to a Southern
city. I need not dilate upon the pernicious effect which this is
likely to have upon the prosperity of the place. I chronicle the
fact as an "awful example" of the curses of absenteeism. The
people felt the sting some years ago. All the land in and around
the town—all the land which had been surveyed—had gone out
of their reach, and they asked the Government to survey a block
at Fannie Bay, in which they might take up allotments for
residences. This request was made in the "flush" times of the
Territory, and it was granted. Ere the survey had been completed, however, commercial dulness had set in, and many of those
who preferred the request had left. The Government therefore
withheld the block from sale. They have continued to withhold it
since, and some of the people are indignant, and they have ad·
dressed to the Minister, through their spokesman, a sounding
staccato "Wherefore?" Most of the houses in Palmerston are
new, and the town looks somewhat piebald. The greater number
of the European offices and tenements represent the white spots—
the black or brown are furnished by the Chinese stores. The new
snow-white houses in the town are so arranged that you fancy
you see them shrinking away from the old and dingy ones, and
that you hear them remarking explanatorily.

"You understand, old houses; we don't object to you—not at
all, bless you; but we must not be seen mixing with you. Society
demands, and so on. You're not in our set, you know." The first
of the set is, of course, the Government Residency. The old one suc-
cumbed to white ants some time ago; the new one is two years old,
and it has inherited the same malady, but in a milder form. The
walls are of soft sandstone stuff, for which there is no geological
name under a multitude of syllables. The building looks fairly well
architecturally, and when the rain comes down there is—well,
there is no necessity to keep tanks outside. The accommodation is
so limited that only two of the Parliamentary party could
sleep in it. Its position is grand, however. From its high level
it overlooks the rest of the town, and makes a conspicuous landmark for a great distance. It is in the centre of a large en-

closure, which goes seaward—steep almost as a wall. Previously to last year this hill was a rough, barren waste, and part of it was an old quarry. Mr. Knight, Controller of Prison Labour, has converted it into a young tropical grove. Fifteen terrace-walks, 200 yards long and five feet deep, have been made, the quarry has been filled up, walks and graduated stepping-stages have been fixed, and the whole has been planted with couch grass and bright blue creepers, and bananas, and numerous ornamental shrubs. There is a beautiful spreading lightwood tree in the centre ; and as this year's plants have beaten their last season's predecessors by successfully defying the white ants, it is not too much to predict that Mr. Knight will have an exceedingly beautiful lasting monument.

The next of the Government institutions which call for mention are the baths, which Mr. Knight has constructed by prison labour on a plan of his own. They are so designed that even the tide-fall of 24 feet does not deprive the residents of the luxury of sea-bathing, out of range of sharks or alligators, with soles unvexed by sharp-edged rocks. Then there is the pretentious, cool and comfortable residence of Mr. McMinn, the senior Surveyor, overlooked by Fort Hill, which, with on top the white railings of the tomb of poor young Bennett, who was murdered by the blacks, you can see from any part of the town. Opposite Mr. McMinn's are the jealously-preserved screw-pines which formed part of the original camp scenery. Opposite to them is the Modern Camp, where the Government bachelor officers live. There is no explanation of the wherefore of the name, and it is misleading. Mr. Cuthbertson, its chief patron, came off to the ship with an invitation to stay at his camp; and it was only when I protested that it would be inconvenient to be camped out in the bush at night surrounded by mosquitos and black-fellows, that he laughingly explained. The camp is in one of the healthiest positions in the town, and it is noted principally for the goodfellowship of its occupants, and the fact that on it have been "raised" the first cocoanuts grown in the Northern Territory. *Such* cocoanuts, too, so large and so juicy; to what we get in the South as like as potatoes are to potato peel. Next to the Camp are the Government workshops and stables, the Customs and the Harbour Master's offices, the Government-bought residences of some of the minor officials, and the domicile of Mr. Knight, a cool bungalow-like place of wood and iron and inter-laced bamboo strips, and with more terraces. It will look like a little Paradise some years hence, but it will hardly ever smell like one. It is right above the Mud Flat. That Mud Flat is odorous and suggestive of piscatorial mortality—of fishy burying-grounds.

Leaving Mr. Knight's, you climb up the steep hill aforesaid, of which it hath been written that a newly-arrived intending settler had left the incoming steamer to seek lodgings in the town one steaming December forenoon. He got no further than half-way up the hill. He then went down again and took his backward passage, explaining that if the Northern Territory was so hot and so steep near the sea he would be anticipating the future by remaining in it farther south. And that would not be fair, he thought. But, achieving the ascent, we find ourselves at the end of the first and main street, and with Government offices on either side for some distance—ourselves in a line with the sea-front terrace, with more Government offices. We take the street first and interview Mr. Whitelaw, the Private Secretary to the Resident the Accountant, and the Secretary to the Hospital Board ; Mr. Lindsay, the junior Surveyor—during Mr. McMinn's absence, in charge of the Lands Department ; Mr. Cuthbertson, his colleague ; the Chinese Interpreter, to whom the Government give £100 a year ; and courteous Police Inspector Foelsche and his courteous family in their private residence, which is under the same roof as, and divided by only a slab fence from, the Public Offices. These offices, by the way, like all the Government buildings, are capitally designed for comfort in this " stifling " climate. What wind there is has free access from a hundred apertures, and it is not intercepted by ceilings. The walls are of stone, and these particular ones are architecturally pretty ; some of the others, to put it mildly, are not. There are no more Government establishments on the right-hand side, but the occupied part of the left—that is the disputed esplanade—has little besides. The first are the Eastern and China Cable Company's offices and officers' residences—the B.A.T. dens is the local name—the second are the S.A. Telegraph people's places—the O.T. huts they are called ; and the third batch are the private residences of the officers of the same. On the terrace you first pass the Gaol, the Courthouse, the police quarters, and the doctor's (Government) residence—filling up all the space to the next street. The only other Government places in the town are the State school (a neat and commodious structure, in which Mr. Kitchin for a petty salary daily instructs a score of children), the site for the new Gaol, the Harbour Master's lately finished new residence, and the Hospital, about which in this spare corner I had better say a word or two. It is by the poor people the best-esteemed institution in Palmerston, and its natural position is most picturesque. It is a mile from Palmerston, and when you get to it, through scrub patches, and—if you follow the beach—by clambering sundry sets of rocks, you approach a grand plot of scenery. There is the sea in the background,

growling its regular deep bass as the puny sands impede its forceful
shoreward march, or lulled to complacency by balmy air and un-
ruffled surface.   On one side there is a deep declivity, scaled by
the aid of rough steps ; the hill as yet unshorn of its rich clusters
of deep green undergrowth and spiral young trees and wiry long-
stretching creepers.   At its foot a Chinese garden flourishing, and
the gardener's hut—though oft the sea in rage has stretched and
stretched to reach and tear it up, it never has succeeded ; and the
rich verdure of the cultivated land continues still to mock it.
Beyond you get a perspective of green trees and high brown
waving grass, with another glimpse of the sea in the far distance,
and in front, opposite to the beach side, unsightly carriage
approaches.   This isn't poetry, but it's truth.

Inside the Hospital is plain but comfortable and cheerful-looking.
There are two large wards, with five beds in each, and plenty of
room for them, and there are besides three rooms for the keeper,
Mr. Mansom, and his wife, the matron ; and a dispensary for Dr.
Morrice, the only duly qualified medical man in the Northern Ter-
ritory.   The building is of stone, with cement floors and iron roof.
The verandah which surrounds it is ten feet wide, and a grand
view have the convalescing patients, for whose benefit it is made.
The rooms are so lofty, and the ventilation is so perfect, that the
Hospital has come to be considered the coolest place in the
Northern Territory.   And I believe that the character is well
deserved.   One ward is, of course, used by patients suffering from
contagious diseases.   At the time of my visit it was unoccupied.
In the other four of the five beds had patients—all, excepting an
intelligent young Port Essington black—people from Adelaide, and
each suffering from some form of rheumatism, in the leg joints
principally.   They all spoke in the strongest terms of praise of
the medical attendance and the kindness of the matron, and the
only sentence approaching to a complaint which they uttered was
one in reference to an extensive leakage which the white ants had
caused some months before in the roof.   They had an idea that
large quantities of water dropping on the floor around them and
occasionally sprinkling their beds did not enhance their chances of
recovery.   As they spoke came a squall and a thunderstorm and a
heavy downpour, and five minutes afterwards we found ourselves
dodging the rivulet running along the floor and its tributary drops
from the wounded ceiling.   But this is comparatively a small
matter, and the marvel is that it should be so old.   The
affairs of the Hospital are managed by a nominated Board, and
generally speaking they are managed well.   Patients who are able
to pay are expected to contribute £2 a week ; those who are not
go in, of course, for nothing but to be cured.   There was once a

Chinese Hospital, but it has ceased to exist; the building was destroyed. I believe the Chinamen contributed well towards its support, and they strongly urge that they should have another. For practically the present Hospital is of no use to them, as the white patients manifest a decided repugnance to Chinamen being in the same ward, though they don't object to blacks. This sounds like a grim satire, but the doctor assures me that it is a fact. Why Chinese should not be allowed to enter it is to me a mystery. Their diseases—at any rate the diseases which would be admitted to a Hospital—are not more virulent than the ailments of the whites—not *so* virulent in many cases; and it seems but fair to ask that the prejudices of the European patients should not be allowed too great effect. But the Chinese want their own Hospital. As they are willing to pay a fair proportion of its cost they will probably have it.

The Hospital and the doctor recall to recollection the cemetery, though there is no necessary connection between the two. The latter is handily convenient to the first, about one mile distant, and two miles from Palmerston, on the course of the telegraph line. It is the subject of one of the local disputations. It is in a wretchedly dilapidated condition, and all the public expenditure upon it seems to have been about .£60 for a wire fence. According to the representations of a member of the District Council, that body put up the fence on the strength of a promise by the Government that the cemetery should be handed over to them to be taken care of. That promise has never been fulfilled, and at present neither Government nor Council exercise any curatorship over it. If a corpse is to be interred the relatives have to hunt up the man who has the key of the cemetery. Sometimes it cannot be found, and on these occasions (I still have the same authority) coffins have been slid between the wires or over the fence. There is no effective register kept of the graves or the names of the persons whose mortal remains they contain, and my informant says he has known sorrowing bereaved ones to plant flowers and weep over grass-grown mounds which they believed contained all that was left of their loved ones, but which really held only Chinese bones. Of course it is very dreadful to think that the bones of Chinamen should mingle promiscuously with European osseous fragments, and there is now a Chinese section in the cemetery.

To the country generally, no doubt the most important institution in Palmerston is the Telegraph department. That portion of it first referred to in my heading is presided over by Mr. J. A. G. Little, who has, besides attending to numerous other duties, to inspect every year the first section of the overland telegraph line, extending 660 miles to Attack Creek. The offices stand at the sea front of a large close galvanized-iron enclosure, and are surrounded by patches of luxuriantly-growing tropical plants. All the buildings are of stone, roofed with galvanized iron, and perfectly ventilated. The fittings of the Post-Office are of cypress pine. They were being arranged whilst I visited the place, as the old ones had been completely riddled by white ants. The appointments of the office generally are well adapted for the climate. Mr. Little is their designer, and his well-performed task was all the harder because he had to fight against the effects of that climate, and to contrive to prevent the ants from getting through the wooden casings and lunching off the letters and newspapers. In the fitting-up of the telegraph-room regard had, moreover, to be had to the fact that some of the operators are bound to be in it night and day without cessation, because of the nearness of the cable terminus. And so it has been made light and cool, and commanding a view of a beautiful landscape. Do these conditions account for the fact that, the colonies throughout, you will not find smarter operators than those at Palmerston? Comfortable quarters are provided for each of the officers, from Mr. Little downwards. Those who are not married have a Chinese servant and black hewers of wood and drawers of water at their beck. The Benedicts have Government houses adjoining these; and if all do not enjoy life it is not the fault of the Government who send them thither. What more could they need than spacious quarters, cool, trellised verandahs in which to lounge and enjoy the sight of moonlit sea and smell of briny breezes, the while the Chinese boy brings them cigar lights and obeys their every behest; good wages, hours not too many, and work congenial? What more except— except a wife? If they want active exercise they may have horses to ride—horses accommodated, with the cattle, in a special part of the enclosure, with its harness-rooms and all other necessary appliances. The animals here enclosed have thriven exceedingly, though they are fed only on the rank native grasses, chaffed and mixed with a little maize. Just beyond the chaff- house are a formidable array of scientific instruments for registering heat and rainfall, and what not? The register is very carefully kept by Mr. Little, who, that the average rainfall throughout may be as thoroughly computed as possible, gives every sugar grower gauges, and tabulates each month the results of their use. Though the section of the Telegraph over which Mr. Little has control is so extensive, his staff of officers and men, including Chinese, is only 52. The mail service has gradually extended in the interior. The latest requisitions are £300 for a telegraph station either at the Shackle or Port Darwin Camp, and £469 per annum for a service from Pine Creek (the terminus now) and the Katherine River. The Overland Telegraph along the 600 miles which Mr. Little travels, he says, is in good order. The white ants now have little power over the posts, for which iron is rapidly superseding wood. He speaks in high terms of all the officers along the line.

Next to the Overland Telegraph quarters are those of the officers of the Eastern Extension and China Cable Company. Both are very similar to their neighbours, except that they boast a capital billiard table and a lawn tennis ground. Mr. Gott, J.P., is the Superintendent, and there are besides himself four operators, one of whom is always at the instrument. The cable-ends come in through a small cabinet close by—the cable is, as every one should know, in duplicate. There are three receiving instruments, so that breakdowns may be prevented. The newest, and the one being used during my visit, was Sir William Johnstone's Patent Syphon Recorder, and the one it most recently superseded was the same inventor's Reflecting Galvanometer. Both are complicated and delicate. To this little room come first the cable messages which convulse the whole of Australia sometimes, and yet, though each operator is duly posted up with the information, there has been only a single instance of one of them betraying the trust reposed in him. That was some years ago, and he never had another chance to betray it. To show how quickly communication is given, the operator sent along a couple of words hundreds of miles off to Banjoewangie, and in a second came back the answer—

"Right you are ; don't mention it."

In the same time from Singapore was flashed through a sentence from a book the operator there was reading—

"They gave him his choice of weapons, from a blunderbuss to a brickbat, and his own distance."

The battery-room has twenty cells to work the magnets and the receiver. They consume a large quantity of bluestone every week. The officers, who have plenty of time on their hands, are noted jolly fellows, who are sent out as especially smart men by the Company from England to remain for a certain time at each of the stations. The white ants have played great pranks in their quarters. They hollowed out a billiard ball, bored through sheets of lead under the verandah posts, and devoured all the door-posts and wooden partitions, leaving nothing but the paint. The Police-station on the terrace is roomy, and excellently situated. The force consists of only fourteen, including the energetic veteran Inspector—Mr. P. Foelsche—Corporal Montague (who has charge of the country head-quarters at the Shackle), and all the men, who as a body are most excellent officers. The day has passed when the Northern Territory force could justly be reproached with inefficiency. It will doubtless have soon to be largely increased, and it might be well if its administration were wholly confined to a responsible officer. There has been a great deal of friction caused on account of a division of responsibility. Considering the peculiar nature of a Police Inspector's duties in the Northern Territory, the marvel is that Mr. Foelsche has been content to undertake them for so many years. However, he has performed them as no man new to the place could hope to do at first, and in other ways he has laid the Government under great obligations to him. At his own expense he has taken and distributed to exhibitions and Royal Societies and travellers thousands of photographs of Northern Territory scenery, and has thus done much to advertise the place. Close to the Police Station is the Courthouse and warden's office, which would do for a second-rate stable, but is wholly unsuited for the honour of Chief Hall of Justice for the Northern Territory. There are great gaping holes in the wooden walls—holes caused by white ants that have also eaten away almost all the wood. After devouring the doctor's house near by, they finished this, and then went for the jarrah and redgum verandah posts, so undermining them that the weight of the roof has had no difficulty in crushing them out of the perpendicular, and itself out of the horizontal. A new Courthouse is a pressing want at Port Darwin.

Convenient to this place is the Gaol, of which Mr. Laurie is Governor, directing the assistant warders. It is a "conglomerate" Gaol, no more like what a prison should be than a chapel is like a cathedral. The whole establishment is surrounded by a nine feet iron fence, over which prisoners can get as easily as an astute lawyer can go through an Act of Parliament. Not long ago an Afghan threw himself over it, and shortly afterwards a Chinaman, who was undergoing sentence, was found out in the street one night. He was asked to explain, and remarked with an air of injured innocence—

"What for you holdee me? Leavee go. I only go out post him letter."

In Court next day he was awarded one year extra for his feat. The same evening, at 6 o'clock, he was over the fence outside again. It would be grossly unfair to blame the warders for these escapes. The Gaol is contrived with such perverse ingenuity that no mortal man on guard can watch all the yards at once, even if he were blessed with the forty-million magnifying vision which Sam Weller thirsted for, unless, indeed, he could bring it to bear from a balloon. Thus one prisoner may go into one corner of the yard, and the other to the opposite; whilst the

warder is watching No. 1, the second may be walking the streets.
It is really of no use for a man to try to escape, however; there
is no place where he could hide or live. He would certainly be
taken in an hour. This, of course, does not atone for the
atrocious badness of the prison accommodation; but there will be
consolation to some of my readers, no doubt, in the knowledge of the fact that £5,000 voted for a new Gaol is
shortly to be spent. The site is a capital one—the beauties of
scenery and architectural uniformity have alike been studied, and
every provision will be made for the comfort of resident
visitors. Coming back to the present Gaol, through which I was
conducted by the Sheriff (Mr. Knight) and the Gaol Governor,
we first entered Mr. Laurie's quarters, which are not much better
than a huntsman's dog-kennel. There is one room only, in
a corner of a verandah, on to which two doors open, and a third
to the Gaolyard. In this one wretchedly dilapidated room,
Mr. Laurie has to eat and sleep, receive and examine his visitors,
hold also his other than official receptions, and transact all the
business of his position. Going thence we interviewed the
prisoners in their miserable cells. I need not detail the actual
miseries of the place. It is always saddening to see men undergoing punishment with the sense of shame keenly manifested;
it is more so to see them without that sense. Both classes were
represented here amongst the imprisoned—nine blacks, eight
Chinese, three Malays, and two Europeans. Of the former, most
clanked along in fetters. The first we saw was a blackfellow sentenced
to ten years for murdering—it was a mysterious case—a white at Port
Essington. He bore a thorough orthodox stage-villain scowl, and—a
heavy set of leg-irons and anklets. Some of the other blacks were suffering for manslaughter; but most, like all the Chinamen and Malays,
for theft. Several of the Chinese were afflicted with a peculiar
disease affecting the joints with swellings, which has almost
baffled the skill of the doctor, and which is often fatal though
not very painful. Gradually the sufferer loses all power over his
limbs, and often dies, especially if he be exposed. Of the Europeans,
the chief is the misguided trooper who stole the gold from the
Southport Post-Office and arrested Chinamen for the theft, getting
a seven years' sentence through the smartness of officer Becker,
and afterwards confessing. He suffers acutely from some sort of
rheumatism, I believe, and seems a thoroughly broken man. The
first cell we came to was of " perished " iron, which would crumble
beneath your grasp. It was 10 feet by 12. In it was a sick
Chinaman, lying on a bench; the next was 12 feet by 5 feet, and
it had but one hard bench, yet in it four men slept. Mr. Knight
has somewhat alleviated the sufferings of the poor fellows by

putting on the cells a double-panneled door, contrived to admit
air in summer and keep it out in winter. The third cell
is smaller than the second, and also has four inmates at
night. Two others have a space 10 feet by 10 feet, and the other
is very like to the rest. The "solitary" room is of double iron
sheets with the centre filled in with sand, which deadens the sound
of the boot-heels and execrations of obstreperous inmates, and
keeps them cool. The sanitary arrangements are well attended to,
and no nuisance whatever is detected by the visitor. Where there
is little provision made for religious services for free men, it cannot be expected that there is any for the imprisoned. That is
true of their position now and always, in the absence of the
minister, which generally is for some months every second year.
The regulations of the Gaol are, whilst stringent, yet framed in
such a way as to show that the framers recollected that those who
were bound to obey them have to work in a climate very different
from that in the south. They are not even so hard as they seem,
for the gaoler is justly very considerate when men are well behaved.
They rise at half-past 5 in the morning, and work from 6 till 8,
9 till 12, and 2 till 5. The outdoor men are engaged in road-
forming and various other public works, and it is suggested that
their labour could be turned to account in the construction of
better wharf accommodation. The indoor prisoners have only to
chop up hard wood for the Government officers' fires, and the
gaoler takes care to keep them hard at work. At 6 o'clock both
classes are locked up for the night, without lights after 8, though
in special cases this rule is not adhered to arbitrarily. I should
have mentioned before this there is a capital kitchen in the Gaol,
in which the cooking is done by an imprisoned Chinaman.
The prisoners do not, like Uriah Heep, read patronizingly moral
lessons to their visitors; they seem mostly wretched, and though
the keeper does all he can for them, he cannot give them the
accommodation which health considerations demand that they
should have.

Next door to the Gaol is the Institute, which, let us hope, will
furnish an antidote to the bane which caused the imprisoned ones
to fall. It was started about four years ago by private subscription
to the extent of £10 spent in books. Several Adelaide gentlemen
helped; but, by-and-by, the undertaking collapsed. It tried again,
fortified by numerous "yellow-backs," and a room in the Land
Office was set apart for them till the new combined Institute and
Council Hall should be built. The tomes on the shelves have
been increased to a thousand, and the income to about £100 a
year. The selection of literature reflects credit on the selectors,
and particularly upon their chief, Mr. W. Cate.

CHAPTER X.—PALMERSTON.

PALMERSTON :—THE BUSINESSES AND BUSINESS PLACES.—THE HOTELS.—
THE DRINK CONSUMPTION.—THE CHINESE QUARTER.—THE
STREETS — THE NATIVE CAMP.—A SATISFACTORY INTERVIEW WITH A
KING.—SYPHILIS AMONGST THE BLACKS.—THEIR RELIGIOUS TEACH-
ING.—THE ONE NORTHERN TERRITORY CHURCH.—THE CLIMATE,
DRESS.—SOCIAL CUSTOMS.

MY first head, so far as it refers to European businesses and
business-places, can be disposed of in few words. Three
large importing stores, in which are vended articles of
almost every kind—from the fripperies of fancy drapery
to billy-cans and sheet-iron, including wine, spirits, and
physic ; a baker's, and butcheries in connection with the two hotels,
both fairly good for this place, but second rate if placed in comparison with an average country public-house in the South. They
are, however, not so rowdy, and their keepers do not consider that
the aim of an honourable ambition is to overcharge a traveller.
The Inspector of the Northern Territory hotels generally (there
are only a dozen) rather strongly condemns the average of them,
and proves by figures that they must make big profits at 1s. a
nobbler, and yet they are not over-anxious to give accommodation
to travellers. I had rather camp out than stay overnight at some
of them. The climate has its effect upon the quantity of potables.
For example, during the September quarter of last year 3,203
gallons of spirits, wines, and beer were imported into the Territory,
the value being £1,195 10s., paying £479 4s. 3d. duty. During
the same time 1,812 gallons were taken from bond for home consumption. This paid £627 1s. 11d. for duty, making the total for
the quarter in duty only £1,106 6s. 2d., or £2,301 16s. 2d.,
besides about £800 (the value of the goods taken from bond), over
£3,000 for intoxicating liquors alone. £1,000 a month for liquors
amongst 500 whites and a little over 3,000 Chinese is a comfortably big figure, is it not? Many of the former and most of the
latter are practically teetotallers. The hotelkeepers' profits on
these lines are, it is estimated, about cent. per cent. at least.
Besides the stores, the bakeries, the butcheries, and the hotels,
there is, I think, nothing worth mentioning except the three
Banks, which are busily engaged at present in cutting each other's
throats, all hoping to drag on till a flush of business comes to the
Territory. The two youngest, a few months old, are the Town
and Country and the Commercial, energetically managed respectively by Mr. J. C. Hillson, J.P., and Mr. Harrison. The pioneer
is the English, Scottish, and Australian Chartered, which, eaten
out of office by the white ants, has had built a spacious, preten

tious, and costly iron Bank on an Indian model. Every part of it
is of iron, and it is, as it looks, light and airy, yet thoroughly
strong. The Managers evidence wonderful faith in the future of
the settlement by having a strong-room large as the powder
magazine for a big mining corporation. It is very thick with stone
and cement; but while it was yet wet the white ants, as though to
mock the builder, came up in thousands right through its centre
in a single night, and he had not been able to get rid of them
when I saw him some time after. Almost the only hitherto un-
enumerated institution of the town is its weekly newspaper, which
is neatly turned out of hand, but small in proportion to its con-
stituency. It is edited by Mr. J. Skelton.

This brings us to the Chinese quarter, which is larger than the
European, and at which I promise you a hearty welcome. Your
shadow darkening the threshold is the signal for the teapot, containing a decoction such as European lips seldom are blessed by
tasting, and the square-gin bottle to be brought out, flanked by
lichee and sundry other Chinese fruits, and all marshalled
in front of you as soon as you have well entered the shop.
Semi-nude Chinamen all round put on their singlets, and twist
their pigtails in captivating fashion, and then come out kowtowing
profoundly to receive you. If you return the courtesies courteously,
you will perhaps be honoured, as yours to command was,
by an introduction to the only Chinese lady in South Australia—a very agreeable, chatty little body, with wee feet and a
tiny baby, pleasant-looking, and prattling as innocently as an
English infant. You would hardly think, my Chinaphobist, that
a Celestial child could be pretty and a prattler, and born without
a pigtail, would you? The stores are of all kinds, including, I fear, a fan-tan shop, which the police cannot discover.
In the mercantile concerns the thing you notice most is the small-
ness of the profits which the keepers make. For 15s. you buy
lacquer-work which would cost you a couple of pounds in Adelaide.
The next thing you observe is the absence of the foulness and
dirt which prejudice had forewarned you to expect. Though the
houses are not so good, you find they are quite as clean and
sweet and wholesome as those of the other quarter. This
is true nearly all through, and the only conclusion I can form, and
yet be loyal to my Chinaphobists, is that the childlike and bland
Celestials were keeping the best side out till the Parliamentary party left. That must be the explanation, I suppose.
The party, let me add, they pressed the acceptance of numerous
gifts upon, and felt greatly annoyed if their liberality was met
with a refusal. That, of course, was not a recognition of the
visitors' position, but simply a politic move, eh? But move politic

or otherwise, the Chinese in this Territory of ours received the Minister, though some of them were aware that he has been one of their strongest opponents in the House, with a cordiality which the Europeans scarcely equalled. I but speak of the Chinese as I found them. Conversation with them has convinced me that there are no men more keenly watching the upshot of the legislative deliberations upon the railway proposals of the Minister than the Chinese merchants and capitalists in the Northern Territory, and the greater men with whom they are in telegraphic communication in the principal capitals of China.

But we have lingered at the Chinese quarter, and so, just noting the fact that they have a little shrine for their Joss, and that they intend to put him by-and-by in a suitable temple, we turn back to the main street this Saturday afternoon—about the busiest time. (The half-holiday with the shops is on Wednesdays.) If more than a score of persons were seen in the street at once, people would probably think that the place had been invaded, and if two-thirds of them were not blackfellows, that—well, that the circumstance was something unusual. The whites are mostly dressed in colours to match, and they look conspicuous ; and the blacks wear little else than Nature's garb, and that little generally a piece of fiery red cloth ; and they are conspicuous too. The picaninnies are covered by nothing but the sky. Some of the women display a bust which an artist might model a Venus from—that of a few might fairly be mistaken for an imitation half-full coalsack. The tibia of both men and women are shrunken and lanky out of all proportion to their otherwise well-modelled bodies. The men generally display them pretty freely, though several are getting accustomed to the European bifurcated garment, yclept trousers. Generally speaking, those who wear it don nothing else, and those who have anything else to wear eschew it. The people are all mimics ; they imitate anything which strikes them as peculiar in a stranger. Such an one, strutting pompously down the street, for example, may find at least a couple of exact copyists of his movements shuffling up close behind him, and a squatting audience laughing and clapping their hands in appreciation of the joke. There interviewed me one night a black named " Billee," dressed in white, with a pith helmet crowning all. The way in which he imitated the Government Resident would have done the heart of Maccabe good. My " boy " was a youngish black named Pickles, because the first act which brought him into the glare of public life was the annexation of a phial of the savoury condiment thus denominated. He was clad in a portion of a Union Jack, and he looked so utterly villainous that I engaged him. I found that he

had sent eight of his kind to their account—one was his own
mother-in-law, I believe. It was interesting at night to have a
murderer grinning at me ; and I felt aggrieved when some weeks
before I left " Pickles " was awarded six months' for becoming
possessed in a questionable way of some wine. There are many
other blacks as bad as " Pickles," but without the especial
weakness which causes him now to be spending six months in
retirement. Though so murderous in their tribal wars, these
fellows are tame enough in the presence of whites, and
really are very useful, though fickle in their fancies, and as
loth to work as an average working man's strike-demagogue.
The young lubras are engaged by the English as washerwomen and
charwomen, and they work very well, I am told. Indeed, altogether they are almost indispensable to the whites. I had already
paid a visit to their camp, whither they repair at night, for fear
of " Mooldarby," when I met King Miranda, and accepted his
invitation to look at it again. On the way down I thought I
would test the truth of a charge of intelligence brought against
him in a passage of a book of travel by an Englishman. This
was our conversation—

" How many people are there under your rule ?"

" Yah !"

" You understand English ?"

" Yessec. Big fellow savee !"

" Well, then, how many people in your tribe ?"

" *My* w-o r-d ! All about."

" My word " is an equivalent for our "good gracious " or something like it ; " all about " signifies " plenty " amongst a dozen
other things. I think, however, the reader will agree that the
famed king of the Larrakeeyahs has cause for a big libel action
against those who write him down as " highly intelligent."

By this we had got to the camp—a beautiful place not far from
Fort Hill. It is backed by precipitous crags o'er which stretch
trailing creepers, binding together in matted fashion gnarled roots
outcropping and interweaving themselves with the luxuriant
masses of green leaves which weight the stalwart trees, causing
them to lean far over the edge whence their roots derive the
nourishment they give them. It is fronted by almost the only
wide boundary of clean seasand for miles around ; it is canopied by
prolific tropical growths. But the beauty is all on the side of
inanimate nature ; and from the sea it is spoiled by the clusters
of heterogenous huts the blacks have built for themselves—huts
compounded of bits of kerosine tin and drift wood, of bark and old
bagging, and one with an old insurance plate stuck upside down

over its portals as a dearly-prized charm to ward off the dread
Mooldarby, perhaps. Some natives, not so highly favoured, have
not huts at all, but shield themselves from the sea blasts by
roughly-arranged big sheets of paper-bark. There you have the
camp. Erections mocking civilization at the back of a most
beautiful groundwork of Nature's best construction; bark piles as
a practical satire upon them in mid-distance, with light and frail
canoes of the same hard by; in the foreground a hard, firm, pretty
promenade, with the natives playing on it, with the sea lapping it,
and sending out little wavelets to sport in the bright, silvery
track which the moon from a cloudless sky has made far out into
the harbour. There you have the camp as we saw it last. But I
spare the reader disagreeable details respecting a people scarcely
more intelligent, so far as the elders are concerned, than monkeys;
nearly all naked; nearly all dirt-encrusted; nearly all syphilitic,
more or less. One little bright-looking and clear-spoken half-caste
boy was a frightful object to gaze upon on this account;
besides himself a tiny half-caste female were the only evidences
of the joint immorality of the whites and blacks. Such
evidences are generally destroyed. For the rest a sentence will
suffice. Wizened old women and haggard old men, prattling but
dull-eyed children, all squatting together with mangy curs; and
young women, some ogling themselves in bits of broken looking-
glass. The younger men especially fashioning spears and canoes
for sale as curios, and offering six days' work for so many pence.
I will not swell out the notes I collected respecting their mystic
beliefs or practices; their curious fashion of bewailing their
bereavements, or disposing of the deceased one's body; their
polygamous habits; or the tribal distinctions so marked that,
whilst circumcision is practised by two of the tribes, the others
laugh at them for practising it—for all this is being done for the
Royal Society of South Australia by Inspector Foelsche, who has
studied the blacks more carefully than any other person in the
Territory. Suffice it for me to add that at present nothing whatever is being done to Christianize them, but a little to debase them
still further. It was different when the Rev. J. A. Bogle and his
successor (the Rev. W. Hanton) lived in Palmerston. I heard
their names mentioned in reverence everywhere I went amongst
the blacks, and that of the former particularly amongst the whites.
Both reverend gentlemen laboured hard to do their dusky
brethren good, with scant encouragement; but a little incident
shows that their work has had some result. Half a dozen urchins
told me they could sing "Missa Hanton song," and they struck up
the "Sweet By-and-by," and sang this other in correct time and
tune, and as to accent much in this fashion—

> A little s'ip was on de sea,
>   It was a pritty sight.
> It sailed a'ong so p'easantly,
>   An' all was calm an' bright.

And so on. I believe there is hope for the young blacks yet. They can be educated as easily as the Chinese, and I cannot say much more than that.

Speaking of religious teaching I should mention that there is only one church throughout the Territory, and that is Wesleyan. It is a small wooden building, reared on brick piles, and untouched by white ants. Some say it is the bricks and others the sanctity of the place that make it proof against the little pests. Unfortunately the climate and the ministers sent up disagree, and there are long periods when there is no one besides the local residents to keep the church going. Mr. Price then conducts on Sunday evenings a church service in the building, in which also a Sunday-school is held. The Rev. W. Stewart is at present in charge of the church. He met me whilst I was coming down.

A reference to the climate may fairly precede a few words about the social life, which it necessarily so much influences. Personally, I found the weather generally better than that south, with cool mornings and evenings, and the intense heat for short periods only. The atmosphere affected by that heat, of course, is humid, and one good effect of that is that there is almost an entire absence of sunstroke. Mr. Little, the weather registrar, assures me that he never knew of such a case during the many years he has lived in the Territory. I had not an opportunity of judging of the reputedly worst part of the year nor of its best, though most of the residents were agreed that the wet season was as bad as any. The year has two seasons—the dry and the wet—from May to September, and from October to April, respectively. The average shade temperature during the former is about 80°, and during the latter 95°, the minimum respectively at night being 56° and 65°. There is no rainfall at all in June, July, August, and September. Of the wet a register has been taken during the last ten years, with the following results':—1872, 54·622 inches; 1873, 72·505; 1874, 51·800; 1875, 56·520; 1876, 60·860; 1877, 60·110; 1878, 61·580; 1879, 60·908; 1880, 68·460; 1881, 45·120; 1882 (to the end of March), about 34. The heaviest rainfall in any one month was 22·790 inches in January, 1880; the highest average is in March. The present wet season is the lightest known for years. The registration which secured the above results was at the Port Darwin Telegraph Station.

With regard to the effect of the climate upon labour, there seems to be a concensus of opinion that Europeans cannot do the hewing and the drawing. That must be undertaken by coloured folk. Mr. Little's opinion upon the subject is as follows:—"With regard to the suitability of the country for European labour the writer can affirm—after four years' experience—that a man cannot perform the amount of constant work that he is capable of accomplishing in a more temperate climate ; but still there is nothing to prevent a moderate day's work being done—and further, there is an almost entire absence of those enervating influences which prostrate the European labourer in other tropical countries, such as India, Java, Singapore, or Africa. Workmen carry out their various avocations throughout the day without taking any precaution to ward off the rays of the sun, the eight hours' system being usually adopted. The climate, in fact, may be said to be more of that type which is generally known as Australian, rather than tropical. It is free from cholera and other scourges of hot countries, and on the whole may be considered healthy. Intermittent fever, commonly known as fever and ague, is prevalent at times, especially in low-lying localities, or immediately after the wet season ; but this complaint is not dangerous in itself, and can often be prevented by a moderate and judicious use of medicine, and a small amount of bodily exercise."

The people have in the matter of dress accommodated themselves to the climate. For the cold weather they wear light-blue serge or tweed ; for the hot white suits. The Civil servants transact the public business very often clad in nothing more than trousers and singlet. The regulation dress for Government House parties and dinners is white trousers, black dress vest, and thin, white mess jacket—a costume which looks far better than the venerable swallow-tail and fixings. At evening parties at private houses people come occasionally in pyjamas. The clothing of the ladies is equally sensible. In the early morning you meet leading residents going through the street in nothing but a serang, and on the first morning I arrived I presented a letter of introduction to a high official who disguised his physical conformation by a bath-towel only. Social customs also have to some extent to adapt themselves to the altered circumstances of the place, and yet, remembering those circumstances, you wonder how so much of society's ceremonies can exist. What, however, would my lady readers think if they had to arrange their company dinners on one special night in the week, because it was the only one on which they could get a joint from the butcher ? Yet that is sometimes the position of the mistress of the house in Port Darwin. The evenings—be the occasion formal or otherwise—are spent outside under the verandahs, and a very sensible practice that is—highly enhancing the visitors' enjoyment. In a place

where the only amusement in any way public from year's
beginning to year's end is an occasional whist-party at the
Government Residency, folks are thrown much on their own
resources for enjoyment. Some keep alive the grand old practice
of scandal-mongering, and it is just now in fine feather.
Palmerston is certainly not the place represented as having

> " No domestic jealous jars,
> Buzzing slanders, wordy wars."

You would hardly think that about fifty of the " society " people
could afford to run two factions, but they do, much to the em-
bittering of the private lives of each. But altogether they are the
most hospitable of people, receiving every eligible stranger with
open arms, and each faction vieing with the other to worthily
entertain him.

CHAPTER XI.—PASTORAL AND GENERAL.

THE] PASTORAL OUTLOOK.—SOME FACTS AND FIGURES.—AN IMMENSE MONOPOLY.—THE GLENCOE AND ADELAIDE RIVERS, AND OTHER STATIONS.—THE SALT TROUBLE.—WILL SHEEP SUCCEED.—ABSENCE OF GENERAL PASTORAL ENTERPRISE.—A PASTORALIST'S SUGGESTIONS.—IMPEDIMENTS IN THE WAY OF PROGRESS.—THE GOLD DUTY.—THE HIGH CHARGES FOR CARTAGE AND FOOD.—THE DEARNESS OF LABOUR AND THE LACK OF SKILLED WORKMEN.—THE LABOUR QUESTION GENERALLY.—EUROPEAN, CHINESE, INDIAN COOLIES.—THE NECESSITY FOR GOLD-SAVING MACHINERY.—ALTERATION IN THE MINING LAWS.—THE CONCLUSION OF THE WHOLE MATTER.—TRAVELLING AS IT NOW IS.—WHAT THE PARTY NARROWLY ESCAPED.—THE DIFFICULTY OF MAKING ROADS.—THE LAST SURVEY RAILWAY A MISTAKE.—AN EASY AND INEXPENSIVE ROUTE FOR A RAILWAY TO THE REEFS AT LEAST.—THE REMEDY FOR NEARLY ALL THE DRAWBACKS.—FINIS.

THE constant complaint which meets you in the country is that there is nothing to fall back upon when the dry weather prevents the prosecution of mining operations. One of the most oft-repeated suggestions has been—that even without a railway the gold country, at least, would have a very fair chance of being developed if there were during the dry months other work than mining for the diggers to do. Hundreds, it is said, have left the Northern Territory because they had no means of earning their bread during these intervals. Leaving planting out of the question, had there been even shearing to be done they could have remained in the country. And they urged with some zest that the Government should compel the lessees of all pastoral lands to stock forthwith, pointing forcefully in support to the fact that whilst every acre of the pastoral areas is held, there are not enough cattle bred in the Territory, or available ones owned by any of the holders, to supply the less than 4,000 residents with fresh meat, which has to come from Queensland. You will remember that the party did not see half-a-dozen cattle all the way through the country. Well, since these representations were made, some of the holders, at least, are assisting in a slight way to remove the cause of complaint. They are starting settling work on their stations, though whether this will grow into a "fall-back" for the diggers is very doubtful. Unless they have sheep, lessees can offer very little work; and it is doubtful whether sheep will thrive so far north for some time. The first experiment to breed them failed disastrously; as will be seen, a second is to be made. A great deal will depend upon whether that succeeds.

The gentlemen I refer to are Messrs. C. B. Fisher and M. Lyons, who hold about 40,000 square miles of pastoral country bordering Palmerston alone, and a great deal elsewhere in the Northern Territory. Of this about 18,000 are comprised in the Glencoe Run, of which I have previously written casually, and which they bought in November last from Messrs. Travers and Gibson. In December, Mr. H. W. H. Stevens, their energetic Manager, took delivery from Mr. Burkitt, the representative of the former proprietors. Since then, Mr. Stevens has let contracts for making various improvements, many of which are in progress, whilst others have been completed. In place of two thatched huts, which were designated by the name of homestead, and a small yard capable of holding only 300 head of cattle, there are now good iron buildings. Large stockyards after the fashion of those in use on the more modern runs in Queensland are in course of construction ; paddocks are being made round the homestead, and others for the reception of stock for weaning. There are now 1,900 head of cattle, and 86 horses on the run. The stock are principally store cattle, but they are to be replaced by others *en route*, the intention being to keep Glencoe as a thoroughly good breeding station. It is by the road somewhat less than 100 miles from Palmerston, and it is in a fair situation relatively to it and to the navigable part of the Adelaide River. The country on this run is some of the best in the Territory. Its plan shows a perfect network of permanent waters and fine shady creeks, with lots of high country for the stock to retreat to in the wet season, and plains extending for miles along the McKinlay River, where they may feed by still waters and in green pastures in the dry weather. The situation of the station is central for all markets in the Territory, and will, in the event of a railway being started and population coming to the country, reap, more than any other pastoral holding, the benefit.

Messrs. Fisher & Lyons have about 21,000 miles on the eastern bank of the Adelaide River, extending from Adam Bay to twenty miles east of the East Alligator, and including it and the other two Alligator rivers. It stretches, indeed, from the northern coast to the Adelaide River, and west and south-west to the Roper auction blocks ; and it and Glencoe, with Sir T. Elder's territory which they bought from him, take up a great deal of the western bank of the Adelaide, the watershed, and I don't know how far beyond. The station on the Adelaide I have already described in my notes on that river. I have simply to add that it is intended that the run shall be used principally for sheep. This is the experiment on which so much depends. Fisher & Lyons have, moreover, a little more than 1,000 miles of the very pick of the Daly country near its northern end, and they will be able to closely approach these as well as the rest of their stations by means of the river vessel to

PASTORAL. **151**

which I have previously referred. As soon as the dry weather sets
in they are going to have a station built on the Daly, so as to be
ready to place there a fair proportion of the mobs of stock they
have coming from Queensland. These comprise 20,000 head of
cattle, 300 brood mares, and 13,000 sheep. Of course, the possession of so much land around Palmerston means a great monopoly
to Messrs. Fisher & Lyons ; but it is to their credit that they have
the pluck to spend so much money upon it. They have shown
the right pioneering spirit, and in Mr. Stevens they have a representative who will make their venture pay if it has within itself
the necessary elements. And no one will be pessimist enough to
say it has not.

With the exception of the pioneer squatters Dr. W. J. Browne,
and Mr. Wallace, and one or two others (including Mr. Gilbert
and Messrs. Tennant & Love on the McDonnell Range country
further south, the latter having 6,000 head of cattle), they are the
only pastoral holders who are spending money on what has been
universally admitted to be good pastoral country—country which
has made all the horses and cattle I have seen "rolling fat."
Amongst the "one or two others" are Messrs. Favenc & Brodie.
Mr. Favenc, with Mr. Briggs, started out some time ago in charge
of what was known as the *Queenslander* Expedition, to select land
for a station, and secondarily to explore the country. Mr. Favenc
has gone on another expedition, to take 1,700 head of cattle to
stock the run they discovered—the Cresswell Downs, about 3,000
miles—and to take a schooner to the mouth of the McArthur, and
to see whether the place is suitable for the erection of necessary
buildings to make a little township. When this is done he intends to explore another large area right up to the overland telegraph line.

Mr. Wallace's station, on the Elsie and Roper Rivers, consists of
6,000 square miles and is 300 miles distant from Palmerston.
There are nearly 2,000 head of cattle upon it and its prospects are
very good, the representative whom I met assured me. Dr. Browne
some time ago stocked the Springvale Station, on the Katherine
River, about 200 miles from Palmerston, on the telegraph line,
with cattle and sheep. The sheep did not get on well at all—a
great many of them died—and the cattle were not in the best
condition. The reason, so far as the cattle are concerned, is the
absence of salt in the water or saline material in the ground.
There is no limestone, and there are no other salt elements. This
applies also to a limited area beyond the Katherine. From the
Adelaide River up to Rum Jungle you see lumps of rock salt
placed before the publichouse doors for the horses to lick ; and
yet on the Glencoe Station, which includes some of this country,

the cattle thrive. As for the rest, by far the greater area has
either limestone or else brackish water coming down the rivers from
the seaboard. There is a salt water well nearly 90 miles
from the mouth of and close to the Adelaide River. On Mr.
Wallace's run there is brackish water, and also on Dr. Browne's
Delamere Downs station, which is 280 miles from Port Darwin,
near the sources of the Victoria River, and to which he sent the
remainder of the sheep (about 3,000) and 1,200 of the mixed
cattle from Springvale. Within the last fortnight I was in the
Territory they brought the sheep back, as they continued to die.
(The cattle, however, throve.) The Telegraph Department bought
what were left, and sent them down to Tennant's Creek (so I am
informed), which, being so much further south, is more suited to
their pasturage.

Whatever the reason, the attempt to breed sheep in the
Northern Territory has hitherto been met with signal failure, and
has involved the men who have made it in serious losses. The
superintending officer of the Telegraph Department (Mr. J. A. G.
Little) showed me some sheep bred near Palmerston, and they
looked hopelessly consumptive—thin, scant-woolled, and scraggy.
The most feasible explanation of the failure which I heard is,
except where there is no salt in the water or land, that at present
the grass is too long and rank for the sheep—that it needs to be
fed down a few times. As the author of an exceedingly
useful book on the Northern Territory (Mr. J. G. Knight) has
written—"There can be no doubt that as the wildly luxurious
indigenous grasses are fed down the character of the herbage will
be completely changed. It is hardly to be feared that the climate
will be found too hot for the growth of good wool, as fine fleeces are
produced in Queensland in corresponding latitudes; but it may
need time, patience, and discrimination before we can find out what
breed of sheep are best fitted for the country. When Port Darwin
was first occupied a number of goats were introduced, but as all
the male ones died it was concluded that goats could not be reared.
More recently another breed of this animal has been tried, and its
progeny are increasing rapidly. [I have already referred to about
a hundred fine ones that I saw at the Howley.] This little
illustration is given merely to show the error of attaching
too much importance to one solitary experiment." So far
as general pastoral purposes are concerned, the Northern
Territory almost all over is suitable for them. There is
throughout a grand interlacing of rivers and creeks, and in most
places where there is not a permanent supply of water the
precious fluid can—for this has been proved—easily be obtained
by sinking to no very great depth. A few Abyssinian wells would

supply all that would be needed at a very slight cost. Though to land fit for agriculture in the Territory the qualification " patchy " must be applied, it is not called for in a general description of the pastoral country. Practically there is grass all the year round on by far the greater area. After that, which is now so harsh and high and dry—though succulent enough to be cut for chaff by the Telegraph Department—is burnt down, in a fortnight or so, in the gullies particularly, a crisp, fresh herbage, high enough for cattle to crop, takes its place ; and so, with this abundance of water and feed, there need be no fear of whole flocks and herds succumbing to hunger and to thirst.

Now, how much longer are the lessees of the big unstocked runs going to leave their lands lie idle ? There are rumours of probable stocking far, and wide, and soon. The holders have been awaiting the results of experiments, it is said. Well, experiments have proved that horses and cattle thrive in the Territory as well as in any other part of Australia. Let them try horses and cattle, then, leaving the sheep at home till the issue of Fisher and Lyons's and other trials with them is known. Or, when the land shall have been fed down a little, let each bring a different class of sheep, and fairly try them and the country. In closing, let me in justice add that though every other class with whom I have mixed here on information bent have had some suggested concession to bring forward, the representatives of the pastoral lessees have not even hinted at one. They urge, however, what they consider to be needed reforms in the land laws. They grumble particularly because so many hundreds which cannot be used for agriculture for years are out of their reach for pastoral purposes ; but when you press them they admit that they have a good deal of land after all. They urge then that their considerations in the suggestion are not personal to themselves ; but they feel how greatly it would be to the interests of the country if they paid rent for the land now lying idle outside the pastoral reserve. And so, I suppose, I may say they are as satisfied as Britons can manage to be under fairly auspicious circumstances.

And now I have to submit for consideration the impediments in the way of the progress of our Northern Territory, through the development of its mining interests particularly.

The gold duty is no small one, and it affects the poor man almost solely, excepting in the case of Companies, and at best it is a tax upon production, and therefore unsound. Whilst I was in the mining districts I obtained from the owners of several of the mines the originals of bank and assay returns for the gold they sent to Palmerston. Here is a sample copy. It is so suggestive of the tremendous handicap the gold-miner has to fight against in one particular alone that I will allow it to speak for itself, merely affixing to it the item of 4d. per oz. for carriage:—" Returns, 83 oz. 5 dwt. of gold, valued at £3 11s. per oz. (equal to that in the Melbourne Mint), £331 0s. 9d.; allowance for silver, 9 oz. 4 dwt., £1 16s. 9d = £332 17s. 6d.; Bank charges, at 3s. per oz., £13 19s. 9d. = £318 17s. 9d.; assay charges at 1s. per oz., £4 13s.; export duty on gold, 2s. 6d. per oz., £11 13s. 2d.; net value, £302 11s. 7d." Putting on the £1 for postal carriage, the gold was worth about £3 5s. an ounce to the Company. This was in June of last year.

Here is a sample Bank account of January 1, 1882:—"By 120 oz. 3 dwt., at £3—£360 9s.; less exchange 2¼ per cent., £9; insurance at £3 10s. (why £3 10s., if it is only worth £3?) per oz. on £420 10s. 6d. at 26¼ per cent. £5 12s. 4d.; freight, 1 per cent., £4 4s. 3d.; export duty, £15 = £33 16s. 7d. of reductions, giving £324 12s. 5d. as the value to the producer, deducting postal charges." He loses 10 per cent. of the value of his gold at Port Darwin. This particular parcel was worth to the owner £2 16s. 8d. per oz.

The high price for cartage between Southport and the Reefs is the next drawback. As much as £80 a ton has been charged in the wet season, when very little carting is done. The average now is about £30. The owner of a battery assured me that its conveyance from Southport cost him about £40 a ton. You can't blame the teamsters for these figures. The road, though better than it was, is bad at best, and always will and must be bad, and goods have often to be unloaded several times in transit; and this again adds to the handicap, for the frequent shiftings cause breakages.

The next difficulty—the high price of living—is partly due to this. The lowest charge for board and lodging—and *such* board and lodging—is 35s. per week. With necessary extras no man pays less on the average than £2 5s. a week. Supposing he lives in a hut and "batches," this is the kind of bill he is confronted with (I quote the prices from an invoice obtained whilst I was in the central mining district, the Twelve Mile):—Fresh herrings, 2s. 6d. tin; beef, 1s. lb.; sugar, 10d. lb.; bar soap, 2s. 6d.; one singlet, 9s.; 50-lb. bag flour, 27s. 6d. (that is £5 10s. a bag); jam, 2s. 6d. a tin; salt, 10d. lb.; preserved milk, 2s. tin; currants, 1s. 3d. lb.; dripping, 3s. lb. Compare these prices with those in the southern capital. For mining tools, &c., the charges are proportionately high:—Steel, 2s. lb.; a hammer, 14s.; handles, 2s. 6d. each; a pick, 10s. 6d.; blasting powder, 18d. lb. Remember, too, that these articles do not pay duty. On the whole I think I had rather be a retail storekeeper on the Reefs, if I wished to make money quickly, than the waiter at an aristocratic hotel. Why, even if a man wishes to write a letter he is faced by a big tax of 5s. a packet for notepaper, which can be got for 1s. in Adelaide, and 1s. for a packet of twenty-five envelopes, which are obtainable for 5s. a thousand there. (These latter figures ruled at Port Darwin Camp on March 23, 1881.) High prices there ever must be till better communication with markets is provided, but such amounts as these seem greatly disproportionate.

Yet, remembering the comparatively enormous risk, I do not blame the storekeeper so much after all, though he is able effectually to dominate the gold-reefer, except the Companies and such men as Jansen at Pine Creek, and one or two others. But let a working miner with a good-looking reef on his property attempt to avail himself of it, and by a recital of his experience you will at once see how it is next to an impossibility that the gold resources of this grand gold country can ever be properly developed under existing circumstances. Half a dozen poor men begin the sinking of a shaft, getting their goods on credit from the storekeeper. When they have sunk 50 feet or so the bills become due, and they have to suspend sinking and open out to get gold to meet them. And so on for each stage, till finally when they have got, after a long time and at infinite cost, to about 150 feet, they are met by necessities for increased expenditure, and they throw up the task disheartened, unable, maybe, to pay even the store-keeper.

Another drawback is the high labour-rate. The highest for working English miners is £5 a week, and the lowest £4 10s. For Chinese the figures are £2 15s. and £2 5s., the general rate being £2 10s. Digressing for a moment, I would just add a few words about the labour question generally. It is the most fitting place to do so. For underground mining I believe there can be many suitable Europeans found. I have known plenty of underground places in the other colonies almost as hot as those in the Northern Territory at the same depths. The reefers themselves agree with me that there is a wide field for European labour in the quartz-mining districts. The principal drawback now is the fever, which afflicts most of the men, but escapes the majority of the teetotallers and other regular livers. The disease is so bad now, because if a man contracts it he cannot consult medical advice; there is no hospital within his reach. With the providing of these benefits the drawback will be considerably modified; with the clearing and settlement of the country it will depart altogether. I believe, however, that in underground mining alone European labour can be generally employed. For the alluvial the Chinese must to a great extent be

depended on, though I have seen them beating and turning a drill
underground almost as well as a white man. Some very grave
charges have been levelled against them. They have been
accused of neglecting to pay miners' rights; of jumping Europeans' claims, or stealing gold from them, whilst the owner was
riding after the Warden for a settlement of a dispute they cun-
ningly raised; of watching prospectors, and when they have found
anything bringing hundreds of their countrymen to work it out;
of inability to discover new fields for themselves; of everything but virtue. This by the miners, but even a leading
Queensland paper, speaking of the Northern Territory, says:
"The Chinese have not formed agricultural settlements, either on
their own account or under the direction of Europeans. . . .
They have done nothing, directly or indirectly, to add to the
prosperity of the settlement. They have scraped together whatever alluvial gold was accessible to them, and we believe that they
have departed from their usual habit to a certain extent,
and found new patches undiscovered by Europeans; and they
have strangled nearly all European attempts at colonization,
miners and traders alike. Nearly all the white men who went to
the Northern Territory have either been ruined, driven out, or reduced to great poverty." This is a gross libel, though it credits
the Chinese for what they are held not to do here—that
is, pioneer work in the discovery of new gold-fields. They
have formed all save four of the agricultural settlements; on all
the European plantations which employ any labour the Chinese
largely preponderate over other people as labourers; so far from
"strangling all European attempts at colonization" they have
assisted them by starting gardens all over the mines; and to
charge them with "ruining, driving out, or reducing to poverty"
the white man is to throw guilt upon the innocent. Ruinous rates
of living, the discomforts of pioneer work in so inhospitable
a region, and the lack of ground for hope of anything better as a
result of the construction of a railway—these drove the Europeans
out of the Territory. The Chinese did not. But for them many
thousands of ounces of gold which are yearly exported
would not be produced. Their bitterest opponents on the
mines admit that they work alluvial ground the whites have long
since abandoned, and, though their peculation must be stopped,
and themselves kept from sharing, without some acknowledgement,
the benefits of Europeans' discoveries, they certainly must be
looked to as the men by whom the poorer auriferous country
must be developed. It should be remembered, when the question
of their swarming gold-fields comes on for discussion, that there
are two sides to it. When the bonus system was in

force, two or three Europeans finding gold in new districts accepted £1 a head from the Chinese to be shown and allowed to work on the locale of their discoveries so that the necessary condition of "payable" might have a chance of being complied with. These Chinamen, whatever their faults or their virtues, should be judged upon their merits. I am no special pleader for them, but I feel bound to protest against the utterly false portraits which have been painted in the colonies of those in the Northern Territory. As to the Chinese in the other walks of life, what Sir William Jervois said of Singapore holds good in Palmerston. When a visitor "gets there he will see the boat in which he lands manned by Chinamen ; his luggage will be taken to the hotel by Chinaman ; when he gets to the hotel he will find the cook a Chinaman, the butler a Chinaman ; and if there is a family he will find the nurse a Chinaman, and every department of life filled by this race." The future population of the Northern Territory will be two-thirds Chinese, I believe. The Hindoo coolies have this to recommend them—they are less intelligent than the Chinese, and more useful as servants because they have no ambition. They come to the country bound to work at exceedingly low wages under agreement with their Government for so many years. They will work their time out like the beasts of burden that they are. Their Government will not allow them to be employed in mines ; and as they will bind themselves for years while Chinamen won't, and work for less than he will where there is free scope for his enterprise, they will no doubt fill the labour-sheets for the plantations, but not the railway works unless I am much mistaken. (I need scarcely add in this connection, that the Indian Coolie Immigration Bill has been passed by the South Australian Parliament.) The Chinese will do the kinds of mining in which the least skilful work is required ; the Europeans will do the rest, and amongst it most of the reefing, as well as the overseeing.

But coming back to the point—the position of the miner. Added to the other drawbacks and the cost of labour, he has, if he be two or three miles from a battery, to pay excessively high prices for the carting of the stone thither. This, then, is his situation : The preliminary work of development over, a mine-owner, assisted by one white and a Chinaman, in six weeks raises 25 tons of stone, which yields 50 ounces. Allowing him £3 an ounce, he gets a gross return of £150. If he has his stone crushed at a battery two or three miles off, the crushing and carting cost him (I have an invoice before me) 75s. a ton, or £93 15s. altogether. To that add £30 for the white's wages and £15 for the Chinaman's, and his expenses for the raising and crushing of that £150 worth of stuff amount to £138 15s., leaving him

£11 5s. for his own wages and wear and tear. So that, whilst in New South Wales or Victoria he would make a handsome profit out of 2-ounce stuff, in the Territory nothing short of 4 ounces will pay. As to other hindrances, I have already expressed an opinion that one-third of the gold is wasted by imperfect saving appliances, and that fortunes may yet be made out of the battery tailings. But that is easy of remedy, and the alterations already indicated as needed in the mining laws could be made if the Mining Board, which has been in such long recess, were resuscitated. The Board, by the way, went into that recess because they proposed to do what the miners now ask so strongly for—to reduce the size of the claims. The proposition, however, was opposed by the very class who now champion it, and the Board, knowing that if they were to meet they would have to confirm their resolutions against this clamour, determined to go into recess, and let the matter rest in abeyance awhile. The whole of the mining laws need very careful revision. They must be special, just as all legislation for the Territory must be. The authorities have not yet seen the absurdity of enforcing the Licensed Victuallers' amongst other Acts—well adapted, maybe, for South Australia proper, but quite the opposite there, where in places it is absolutely impossible to obey the Act. But they will see it, and they will see many scores of minor points, and if there is to be no railway they may as well rest content with seeing them. In any case they might wisely, I think, offer bonuses for deep-sinking, for the discovery of new gold areas, for the first 100 tons of tin and copper, and £150 or so for comparatively small quantities of different kinds of tropical produce. This latter would bring small capitalists into the field—comparatively poor men who cannot aspire to so great an output as 150 or 500 tons of sugar to secure the premium now offered. Holders of mining claims should not be allowed to shepherd them without working them, and the size of each claim should be reduced one-half. They are now altogether too large. A point which investors themselves must attend to is the obtaining skilled management for their ventures. The deeds done under the name of mining in this Northern Territory make a practical man either wax witheringly sarcastic or weep.

And these, roughly stated, are all the principal impediments, Under the general heading some people seriously class white ants, but though they were a serious nuisance once, the days of their power are, I believe, fast being numbered. Their influence over acclimatized vegetation has already been virtually overcome ; when settlement thickens they will have to go back into the bush. Legislation cannot affect them much, and it is a question whether it can remedy the really grievous hardship of which first of all the visitor to the Northern Territory sees plain evidence—the withering blight of grasping absentee owners of Palmerston itself.

Before I write anything about what the reader will have seen I am convinced must be carried into effect ere the Northern Territory can advance appreciably—namely, a railway to the reefs at least—I will give an idea of the difficulties of travel from Palmerston thither by the present only means—the road. Though in one or two of these sketches I have mentioned incidentally the wretched condition of that thoroughfare during the wet season, I never had the opportunity of seeing it at its worst or of describing it thus. The Parliamentary party had wonderful luck, and as they travelled serious obstacles were mysteriously removed. The very clouds held back their heaviest downpours till the travellers were safely camped, and it is no wonder if they somewhat discredited the sensational tales told them of floods and bogs. But at the last moment I have been favoured by Corporal Montague, who began the down journey the day after the party finished the upward one, with a recital of his experience, which proves that the distinguished visitors had a narrow escape from a most unpleasant predicament ; that throughout they had wonderful good fortune, and above all what serious difficulties there are in the way of communication between Palmerston and the interior. The reader's attention will at once be drawn to the significance of the testimony as showing the difficulty in maintaining roads subjected to such tremendous strain, and if he will keep in mind the route traversed by the party he will have no difficulty in fixing the position of the points named relatively to the gold-mining centres. The Corporal writes :—" It may perhaps interest the Ministerial party to know what they would have encountered if they had been a couple of days later on the road. The Stapleton had swollen considerably, and the Adelaide was rising high. The whole of the Adelaide Plains were under water. At Burrell's Creek the overflow formed a rapid stream down the road, and very deep. The road was washed full of holes, into one of which one of us fell, horse and all. The packhorse got bogged up to the girths twice in a quarter of a mile, and had to be unloaded and dragged out on to firm ground. Bamboo Creek at the crossing was nearly six feet deep, and running very swiftly. With the assistance of two Chinamen and a long rope we hauled our six horses over, and then got our things to the other side, where we had to dress standing up to our knees in water. We had no sooner crossed than a heavy downpour of rain set in. The road along the flat near Mount Darwent was all under water, and very rotten and boggy. Near Bridge Creek the whole flat was covered about a mile nearly up to my knees in the saddle.

The creek itself was overflowing its banks. The Howley was level with the bridge, and running over the confines of the bank a sheet of water. In a flat to the north side of the bridge the deepest parts of the flood-waters were about six feet. At the foot of the rise there was over three feet of water on the road. Yam Creek, at the old bridge, has been about twelve feet deep, and Brock's Creek from fifty to sixty yards wide. Old trees weighing half a ton are washed right across the road, on which they now lie, and large holes have been made in it in places. Crossing one creek alone took us two hours." It is thus every wet season, and without saying any more on that head I will leave the reader to draw his own conclusions as to the possibility of keeping roads in good repair under such circumstances—to ponder the question whether the cost of it if it were possible would not be much more in a few years than the whole expenditure upon a railway. In the latter speculation he will not lose sight of the fact that the road would be no source of revenue to the Government; the railway beyond question would. He must remember, too, that while traffic on a road would be stopped four months in the year, the railway would always be available. That is, of course, providing the proper route were chosen. There is in the Northern Territory—you will find it everywhere you go —a deep-seated conviction that everything has not been "jonnick" about some past railway surveys; that those conducting them have had to survey as directed rather than as their better judgment suggested. As to the 1880 survey for a railway to the Reefs, while they manifest the greatest regard for Mr. Stewart, who conducted it, and appreciate his ability, they question whether he was allowed free choice or full scope. At any rate, old bushmen and miners and others who know the country thoroughly well condemn most uncompromisingly the route he proposed. It is admittedly a comparatively short one, but there you exhaust its merits. It does not even tap the mineral country on which the recorded slight attempts at development have been made. These are its sins of omission. As to the others, it goes too far east; you can see it for yourself by tracing its course on the map. You would see it much more clearly had you gone through the country. It leads through swamps and marshes, places where the line would have to be built on piles, or else completely covered by water during certain periods of each year. It would necessitate the construction of enormously long and, of course, expensive bridges across the rivers and creeks. It would no doubt exhaust every penny of the fear- fully high estimate of cost of construction. These facts have strongly presented themselves to a trustworthy competent

expert, who knows more about the interior of the Northern
Territory than perhaps any other man (with a single exception)
there. The gentleman to whom I refer—Mr. David Lindsay—in
his capacity as Government Surveyor has minutely examined all the
country for hundreds of miles, and he has given especial attention
to the subject of a railway route. The result of his study he has
given in a rough sketch of his scheme to the Minister of Education. The route he proposes would be a distance of about 155
miles from Palmerston, or some 20 miles more than the length of
Mr. Stewart's line, but the cost of construction would not (if well-
informed enquirers may be trusted) be more than £5,000 or £6,000
per mile at the utmost. Mr. Lindsay's line crosses high level country,
avoiding submerged plains, and the heads instead of outflows of rivers.
The Adelaide, for example, could be safely spanned by a bridge 150
yards long instead of 1,000, as contemplated by Mr. Stewart.
From Port Darwin to Rum Jungle the line I have just indicated
would pass through the land which was surveyed by Mr. Goyder
(I omit the numbers of the sections for an obvious reason), and
granted to whomsoever would take it under the lot system conditions, and excepting where it followed the road or telegraph-
line reserve compensation would of course have to be allowed to
the owners of the properties crossed. From close to the Rum
Jungle, however, there is no surveyed land, and the Government
have already had the forethought to withdraw from offer all blocks
which might be traversed by the railway in this direction, so that
the amount to be paid for compensation will be, or should be, a
mere trifle. Some notable Territorians are sanguine enough to
believe that as the line approaches central sites they would, if
they were surveyed into township blocks and sold, yield sufficient
funds to enable the construction of the railway to be consummated
without the expenditure of so much as a farthing from the
Treasury coffers of South Australia proper. As bearing indirectly
upon this point it may be added that Mr. Lindsay claims for his
line another advantage over the other—that it will pass through
good agricultural land, will go close to the first acknowledged
gold country (the Stapleton), on to the next (the No. 1. Depot),
past Bridge Creek Gold-field, the Britannia and John Bull mines,
within five miles of the Howley Reefs, over others, and the alluvial
diggings at Sandy Creek, as well as close to the numerous gold
claims at the Twelve-mile, and through the heart of the proved
tin land. Experienced men attest that the country the line would
follow generally presents no engineering difficulties whatever, as it
keeps to the level high ground. "Stewart's Line," says Mr.
Lindsay, "for miles is subject to inundations, and he has bridges
over the Brooking, Mitchell, and Adelaide Rivers and Lloyd's

Creek, all of which save one are missed in my route ;" and at this
stage I leave Mr. Lindsay and Mr. Stewart to fight the matter out
between themselves, just adding that a third surveyor has now
began a fresh survey.   The reader may think that the estimate
of £5,000 a mile is too low ; that it would take far more than
£775,000 to make to Pine Creek a railway which shall serve all
the mining country and help the navigable rivers to take down
the pastoral and agricultural products to the seaboard.   They will
tell me that the white ants will eat what the floods and the soaking
baking heat leave of the wooden sleepers ; that iron ones must be
used ; and that they will run away with a mint of money.   But
these are exploded notions.   Every one who has travelled the
Territory with an observant eye, every experienced resident there,
will endorse what Mr. Knight—himself a civil engineer, albeit
a Government servant—has written in his little book   on
the Northern Territory :—" As to the question of sleepers, a long
residence in the Northern Territory, and an intimate acquaintance
with its timber, enable the writer to state with some authority
that an ample supply of durable indigenous wood is obtainable.
Ironbark, paperbark, bloodwood, and cyprus pine resist the ravages
of the white ant ; while stringybark, which is most abundant, is
only piped by this destructive pest, after which it abandons the
tree,   leaving sound sufficient wood for sleepers, fencing, or ' cordu-
roying.'   The timbers herein mentioned have been used in building
the existing bridges and are available for ordinary bridges, culverts,
&c."   So much for the construction of a railway.   The prime consideration of course is whether it would be politic to make it.   All
my enquiries and observations relating to the various resources of
the country lead me, at any rate, to respond to the question with
a most emphatic " Yes."   My readers have had in these
sketches, as succinctly stated as manifold difficulties would allow
me to state it, the evidence for and against.   What say they?
Let them remember, as the first important consideration, the
possibilities in the way of population.   What manner of people
will the Government have to cater for ?   The whole conditions, I
believe, in this as in other matters, will be widely different from
those in these lower latitudes or many degrees north of them.
Space will not permit me to do more than merely suggest this for
thought, or to do more than indicate that in addition to subserving
directly the interests of the miners, the agriculturists, and the
pastoralists (so far in the latter as horses and cattle are concerned),
it will bring within reasonable distances of the seaboard and the
rivers leading thither the country to the south where sheep also
can thrive.   A wool export from the Northern Territory is by no
means a chimerical notion.   May I say the same of the utilization

of the country as a remount station for the Indian Government?
And, finally, without a railway I cannot see how the Territory
will be a good field for enterprise. Without it must remain almost
in statu quo. The development which has been achieved already
has been made in expectation of the time when a railway shall
attract population and cheapen labour. Unless that labour be
cheapened—unless, too, the cost of carriage be reduced 75 per
cent.—the growers of sugar, rice, and other tropical products there
can never hope to compete with planters elsewhere, who, with
facile means of carriage, pay a merely nominal wage to their
labourers. This is the position of the plantation-owners even
on the seaboard within hail almost of Palmerston. What can
they do, whilst they pay £1 a week for workmen? What can they
do, even if they get Hindoo labourers at five shillings a week, with
no railway to attract a population large enough to make it worth the
while of steamers to call there more than once a month and take
away their produce? Or even if they go to the expense of pur-
chasing or chartering vessels to do this, see how they are handicapped by the high prices of everything—prices which will recede
only before better communication, and the competition which
will accompany the population it will bring. And this applies
only to the seaboard or places within say twenty miles of it. It
affects not at all the interior, with the gold country, the pastoral
and the agricultural areas. As to them all as yet only the most
pitiful apology for development exists, and ever must exist in
slightly modified reality so long as the present compelling conditions remain. If they *are* to remain, the Government may as well
let the Northern Territory drift, and confine their attentions to
the Southern. But if they *do* let it go, they will have cut from
them one of the most valuable possessions any colony might envy.
The gold which now, though abundant, is so hard to get, and of so
little value comparatively when got; the tin, which, if easily
accessible, would form such a valuable article of export; the rich
lodes of copper, which cannot now be looked upon with practical
intentions—*all* the varied mineral deposits will not much longer
be allowed to remain undisturbed. Some one somehow will
disturb them. The most effective *how* is the construction of a
railway first. His Excellency the Governor said recently:—
"There are three things required as important elements in the
development of the Northern Territory. One is the supply of
Hindoo labour for agriculture; another is the supply of Chinese
for the working out of the railways and the legitimate business of
the country, and the other is a means of communication to bring
down the mining and other products from the interior to the
seaboard." An expenditure of private capital has rightly been

suggested as an addition to the "things required" as here enumerated, and let me add there is one more want—the want of
practical men to superintend the expenditure of money and the
work on which it is spent. Hitherto this prime necessity has to
a great extent been ignored, in mining particularly. Men with
good address have won the votes of Companies for managership,
men either unconscientious or without knowledge of mining,
practical or theoretical ; knowing no more how to open up lodes or
develop ground than a clergyman knows or should know of the
mysteries of cardsharping. The results are bungled work, squan-
dered capital, disheartened speculators, and strong scepticism
respecting the resources of the Territory. It will take hard,
honest, and intelligent work to overcome these things. But the
Northern Territory has a geographical situation more favourable
perhaps than that of any other part of our continent. Port
Darwin must by-and-by be the "depot of Eastern commerce for
Australia," if not eventually the gateway through which travellers
from China, Japan, our bigger colony—India, Europe, and the
United Kingdom shall pass on their way along a transcontinental
line to the southern capitals. This latter idea may seem Utopian,
but will it be, think you, a decade hence ? However, leaving that
out of the question now, let me plead, in justification of the very
full references I have given to the various matters connected with
the Territory, the great prospective importance of the place. As
another writer says—"When it is remembered that the area of the
Territory is considerably greater than that of South Australia
proper, the importance of knowing something about this great
adjunct to the province will be apparent to all thoughtful minds. It
cannot for ever remain unsettled or unproductive, nor will its
destiny be far different from that of the other sections of South
Australia. It must become populated, and it must in due time
raise its proportion of staple products, not merely for home
consumption but for export."

A P P E N D I X.

PROFESSOR TATE'S OFFICIAL REPORT.

By the courtesy of the Minister for the Northern Territory, the author is enabled to include as a valuable appendix a statement of the professional opinion of Professor Tate upon the country. It embodies the results of the observations of the Professor during his visit with the Parliamentary party :—

May 13, 1882.

Sir—In submitting to you the following report, based on personal observation, of the mineralogical, geological, and botanical features of the Northern Territory of South Australia, I beg, in the first place, to thank you for the high compliment which the appointment conferred upon me ; and, secondly, to express publicly my obligations to the Council of my University for granting me the necessary leave of absence to accompany you on your official visit to the Northern Territory, to assist in the task which has been so energetically and successfully accomplished by you. Whatever may be the immediate results of this report, yet I do not hesitate to say that information on some matters therein contained ought to have weight in determining the directions which development of the resources of the Northern Territory must assuredly take. The geological phenomena of the Northern Territory are such as to determine, to a large extent, the nature of the future industries ; and though we need not enquire into the causes of this effect of geology, yet the force of my statement will be seen to have foundation in fact as I proceed with my report. Particularly, in this connection, is it to be regretted that I had so very few opportunities for extended and specific observations, and in consequence the geological work is for the most part a recommoissance while in the saddle, and more frequently than otherwise under the most trying circumstances, to which you yourself can testify from your own experience. Nevertheless, the general features have been, I think, correctly read, certainly as far as regards the prevailing character and area of the metalliferous rocks and their relationship to those barren in minerals. By consulting the writings of explorers who have visited the Northern Territory, and by information communicated by Government officers and others who have recently traversed previously unknown ground, I have been able to supplement the facts acquired by my own personal observation, the outcome of all of which is the geological sketch map and mineral map accompanying this report. *Surface Configuration and General Botanical Features.*—The country traversed, from Southport to Pine Creek, consists for the most part of parallel ranges of hills of moderate elevation, having a general trend of north and south in the northern part, and of north-west and south-east in the southern area. Intervening between the ranges are broad plains, which are, however, occasionally interrupted by low spurs and ridges of rocky ground. The road follows the low ground, and the incline from Southport is very gradual, being about 50 feet per mile. Pine Creek, the most southern point reached, is 755 feet above Southport by aneroid measurement, or about 800 feet above sea-level at ordinary low watermark. Yam Creek is 730 feet above Southport. Immediately to the west of the telegraph line from Yam Creek to Pine Creek there confronts the traveller the bold picturesque escarpment of the " Sandstone Tableland," which is the northern edge of the great plateau of Central Australia, with which it is physically and geographically connected. This precipitous rampart of sandstone has, near Yam Creek, where I studied it, an elevation of about 600 feet, or of about 1,400 feet above sea-level; but at the point Leichardt descended from it, into the valley of the S. Alligator River, it is 1,800 feet high. The character of the landscape, as far as it depends upon trees, shrubs and grasses, presents along the whole route very little variation ; and it is only by the margins of some of the sluggish watercourses that the vegetation assumes a tropical aspect. In the jungles, always of limited area, such as at Fannie Bay, near Palmerston, at Rum Jungle, at the Stapleton, and those on the margin of some of the tributaries of the McKinlay River, there abound bamboos, reaching to 40 feet and 60 feet high, screw pines, umbrageous fig-trees, tall eucalyptus, and the paper-bark melaleuca or tea-tree, amongst which climb certain convolvulaceæ, true vines, sarsaparilla vine, &c. The rest of the country is grassy and lightly timbered. The flats, the soil of which is a stiff clay, have much grass and little timber ; the slopes of the hills are covered with a pisolitic-iron, quartz-sand, and gravel ; and as we recede from the swampy ground the grass becomes shorter and scantier and the trees closer and smaller. The timber is of a scrubby kind, the chief constituents being two or three eucalypti (E. clavigera, &c.), iron wood (Erythrophlæum Louchcrii), and Grevillea-chrysodendron. There is a general abscence of shrubs ; and the grasses, which make up the rest of the landscape, if we except the grotesque ant-hills, which almost equal in height the trees amongst which they occur, are comprised of about three species.

Geology.—The general geological features may be summarized as follows:—1. The coast cliffs of Arnheim Land are composed of sandstone and calciferous sandstone, the lower beds of which conform with the denuded surface of the metamorphic slates on which they rest; but with increasing thickness the horizontal stratification is gradually approached. Sections displaying the junction of the two dissimilar formations are those of the scarped face of Fort Hill, at Palmerston, and Talc Head, on the west side of the entrance to Port Darwin. 2. Beyond the confines of the formation of the coast cliffs there is an extensive and well-marked region, which may be named the region of the river basins of North Arnheim Land. Here the prevailing rock is of the metamorphic class, being either a micaceous or a talcose slate, with which are interstratified quartzites and felspathic sandstones and grits. The latter series constitutes the hilly country, whilst the former has been more extensively denuded to form the intervening depressions of the surface. The axes of the ranges and of the plains, where unaffected by igneous intrusions, coincide with the direction of the strike of the rocks. 3. Intrusive rocks, as granite, diorite, and porphyritic felstones, occupy here and there, in the midst of the metamorphic rocks, not inconsiderable tracts of country. All these are of later date than the metamorphic rocks, but older than the "desert sandstone." 4. The table land of Central Australia constituted of sandstones and gravels horizontally bedded, terminates in South Arnheim Land in a bold escarpment, as already referred to. Its position in the stratigraphical scale is presumably upper miocene, but, for distinction sake, the formation has received the name of the "desert sandstone." The line of escarpment within the area under review approximates in outline to the letter V, the apex of which is at about twenty miles north from the crossing at the Katherine River, and the ends of the two limbs near to the mouth of the Alligator River on the north, and at about the limits of the tides on the Daly River on the south-west. The base line of this triangular space is occupied by the coast cliffs, which are undoubtedly outlying portions of the "desert sandstone." The area within these lines is the region of the rivers of North Arnheim Land. This vast sheet of "desert sandstone" is barren of useful minerals, and conceals from view the productive metamorphic rocks which underlie it. The "desert sandstone" is reported to contain layers of coaly matter, quite within the range of probability; but it is extremely unlikely that coals of passable quality occur. It is a question well worthy of investigation if the bottom gravelly beds of the formation do or do not contain detrital gold, though its presence is somewhat incompatible with the probable origin of the materials composing the "desert sandstone." inasmuch as the detritus of the local metamorphic rocks has not apparently contributed to its formation. The metalliferous area is included within that of the metamorphic rocks, the boundaries of which are defined by the inland escarpment of the desert sandstone and the coast cliffs, as previously described. It is worthy of notice that the schistose formations which lie to the north of the granites on the River Finniss seem to be non-metalliferous, whilst similar formations between Bridge Creek and Pine Creek are exceptionally metalliferous; and from the circumstance that the strike of the beds is not coincident, it is not improbable that the rocks of the two areas belong to different periods. In no case has it been proved that the igneous eruptions have directly contributed to this wealth of minerals, though it might have been so inferred from the prevalence of granite and diorite in the richer parts of the metalliferous area. Whether or no the richer alluvial gold drifts of Yam Creek and the Margaret have been derived from reefs included in the diorite, or in rocks in contact with it could not ascertained. At any rate, no reefs have as yet been discovered in that rock or in near proximity to it. On referring to the accompanying mineral map it will be seen that the metalliferous deposits are situated for the most part within a few miles east or west of the telegraph line ; but we must except those which are on the line of road from Port Darwin Camp, *via* Twelve-Mile McKinlay River, to Pine Creek. This detour will be seen to coincide with the north-easterly projection of the " desert sandstone," and with the line of outcrop of granite which is traversed by the telegraph line between Yam Creek and Pine Creek. The rock formation over the whole of the metalliferous area is almost entirely of metamorphic origin, and there cannot be a doubt that much, if not all, of the outerlying area, extending probably to the escarpment of the great tertiary plateau, is of a similar character, here and there doubtlessly broken through by eruptive rocks. We have thus a very extensive metalliferous country awaiting exploration. Year by year the area of the mineral-bearing ground is extended by discoveries beyond previously known limits. A little while since Mount Wells was proved to be stanniferous, and later the more distant diggings at Chinaman's and Saunder's Rush have considerably enlarged the known area of the auriferous country. Though the metamorphic rocks occupy a circumscribed area, approximately an equilateral triangle, yet that area is absolutely large, as it contains 7,800 square miles ; and should the portions not hitherto prospected prove to be as metalliferous as the known tracts, then may be realized that prosperity which has been so long hopefully anticipated. The circumstance that the telegraph line has followed the " run of the metal" is explained by the fact that the telegraph road, by opening a way into the interior, has served as a base line for exploration. Beyond the Driffield all exploration in a southerly direction will be barren in results ; possibly, however, there may be some small inliers of metamorphic rocks in the deeply excavated channels of some of the rivers flowing southward. Such probable inlier is on the Katherine, some forty miles north-east from the telegraph line. It is a fortunate circumstance that the general direction of the northern portion of the projected transcontinental railway, as determined by topographical features, will traverse the whole of the mineral fields, so that an independent line of railway constructed to overcome some of the difficulties which impede mining development may in the future become an integral part of a great railway system. For immediate purposes it need not be carried further than Pine Creek, and most certainly not beyond the Driffield.

Gold Reefs.—The gold-fields extend from the River Stapleton, *viâ* Bridge Creek, the Howley, Port Darwin Camp, Twelve-mile McKinlay River, and the Union to Pine Creek, a distance of sixty-five miles, and thence to the Driffield, thirty-five miles further. The last-named district was not visited by me, but all the chief workings in the others were inspected ; these are coloured in gold on the accompanying map of the metalliferous district. The width of the auriferous country as at present known is only a few miles. The chief centres of gold-reefing are the Howley, Twelve-Mile McKinlay, the Union, and Pine Creek. The quartz veins are included in the felspathose sandstone forming the high ground ; and because they intersect the " country " at angles approximating to the strike of the rocks they have contributed to the ridge-like form of the ranges. In some cases the crest of the range coincides with the outcrop of a quartz vein of two feet or so in thickness ; this phenomenon is well-exemplified at the Union, where one reef is traceable along the summit of the range for over two miles ; in other cases, a close series of strings of quartz determines the out-line and direction of the ridge. Many of the hills carry one or many quartz reefs, the majority of which are auriferous ; most par-ticularly are the smaller veins and strings rich in gold. From " prospects " taken at random, I have no reason to doubt the statements made that the yield from them is from four to six, and even twelve, ounces per ton. Were these reefs located in a country better circumstanced, they would have been made to yield hand-some profits. An unfortunate feature of most of the auriferous lodes is that the gold is compressed into a small compass ; whereas, if it were disseminated throughout a wider and more solid body of stone, there is no doubt it would be easier and more profitably extracted, and offer less uncertainty as to its permanence. Quartz-reefing is chiefly carried on by small parties, whose capital is their bone and sinew. The returns for a time are large, but, on encountering water or other impediments, which bring down the earnings, the reef is abandoned in order that the same process may be repeated elsewhere. In this way the multiplicity of auriferous reefs has been a comparative disadvantage, as very few of them have been followed to any depth. The mining operations are of the simplest kind. The quartz is raised to the surface in buckets by hand windlass. There are only two pumping-engines on the whole field. The period at which the bulk of the quartz veins can be advantageously worked will not entirely depend on their yield, but will be more or less influenced by the general price of labour and the materials in the district. The supply and consequent price of labour is materially influenced by the distance at which the gold-fields are situated from the great centres of trade. The history of gold-mining in Victoria offers a striking illustration of these axioms. Year by year the amount of gold derived from the working of gold-quartz has gone on gradually and rapidly increasing, as, by the introducton of efficient and powerful machinery, ores of a very low produce are treated with advantage ; but in this connection it must be observed that to obtain a satisfactory profit it is necessary not only that large quantities of ore should be treated, but also that the greatest economy should be observed in every department of the manipula-tion. To develop the gold resources of the Northern Territory it is necessary that more capital be introduced, to be chiefly applied to improved machinery for the extraction of the gold; and to cope with water ; more experienced and honest management be secured, and a reduction of working expenses be effected. The batteries which I examined are discreditable ; they are all the same pattern, and no attempt has been made to adapt them to particular requirments. There is a total absence of labour-saving appliances. All the batteries which I saw at work are in the highest degree wasteful ; the slimes in every case are highly charged with amalgam ; and no attempt is made to save the auriferous pyrites, as indeed no appliances are in use for their treatment. I do not hesitate to estimate the loss of gold at from 50 to 75 per cent., involving among other disadvantages a loss of considerable revenue to the State. If to the above fact we add that the price of carting and crushing has been hitherto at the rate of £3 10s. to £4 per ton, and that the wages of the skilled miner are £5 per week, and that the gold realizes only about £3 6s. per ounce, there can be no reason for wonder that quartz reefs carrying an average of 3 oz. of gold per ton are barely remunerative. It must be obvious that unless the quartz is really good our gold mines could never have kept so many men employed with these expensive appliances for so long a time. I have diligently sought for and enquired after memorials justifying the expenditure of those large sums of money which were raised some few years ago in Adelaide for the purpose of working the auriferous reefs in the Northern Territory; but it is with a mingled sense of shame and pleasure that I have to record that they exist only in the shape of a few primitive stamping batteries. The very limited exploitation that had been done on a few mines is hardly deserving of being placed to the credit of the enterprise. The sense of shame is experienced when we consider the misapplication of capital by the local managements; that of pleasure on finding that the disrepute into which this auriferous field has been brought cannot be attached to the gold properties themselves—indeed, those of the abandoned mines which have subsequently been worked by private capital have proved remunerative. It is a notorious fact that few, if any, gold properties in the tropics have been made remunerative under skilled white labour—and no wonder, if it be conceded that a tropical climate is unsuited for Europeans to work in. But mines employing native labour, with a minimum number of European overseers, compatible with successful and economic exploitation, have yielded steady profits to the proprietors. The St. John del Rey Mine, in the Brazils, makes a noble profit with a quarter of an ounce of gold per ton. To reduce the working expenses of our gold mines it is imperative that we employ cheaper labour—that of Chinese or negroes.

Alluvial Goldfields. — These are located in the immediate vicinity of the auriferous reefs, and occupy the lower slopes and bottoms of the short gullies which feather in and out among the ranges. There the "pay-dirt" lies on the surface, or rarely at a greater depth than two feet. It is obviously of local origin. Here and there the gold has been retained in pocket-like depressions fronting rocky barriers across the gullies, from which considerable stores of the precious metal have been obtained. The main lines of drainage into which these gullies lead have not been systematically prospected, and it is a moot question whether or no the broad valleys have "pay-dirt" beneath them. The ground may easily be tested, as there seems to be a very limited depth of drift-deposit filling the depressed surfaces—indeed, the slight rises on the plains are all composed of bed rock. The deepest accumulation of drift that I saw on the south flank of Mount Carr, where it is cut through by the Adelaide River, is not more than twenty-five feet. The bed of the river is composed of metamorphic rock. But as long as rich gold shall continue to be found in shallow ground, as long shall we despair of the deep ground being tried, or the auriferous reefs being energetically prospected. Although some

of the diggings have yielded well, I cannot regard the Northern
Territory as much of an alluvial field. The limited areas of the
diggings and the inability to work them, through lack of water, for
more than a few months in the year, foster a nomadism among the
miners which is inimical to. permanent settlement of the country.
Considering the primitive methods employed for gold-washing (I
saw in use only the tin dish and small cradles), I have no doubt
that the employment of more efficient appliances will result in
very much larger returns of gold than have hitherto been obtained ;
even the residuum of the deserted goldfields may be again gone
over with profitable results.

Tin.—Stream-tin was seen *in situ* at two places ten miles
apart in a straight line. These are shown by red streaks
on the mineral map, but samples of tinstone were inspected,
which were reported to have been obtained at other localities
than those visited. The first site is the gravelly bed and
east bank of one of the tributaries of the McKinlay River.
Good prospects were obtained here. The tinstone is well
rounded, but the pebbles do not exceed half an inch in
diameter. As prospecting was limited to two holes near to
each other it is impossible to arrive at any approximate estimate
of the quantity of stream-tin that is here present. One excavation
is 20 feet by 30 feet, and 6 feet in depth, from which, it is said,
11 cwt. of tinstone was taken. On following up stream the
rocky walls come together at a distance of 200 yards, but what is
the character down stream beyond the excavations could not be
ascertained. The gravel in the bed of the creek is well rounded,
and consists of silicious talcose slate and hornblendic schist,
identical with the material composing the rocky walls of the gorge.
No trace of granite *débris* was observed, though searched for. The
other site of tinstone was near the head waters of a stream which
drains a boggy flat, and flows north along the east flank of Mount
Wells. The bed of the stream is at first gravelly, and here fair
prospects of stream-tin were obtained. Other holes, embracing a
distance of about one quarter of a mile, yielded similar results, but
from this point the fall is rapid, and the detritus is in the form of
large boulders only. Unless tinstone occurs in the quieter flow
in the lower ground, beyond the limits of exploration, I am afraid
the present discovery is of little value. The tinstone at this
locality is small and angular, and shows the fine ruby colour
characteristic of the purer state of the mineral. From the
physical features of the country, and the condition of the mineral,
it is evident that the tinstone has been derived from the adjoining
slopes, which are composed of a sub-metamorphic micaceous sandstone. These stream deposits are of comparative small importance

in comparison to the supply to be derived from stanniferous lodes, but they will doubtlessly afford employment to a number of the poorer miners for some time to come. The formation most abundant in tin veins is the granite, but in neither of the two deposits of tinstone did I find evidence of such an association, nor is it definitely known if stream-tin has been found in the *débris* from the known granitic masses.

Copper.—The existence of ores of this metal in the Northern Territory is beyond dispute. The sites of the discoveries are shown by blue colour on the mineral map ; these are a little south from Pine Creek, in Cruikshank's Gully, and at another point near the Howley Battery. The prospects are, in each case, in the highest degree encouraging ; but, apart from the question as to the quality of the copper in these ores, their utilization under existing surroundings must not be attempted. Other minerals are galena (not seen *in situ*) and hæmatite, in massive beds.

General Conclusions and Recommendations Touching the Mineral Resources.—The develpoment of the mineral resources is but in its infancy, and I believe that rich stanniferous lodes will yet be found, whilst the prospects already unearthed indicate the presence of good percentage copper ores. Rich auriferous lodes abound over a large tract of country. Hitherto adventurers have made a show of developing the mineral resources, but their action has been protractive rather than otherwise, whilst the honest efforts of the nomadic miner cannot count for much. It is my honest conviction that, with improved machinery for the extraction of the gold and to cope with water, more experienced and honest management, a reduction of working expenses, and above all the introduction of more capital, the gold reefs can be worked profitably and to considerable depth. To hasten the advent of all this, however, there must be a railway to cheapen carriage and make the country accessible to mining and other speculators, and that railway may also be the means of opening up the copper deposits known to exist along the route to Pine Creek. To ensure occupancy and development of the mineral properties, the conditions under which they are held should be rigidly enforced. In the future all mineral rights should be reserved by the State, and the right of search for, and the mining for, minerals upon private lands, under equitable conditions, should be made statutory. As a revenue should accrue direct from the exploitation of minerals, a royalty on the net produce should be exacted, or commuted for by an annual rent, at the option of the lessees. The export tax on gold should be withdrawn, but the alluvial miner should be required to take out a licence at a nominal fee. Alluvial digging is only pioneer work, and should be strenuously encouraged, as leading to permanent settlement—by it the poor miner may acquire sufficient capital to open out additional sources of revenue to the State of a more enduring nature. I recommend the appointment of a warden skilled in geological and mineralogical surveys, and one competent to make chemical analyses, both to reside within the mining district. Apart from their judicial duties, they should be required to geologically survey the country, to impart information touching the nature of mineral specimens, and in all possible ways further the mining interests of the colony. The question of the employment of a drill for determining the character of the deeper parts of the auriferous lodes is one that may be left till the advisability of Government interposition arises.

Agricultural Resources.—So very little has been done to test the agricultural capabilities of the country that the question, "Are the climate and soil of the Northern Territory suitable for the growth of tropical plants of economic value?" is still open for discussion. The soils of the valleys and of the hill slopes are, in my opinion, ill-suited for agriculture ; and, with a few exceptions, the land seen under cultivation was only that reclaimed from the jungle. The chief of the exceptions to which I allude is the soil formed by the decomposition of the diorite rock, massed between Port Darwin Camp and Yam Creek Telegraph Station ; it shows great capabilities, if I may judge from the healthy growth of the great variety of culinary and fodder plants under cultivation by the Chinese. Corroborative evidence of its richness is afforded by the reappearance of the graceful palm, Kentia acuminata, and, if it really be that species, in a more luxuriant state than it assumes in its northern stations. It abounds about Fannie Bay, near Palmerston, and occurs at intervals as far south as the Stapleton ; thence its place is taken by the fan palm, Livistonia humilis, which is less choice in its habitat. My opinion of the unfitness of the country generally for agriculture is based on observations. 1. On the nature of the soil ; 2. On the general character of the indigenous vegetation ; and 3. On certain meteorological phenomena. The "desert sandstone" tableland I leave out of consideration, as it is conceded by all who have traversed it that, with the exception of isolated tracts of the basaltic formation, agricultural operation is impracticable. The prevailing uniformity of rock structure makes it easy to generalise upon the capabilities of the soil. Thus we have a dry, gravelly, iron and quartz *detritus* on the slopes of the metamorphic sandstone ; stiff clays with humid surfaces on the metamorphic slates ; barren sands upon the granitic surfaces—all of these are completely worthless for agriculture. Whilst the soil upon the coast cliffs is generally condemned, Captain King, in his narrative of a survey of the coasts of Australia (1818-22), writing concerning Raffles Bay, says, " The soil in some parts might be called even rich ; there were, however, very few places that could bear so favourable a character," vol. I., p. 85. And again, " The land about Port Patterson appeared to be barren and arid," vol. I., p. 271. Captain Stokes, in his discoveries in Australia, expresses the same opinion regarding the Port Essington District. At p. 386, vol I., he writes, " Generally speaking, however, there is a great deficiency of land fit for cultivation ;" and again, " The capabilities of the soil, though it has by some been pronounced totally unfit for agricultural purposes, are still supposed by others to be great, and it is believed that rice, cotton, indigo, &c., might be raised," loc. cit., p. 389. Alluding to the same area, Jukes, in the voyage of the Fly, vol. I., p. 351, says, " The soil generally seemed of the poorest and most sterile description." There are patches of good, if not rich soil, most undoubtedly ; but in the aggregate they form a very small fraction of the region of the northern rivers. The opinions touching the capabilities of the soil about the tidal portions of the rivers are very conflicting. King describes the soil abutting on the Alligator and Liverpool Rivers as a sour stiff clay—Op. cit. I., pp. 104 et 259. Stokes says, " While the banks [of the upper part of the tidal portion of the Adelaide] were low —a circumstance very favourable for irrigation and the cultivation of rice—Op. cit. I., p. 415, Jukes writes, "That rice might probably be raised in small quantities on the borders of the lagoons "—Op. cit. p. 361. I have reproduced these observations because they have reference to portions of the Northern Territory with which I am unacquainted. The meteorological poenomena, which must have a depreciating influence on the value of certain soils for particular crops, are—(1) The intermittent character of the rainfall at the chief period of growth. Many successive days of unclouded sky and hot winds during the wet season must have a deterrent effect on the growth of succulent plants and shallow rooting annuals in particular. (2) The rapid diminution in the amount of rainfall, proceeding in a southerly direction, thus starting with a yearly average of 76·89 inches at Southport, it gradually decreases at the rate of about one inch to every five miles, to 39·23 at Pine Creek. (This will be seen on a reference to Mr. Todd's reports.) The pro- ductions of the soil of the Government Gardens at Fannie Bay, reclaimed from a dense jungle, afford evidence that a great variety of useful plants may be successfully grown under similar con- ditions of soil and situation. But, as I have just shown, the climatic conditions change so rapidly as we recede from the coast that I am dubious, even other things being the same, whether equal results will be gained in the more inland tracts. If we turn our attention to the dominant vegetation we find that it implies, if not sterility of soil, then certainly the absence of those points of character indicative of permanency of atmospheric moisture, and conversely general exposure to the sun. Thus we note the absence of dense lofty forests, scarcity of ferns and epiphytic orchids, no lichens, no liver worts, and only four species of mosses having a very limited range of distribution. However, I believe that in several parts of the colony various species of Gossypium (cotton-plant), rice, and indigo could be cultivated, and a fair or even prolific crop obtained. Indeed, good cotton has been produced within the Murray basin (see F. von Mueller, "Select Plants for Cultivation," p. 99, 1876). The rice-plant is indigenous to the Northern Territory, having been found by Baron F. von Mueller in the marshes about Hooker's Creek, by Mr. Wilson in the marshes of the valley of the Norton-Shaw River, and by Mr. J. A. Giles in the valley of the Birdum Creek. The tamarind is also a native, having been noticed first by Leichardt at Port Essington, and subsequently by Mueller on the cliffs at the entrance to the Victoria River. Another useful plant indigenous to the country has been overlooked. It is Tacca pinnatifida, from the tubers of which the main supply of Fiji arrowroot is prepared. I noticed it growing in rather humid gravelly soil here and there from Palmerston to Pine Creek.

Pastoral Resources.—The humidity and high temperature of the air during a portion of the year cannot be conducive to the rearing of sheep within the region of the northern rivers. Jukes says, "Sheep, if they lived at all, would soon have their woolly coats changed into hair."—Op. cit., p. 361. Landsborough writes that "The kangaroo grass, though of itself possessing excellent properties [the species of Anthistiria referred to is probably A. ciliata, one of the chief constituents of the herbage on the plains between the Adelaide River and Bridge Creek.—R. Tate] is so certain an index of humid soil, which is on the whole unfavourable to sheep, that I cannot agree with many squatters in their estimate of the country on which it is found."—Narrative Explor. Gulf of Carpentaria, p. 36. What is true with respect to the unsuitability of the climate for sheep will be true in a less degree for horses, both of which, however, may find more congenial conditions on the tableland country, especially along the courses of the southern creeks, which are well known for luxuriance of vegetation and richness of soil. These creeks take their rise in basaltic formation, and it is to its presence that is due the oases in an otherwise desert country. Landsborough, in describing the Barkly tableland, which is drained by the Herbert, says—" In the course of the day we had travelled thirty miles, chiefly over fine country, doubtless destined to rank as a first-class sheep run "—Op. cit., p. 53. Tropical South Australia has truly been said to be a land of grasses ; the number of known species is about 130, and of these I collected over 50 between the Adelaide River and Pine Creek. But only some four or five are constituents of the grass plains and adjacent hill slopes. Some flats are almost exclusively occupied with Anthistiria, or with Andropon triticeus, or with another congeneric species, whilst not infrequently the three are found in company. The two latter grasses acquire on the flats a height of from 6 feet to 8 feet, and exceptionally attain to 14 feet ; but on dry hill slopes the same species dwindle down to two feet or less. The exuberant growth of grasses in the plains of the basin of the northern rivers should be capable of keeping alive large herds of cattle ; but I very much doubt if there are all the requisites for the production of marketable beef. I have observed that there is an absence of the rich fodder grasses, and the much valued kangaroo grasses (Anthistiria ciliata and A. frondosa) are only locally abundant in the country traversed ; whilst Andropogon triticeus or tall speargrass and its congener, A. Australis, seem to me ill-adapted for fattening stock. The tall speargrass is everywhere abundant in the open country, its hard and cane-like flowering stalks growing to 14 or 16 feet in height ; the other common grass, A. Australis, is not so strong a plant, but is equally deficient in succulency and leaf. The density of the growth of the grasses on the flats defies all opposition to the establishment of other herbaceous species ; but when external agents exercise their sway, then a herbage of panick grasses and some sedges take possession of the soil—the former on the drier ground chiefly, the latter on the more humid surfaces. Whether or not this improvement can be maintained without the intervention of man and domestic animals, or can be extensively brought about, is a question which I doubt if any one can yet give answer ; but, nevertheless, it is true that such a change has supervened over very limited areas, where the balance of nature has been disturbed and maintained by the agencies referred to.

I have, &c.,

RALPH TATE, F.G.S., &c.,
Professor of Natural Science in the University of
Adelaide.

BANQUET BY CHINESE IN PALMERSTON.

One of the most pretentious displays of the hospitality of the Chinese residents in the Northern Territory was given on Tuesday afternoon, March 21, when the Parliamentary party and leading representative residents of Palmerston responding to their invitation attended at Pickford's Hotel what was in truth a grand banquet. The edibles were served mostly in English style, and knives and forks took the place of chopsticks, but some of the appointments and the scene were truly Oriental. The Government Resident occupied the chair, but his *vis-a-vis* was a very intelligent Chinese merchant, who spoke English with as much fluency as foreigners from other countries than China generally attain unto. When the time for toasting came the duty was heartily undertaken alike by Celestial and European. The tribute to Her Majesty was loyally paid, and after it had been recorded,

Mr. PRICE, S.M. (Government Resident), proposed "The Emperor of China." He sturdily combated assertions unfavourable to the good behaviour of the Chinese. He asserted that the alarm which some people felt at their great preponderance in number over the Europeans had proved to be utterly groundless. As a matter of fact when shipload followed shipload of Chinamen they went peacefully into the gold country, and caused no disorder whatever. They had caused no extra work to be thrown upon the police; they had been law-abiding in every way. When they first came they were untaxed; but after the Customs duties were imposed they readily contributed their full share to the revenue without a single grumble. It had been said that the Chinese escaped their fair share of taxation, but the fact was that they not only paid the gold duty equally with the European, but they also paid duty on rice, while flour came in free. He was glad to be able, in the presence of such distinguished visitors, to bear testimony to the good character of the Chinese as a body throughout the Territory. (Cheers). It had been said as an argument against the Chinese that they took their gold out of the country, and did not remain to develop its resources; but he contended that a European making a fortune by gold-digging would not be content to spend the rest of his days in the Territory; and so the two races were equal in that respect. The rate of recorded crime had not perceptibly increased since the Chinese came amongst them, and he was doubtful whether the new gaol—though he had recommended its construction—would be needed for a while. He bespoke for the Chinese, for their courtesy and good behaviour at all times, the fair play which true Englishmen gave to every man everywhere. The Chinese had opened their ports to us, we had opened ours to them, and we should remember, when honouring their enlightened Emperor, that whilst our forefathers roamed the woods unclad the Chinese had attained to a comparatively high degree of civilization. (Cheers.) They had accepted so much the changed condition of things that their old traditions—their old exclusiveness—was fast breaking down; and one proof of that was that an Englishman could now safely travel through any part of China. He hoped that equal facilities would be given to Chinese travellers in every country boasting English rule. (Cheers.)

Mr. PRICE, after the toast had been drunk, read the following significant address, prepared for presentation to the Minister and his party, as the focus of Chinese opinion in the Northern Territory :—" On behalf of the Chinese residents in the Northern Territory of South Australia, we desire to express our pleasure and satisfaction at meeting you as representatives of the Parliament governing this fine colony, and further to assure you of the respect we have for the laws of your country. The Chinese are a peaceable race, and wherever they have settled out of their own dominions they have always endeavoured to keep and respect the laws of the lands in which they have lived ; and though in some colonies our countrymen have been abused by the lower classes, we are glad to notice that the educated and well-instructed people have treated us with that generosity which is extended to other nationalities. We view with satisfaction the fact that your Parliament in its wisdom have decided not to restrict the immigration of our race to this portion of Australia. We claim that had it not been for the influx of Chinese to the Territory it would not now present the encouraging position which it maintains. As we think we have assisted in the development of the mining in no small degree, we think we are entitled to point out to you that the imposition of the export duty on gold is most oppressive and unfair, and we would urge upon the Government a reconsideration of this question. We would also suggest an alteration as to the collection of miners' rights. It has frequently been urged that we are a migratory race, but hitherto no inducement has been held out for us to settle in this country. Had there been, many of us, no doubt, before now would have been cultivators of the soil instead of being mere labourers on your goldfields. As we well know that vast portions of this settlement are good for agriculture, we would like opportunities of settling, and making permanent homes. If grants of 50 to 500 acres could be made to us on easy terms of purchase, cultivation of tropical products would be entered into, which would ultimately prove of great benefit to the entire community. And, again, we would further urge that if we become investors and

settlers, we should be entitled to a voice in choosing the representatives of the country in your Parliament."

The Chinese Vice-Chairman then, in a graceful and perfectly
grammatical little speech, proposed the health of "The Minister
for the Northern Territory and the Ministry."

The Hon. J. L. Parsons, in responding, expressed his pleasure
at the compliment paid to him, and said he accepted the magnificent reception given to the party that day and at other times as
an expression of the desire of the Chinese settlers to recognise and
respect the institutions and the laws of the Australias, which so
many of them had made their adopted home. The desire of the
Government was to so manage the affairs of the northern portion
of the colony of South Australia that its resources might be
developed, and that those who had cast in their lot here might
share in that prosperity which would be the result of increased
capital, and of course an increase of industrial occupation. He
need hardly say that so far as the present Ministry were concerned
they had given special attention to the Territory. It was only
fair to say, too, they had had the advantage of some others.
They had to deal with the Territory at a time when a large
amount of attention was being directed to it. (Cheers.) Just at
that time there was one of those tides in the affairs of nations
through which they were enabled to deal with the Northern Territory in an entirely new and different way from those their predecessors in office could adopt. (Cheers.) They were enabled at
once to inaugurate a bolder and more progressive policy, and the
presence of the Parliamentary party was an expression of the
opinion of South Australia that the people of the Northern Territory were worth visiting; that they had large resources; and
that it was the duty of South Australia proper—or the mother
colony—to do all they could to make that Territory attain and
keep that position of importance which it was bound to hold in
future. (Cheers.) He considered that whoever might have been
Minister of Education for the time being would have done less
than his duty if he had not during the recess visited the Northern
Territory. Since the party had been there he hoped they had
impressed the residents of the Northern Territory with the idea
that, while glad on all proper occasions to enjoy themselves, they
commenced their stay with business and work. (Cheers.) Since they
had landed they had gone through what was called the mineral
portion of the Territory as far south as it had been developed to
any extent. They had met with a great deal of kindness, received
great hospitality, and throughout the whole of their travels had
been readily furnished everywhere with reliable information, so
that they had every opportunity of forming an independent

judgment upon the natural resources of the whole of the Northern Territory. He believed that they would all return to Adelaide with the feeling that not half of the wealth of the country had been told them, and that in future debates in the Parliament on Northern Territory matters there would be a very large amount of interest and also a large amount of belief in its future that had been sadly lacking in the debates and legislation of past years. One of his main objects in coming to the Northern Territory was to be able to give his colleagues an intelligent opinion based upon observation of the best way of opening up the interior, because he felt that it was absolutely impossible, even though the gold-fields and reefs were of exceptional richness, that they could be profitably worked whilst their development was so handicapped with the enormous expenses of wages and of food. (Cheers.) The country must be opened, and he had come up to see whether its circumstances warranted the construction of a railway. (Cheers.) That was proposed some years ago, when a surveyor came from the South, and a survey was made. He felt now that in going South he would be able to press, as a result of his observations, upon his colleagues the claims of the Northern Territory in connection with the transcontinental railway. He had in view to recommend to them that at any rate for 150 or 200 miles south the railway should be constructed. (Loud cheering.) Of course he was only one of six, and the Cabinet and the Parliament might be of a contrary opinion to his own. It was for the Parliament to decide whether or not the railway should be made, but he certainly would recommend it. (Cheers.) He believed that his colleagues would be disposed, at any rate, to listen to his advice, and they would be fortified by the views of the gentlemen who had accompanied him. (Cheers.) Referring to the address, he wished to say that the Chinese were, in his opinion, a very peaceable race, and he heartily endorsed what had been said of their long history and the long-enduring civilization they boasted. He had always respected and reverenced the integrity of the Chinese Empire. They could boast of scientific men, philosophers, and philosophic systems of morality when our ancestors were wandering about in barbarism. No one could look at the Chinese Empire and no one could regard its history without feeling that, as in the past, so in the future, both by numbers and also by intelligence and activity, the Chinese were bound to be a great factor. (Cheers.) So far as the gold duty was concerned, it had been one of the first interests of the State to derive a revenue, and at the time the Bill was passed its object undoubtedly was to make the large Chinese population contribute in a direct way to the revenue, in return for the protection of life and property they enjoyed. He admitted that a tax upon product was bad in political economy, and he thought if they were to reduce the duty to a nominal sum so as to secure a record of the amount of gold raised in the Territory it would be very easy to make up the deficiency in some other way if necessary. (Cheers.) The miners' rights he also thought might be issued quarterly, so as to avoid a hardship which had been pointed out. (Hear, hear.) There must be some mistake in the minds of the Chinese with regard to the cultivation clauses. He hoped it was thoroughly understood that with the payment of 7s. 6d. per acre and the cost of survey the obtaining of land was as open to the Chinese as to any one else. There was also the Plantation Act, by which by the payment of sixpence a year and the fulfilment of the cultivation clauses land could be obtained for the growth of tropical products. There ought not to be any difficulty in the way of those who were prepared to invest their capital and take up land. He was pleased that he had come to the Northern Territory, and he would ever cherish pleasant recollections of it and its people. (Cheers.)

Mr. T. BURTT proposed "The Parliament," and urged that as the Chinese contributed their fair share of taxation they were entitled to representation in Parliament.

Mr. BRIGHT, M.P., in responding for both Houses of Parliament, referred to the Council's action in negativing the proposition to place a poll-tax on Chinese coming to the Northern Territory as a proof of the necessity of a second Chamber to check hasty legislation. He felt it a duty to come to the Northern Territory, and see it and its wants for himself. He had been pleased with his visit, and he would be able on his return, when matters affecting the Territory were brought before the House, to deal with them more intelligibly than if he had not paid the visit. For example, if a proposition were made for representation of the Territory he would not oppose it. He saw the important aid the Chinese had given in the development of the place so far as it had been developed. The European population, he understood, were dependent upon the Chinese for even their supply of fish as well as vegetables. (Hear, hear.)

Mr. FURNER, M.P., was extremely gratified with his visit. As to the influence it would have upon his Parliamentary action, he would be most happy to do simple justice to the Northern Territory in the matter of local representation. The interests of this portion of the colony were too great to allow of its being simply tacked on to another district, and he thought it should have ndependent representation. (Cheers.) He had taken especial nterest—because he represented a large mining district—in the mineral deposits of the Territory, and he was greatly pleased with what he had seen in relation to that industry. With regard to the gold duty, he coincided with the opinions of the Minister ; and concerning the point raised by Mr. Burtt with reference to the representation of Chinese in Parliament he need only remind their hosts that they had but to pay the naturalization fee of 10s. to be entitled to the privileges of British subjects. (Cheers.)

Mr. BAGSTER, M.P., spoke appreciatively of the hospitality which had been extended to the party equally by Europeans and Chinese, expressed his idea at the importance of the work the party had accomplished during their trip, and his hopefulness of great advantage accruing from it to the colony.

Mr. PRICE proposed "The Vice-Chairman," remarking that not only were the Europeans indebted to the Chinese for their fish and vegetables but for their beef also, in times past an unknown luxury. But for the Chinese consumption the cattle would not be imported from Queensland. He expressed the opinion that the trip now closed would be of immense advantage to the Territory. Partly through it, as it called attention to the resources of the place, the Territory would soon be looked upon by South Australia not as a white elephant, but as a bright gem. (Cheers.) People talked of a separation of Northern from Southern Australia, but he did not believe that anything of the kind would take place. Before long South Australian money which went to Mauritius and elsewhere would come to the Northern Territory for sugar and other tropical products. Year by year during his six years of the Government Residency he had looked forward to this : and he saw the first dawn of its fulfilment when the Minister controlling the Territory spoke of visiting it. The place only needed to be seen to be appreciated. (Cheers.) As to the railway and what Mr. Parsons had said about it, he felt sure that if the Minister recommended the railway they would have it. (Cheers.) He believed the Parliament would uphold him, and that the Transcontinental Railway of South Australia would in time be quite as great and important as that connecting the Atlantic and the Pacific. (Cheers.) The world was north of South Australia, and they would have to work towards it and not from it.

In conjunction with all the company Mr. Price gave the sentiment, " May God speed the party on their return journey," and the honouring of that and several other toasts concluded the business of the engagement so gracefully arranged and so well carried out by the Chinese.

THE EUROPEAN BANQUET.

Closely following the dinner given by the Chinese residents of Port Darwin, on Tuesday night, a public banquet was given to the Parliamentary party in Parker's Hotel. Mr. Meldrum presided, and Mr. Gott filled the vice-chair, and the party included the Government Resident and all the other leading residents.

The usual preliminary toasting having been performed, the CHAIRMAN proposed "The Ministry." He considered that the visit of the Parliamentary party to the place was the best assistance South Australia had ever given to the Northern Territory. As a man who represented a Company which had invested large sums in mining he expressed the belief that if there were better communication between the Northern Territory and Adelaide, the next thing most wanted—cheap labour—would be supplied. Miners receiving £5 a week for their work would cripple any Company, and under such circumstances proper development would be impossible. The present Minister was the only man who had ever yet held out to them any hope of their getting their much-needed railway.

The Hon. J. L. PARSONS, Minister for the Northern Territory, in responding and referring to the history of the proposition to visit the Territory, said that when he had decided upon making the visit himself he felt he could not do better than ask other hon. members to accompany him, and have all the facilities the Government could offer to aid them. The proposition was received in some degree by the Press of South Australia with doubt as to its propriety, and some articles had been written reflecting upon the expenditure of public money upon such a visit. But the party had come and gone through the country, and he was now more satisfied about the wisdom of that proposition, and as to the results the visit would have, than he had in regard to anything else that he could connect with his Ministerial experience. (Hear, hear.) It was quite true that the visit had been somewhat hasty and a little hurried. They had had to pass through the different parts of the Northern Territory rapidly; but from the fact that they were expected, and that it was a Parliamentary party in particular, they were brought into contact with every intelligent, thoughtful, and industrious man in the Northern Territory, and he believed that on returning to South Australia they would be able to say that there was not one who had got his hand and his heart and his pocket interested in the Northern Territory that they had not met with, and whose opinions they had not heard. For the future legislation of the colony they would carry back an amount of information gathered partly by observation and partly by report to tend to a more successful and more progressive policy than had obtained for the past few years. Reference had been made sometimes to the connection of the Northern Territory with South Australia. That Territory, it should be remembered, was a gift of the Imperial Government to South Australia, and whilst he had heard some hard things said about South Australia since he had been amongst them he asked than to bear in mind that the colony, herself young, busied with the settlement of her own great concerns, accepted the trust and had not shrunk from the responsibility. She had added to her public debt, and maintained ever since everything that was necessary for the protection of life and property, and had done that in the face of great obstacles ; and he hoped that the people in the Northern Territory would admit that South Australia had in every way proved herself a true parent to her Northern Territory. (Cheers.) He was very much pleased at the cordiality with which the toast of the Governor had been received. There was no better friend to the Northern Territory than Sir Wm. Jervois. There was not in Australia any more far-sighted statesman than he. Shortly before the party left Adelaide, the Governor, conversing with him about the trip, had shown conclusively that from the time of his appointment he had had a true conception of what would undoubtedly be the ultimate position of Port Darwin. (Cheers.) It was bound to be the key to the whole of Northern Australia. (Cheers.) In his Parliamentary career he had more particularly connected himself with the question of education ; and it was chiefly owing to the interest he had taken in that subject that he held his position in the Ministry ; but he had not been in office more than a few weeks before the importance of the Northern Territory forced itself upon his attention, and he felt that there was in connection with that dependency a magnificent future. (Cheers.) The opinion he had before he visited it was based on reports concerning it. He had now seen the country for himself, and on whichever aspect of the Northern Territory he looked he saw the materials out of which a prosperous and great nation were to be built. The waste grasses of the public lands of the Northern Territory were of incalculable value. He was taking back with him samples of excellent hay and chaff made by the Overland Telegraph Department out of those grasses for feed for the horses. He was taking down with him specimens which would be shown to the Parliament and people of South Australia of the gold wealth of the Territory. He felt that if during his visit through the mineral country he should be able to obtain from the various reefs specimens that he could show to the members of Parliament they would be much more eloquent and forceful than any speeches he could make; and on the different reefs, the proprietors, recognising the importance of the opportunity, had given him, for the public interest of South Australia, specimens of which no gold-producing country in the world need for a moment be ashamed. (Cheers.) He was also pleased to say that, so far as his own judgment went, there was in the Territory land suited for the growth of any product suited to a tropical climate. Some of the swamp lands through which they had passed would grow swamp rice, maize could be grown anywhere, and on the higher lands the hill rice could be grown successfully. The Government Garden was an evidence that almost anything planted and tended with care in this climate would grow to perfection. (Cheers.) He felt that the immediate successful future of the Northern Territory was wrapped up in the successful production of sugar. In the Government Garden there was at present growing some of the most luxuriant cane that any sugar-planter ever saw, and any Company possessing a few hundreds of acres of such a crop would feel that it had a good promise of dividends. (Cheers.) Across the bay there was a Company which had spent a large amount of money, and which, perhaps, had not the same good luck that might have been desired, and not commensurate with the pluck and enterprise it had displayed. (Cheers.) But it was his good fortune to be on the DeLissaville Plantation the previous day and to see manufactured the first sugar ever grown and produced in South Australia. (Cheers.) It was taken from the vat where the juice from the canes crushed some weeks ago from the Government Garden had been placed awaiting the arrival of the party, and the sugar was made under their own observation. He was taking down a small packet to Adelaide to show with the other specimens, and he hoped that it might be taken as the *avant-courier*—the precursor—of thousands of tons to be profitably grown and manufactured in the Northern Territory. (Cheers.) In addition to the gold deposits, he believed (without speaking at all confidently, because, although he had visited Bamboo Creek and Mount Wells, and saw tin taken up, he wanted to speak with all caution) that there was undoubtedly stream tin in all parts of the mineral country, and behind that stream tin there must be lodes. It required prospecting and the expenditure of money, and that done he believed that there would be a large tin-mining industry in the colony. (Cheers.) With regard to the question of Parliamentary representation for the Territory, provision would be made in the new Electoral Bill for that representation, and it should be given them without their being tacked on to another district with which they could have no identical interest. (Cheers.) On behalf of the Government he thanked the people of the Territory for the great kindness and courtesy they had shown, and for the facilities they had afforded him for obtaining information. He had not had an idle time. He had had hardship and inconvenience; but when he returned he would carry with him nothing but pleasant associations in connection with the Northern Territory.

The VICE-CHAIRMAN proposed "The Parliament of South Australia."

Mr. BRIGHT, M.P., said in reply that the resources of the Territory had far exceeded his expectations. Even the roads he had travelled over were better than those not many miles from Adelaide. He believed that the principal want of the Northern Territory was suitable labour, for what was the use of having valuable land if they had not the means to develop it ? European labour was altogether unsuitable for the requirements of the place. No mines in the world would pay when wages were so high as £5 a week. To get more suitable labour he would do his level best. (Cheers.) He expressed great surprise at the extent of the work which had been done at DeLissaville, and the opinion that the sugar he had seen manufactured there would be a credit to any part of the world. If anything could be done by Parliament he was sure that they would not withhold a hand to assist those who endeavoured to assist themselves as the pioneers of industries in the Territory had done. (Cheers.)

Mr. FURNER, M.P., spoke in glowing terms of the impression his visit had made upon him. He had noticed with pleasure the luxurious vegetation—grass 14, 15, and 16 feet high. The inference was that land which would grow that would grow anything else suited to the climate. Most of the journey, of course, lay along the course of the road, which was on the ridges; the land where they had to cut across country was not generally so good; but the Rum Jungle (Poiett's & Mackinnon's plantation) was some of the finest land he had ever seen in the colony, and such land ought to produce tropical plants in abundance. He was delighted with his visit to the Delissaville Plantation on Cox's Peninsula, where the land seemed to be wonderfully rich, and though some adverse opinions had been expressed respecting the character of the soil, he believed the estate was a magnificent one. (Cheers.) With regard to the railway, he entirely agreed with the remarks of the Minister, and he pledged his word that he would go back to Parliament fully prepared to advocate the construction of a railway south from Palmerston. (Cheers.) He had no doubt upon the point. The country was of such importance, the character of the land of such a nature, and the minerals of such extent as to warrant the commencement of the work. (Cheers.) He now quite agreed with what Sir William Jervois had recently said of the Territory in its relation to South Australia, that "the tail would waggle the dog." He had been remarkably pleased with his visit to the Gardens; and that in two years an almost impassable jungle should have been so transformed was wonderful. The growth was absolutely beyond belief. He fully believed that Port Darwin must necessarily become an important outlet for the northern part of Australia—if not the most important for the whole of Northern Australia. (Cheers.) It was necessary that something should be done in the way of a jetty or wharfage accommodation. Details must be left to the engineers.

Mr. BAGSTER, M.P., referred to what he considered to be a successful issue of the trip. The pastoral, agricultural, and mineral resources of the place had all been made patent to them, and the only matter in which they were unsuccessful was the intended trip to the Daly. That they did not visit the Daly, however, was not their own fault. They honestly attempted it. He doubted whether it was, taking other possible occasions into consideration, the wind and waves and rain which prevented that visit so much as the want of a suitable vessel in which to make the trip. If there should be on the next Northern Territory Estimates a line for a proper Government vessel at Port Darwin he would support it. As to the railway, he thought the time was fast approaching when South Australia would be connected by a line to the Northern Territory. (Cheers.) Local representation for the Territory he was strongly in favour of. (Cheers.)

Mr. V. J. SOLOMON proposed—"The Pastoral and Agricultural Interest." He considered the plan which had been adopted in the Territory of granting leases to pastoral tenants, with a long term of tenure and a long time to stock, was a great mistake. To give pastoral lessees three years to put cattle on their country was almost an encouragement to dummyism. Every square mile of country put up in the Northern Territory was now held by these lessees, and yet not 100,000 head of cattle were placed upon it. He pressed upon the Government the necessity of endeavouring to force the stocking of the land. At present the actual pastoral interest was represented by three or four small squatters, and the people were entirely dependent for their supplies of fresh meat upon a few Queensland "cockatoos." It would be better if the Government gave the land for nothing if they could get it stocked. The agricultural interest—as represented by small planters on Cox's Peninsula—had not, he thought, been fairly treated by previous Governments, and he referred incidentally to the fact, that of the whole 70,000 or

80,000 acres of land given them under a special Act only the DeLissa proprietors had done any real work upon it. It almost seemed as if there were some dummy Companies about. (Cheers.) The system of giving these big blocks was a mistake. What was wanted was real encouragement to bona fide settlers, and a land law which would permit any working man with strong arms and health to take up a block up to about 500 acres, and by cultivation and other improvements to secure its freehold. (Cheers.) That would be far better than encouragements to large Companies to take up land as a huge speculation. It would be a great advantage if £20,000 or £30,000 of the revenue now being derived from the Northern Territory were divided and offered in four bonuses for different kinds of tropical products. This would be a tangible encouragement to small growers. At present the only bonus was that for sugar—500 tons, to gain which would involve an expenditure of from £20,000 to £25,000. Almost the whole of the land down to the Rum Jungle had years ago been frittered away in blocks averaging about 320 acres, which were sold, with a town block given in, for £50 each—not enough to pay the cost of survey. The effect of that foolish policy was sorely felt now. He did not think the Northern Territory was indebted to South Australia proper, but to the strong arms and clear heads and energy of its pioneers. He suggested that the reserved suburban blocks near Fannie Bay should be offered for sale before the rush came, so that the original settlers could obtain a place to build residences on.

Responses were given in due course, and so closed the last public act of the party in the Northern Territory.

THE HOMEWARD JOURNEY.

THE homeward journey was made on board the steamship Tannadice (of the Eastern and Australian Mail Line), whose commander, Captain S. G. Green, is deservedly one of the most popular of popular masters. The Tannadice is a new vessel, built under the direction of Mr. R. Wildridge, her present chief engineer; and she is one of the smartest of the fleet which are now engaged in connection with the South Australian Mail Service with the Northern Territory and also in the China trade. Her burthen is 3,000 tons register, and her owners are shrewdly awaiting the upshot of events in connection with our northern possession. They have unlimited capacity for serving us in all respects.

The voyage from Port Darwin to Sydney was so unexciting that it would have been monotonous were it not for the numerous devices of Captain Green to "keep things going," as he would put it. Moreover, we had on board the most nervous mortal in man's shape that ever I met. He was a high official, holding some semi-military rank, too. He joined the steamer at Hongkong; but several days before she sailed he looked up the agents, and made searching enquiries respecting the Captain's character, ability, and so on. He would see him before he would ship, he said. At last he had an introduction. Said he—

"H'm. Captain, are you? Young, eh!"

The Captain with due humility said that he was born young, and he really could not help it.

"Well, Captain," spake the high official, "I'm wanting to go to Sydney with you; and I've been studying the charts, and I see there are lots of reefs and sandbanks and rocks in the way. You're sure you understand your business, and there's no danger of your running your ship on 'em?"

The Captain would try hard not to do so.

"Well; I—I think I'll trust you."

They started. The first night on which they had got well away from the land, a bank of light clouds appeared on the horizon.

"What sort of weather will it be to-night?" was the question our friend put to one of the officers.

"W-e-l-l; I—I don't know." (He knew his man.)

"Steamers ever get wrecked here?"

"Y-e-s. Typhoons, monsoons, and so on, you know."

"Bless my soul! What are we to do, then?"

"Only one thing; vessels sometimes put back to harbour."

"Well; why on earth doesn't the Captain put back?"

" Doesn't like to run the risk and expense."

" But I will protect him. My Government will. I'll give him a guarantee at once."

He left ; and by-and-by he met the Captain. "Captain," said he, " on behalf of the passengers, I must ask you to put back into the Celebes, and anchor."

" No ; I can't accept the responsibility."

" But I'll protect you. Here's a written guarantee on behalf of my Government." And he pleaded like a " jury" lawyer, but unsuccessfully. He hied to the officer again, and frantically deplored the obstinacy of the Captain.

" Can't be helped now," said the officer. " You see that light ? (pointing to a small bush fire on the nearest land.) That's from the last land on the China coast. No more ports till Port Darwin."

" Well ; put in there. Why can't the Captain do that ?"

" He dare not."

" Why, dare not ?"

" Because there are fierce blacks there, and if he goes near, they will come down upon us and attack us."

" Well ; what if they do ? I have a six-shooter, and I guess I can protect the saloon." And he entered in his diary, which he published—" The Captain, with stormy indications and danger, did not put back to port because he was afraid of being attacked by the blacks." Of course, there was no storm, and of course, there were not any blacks. Though the next day was as fine as any day you would wish to see, the nervous man interviewed the officer again, watching the Captain's departure for a moment—

" Now tell me candidly," said he, "*do* you think there is any danger of the ship *capsizing?* She hasn't got much on, you know."

By-and-by there was some trouble with the machinery, and on his persistently enquiring the cause, he was told that a *rat had got into the piston.* When I went on board he said to me :—

" Gross negligence aboard this vessel. Rats allowed to get into the piston. Going to send about it to papers."

And he sent too. Next day the cigar-light stick was set to smoulder in its case on deck. He hadn't seen cigar-light sticks before; and edging up to me, he asked in a tremulous voice :—

" Bad weather, d'ye think ? I see the Chinamen have brought the fire-stick to propitiate their Joss."

This sort of thing lasted all through the trip. Each night our nervous friend would come to the cabin with a sepulchral—" D'ye think it'll be safe to go to bed to night," and if the sky was aught but very clear—" Tried your life preserver on ?" The climax was

reached when we entered Sydney Heads on a beautifully bright
day at noon. Our friend came up in that graveyard-reminding
way of his, and said—

"Don't you think we're going dangerously near those Heads?"

We put in at various ports, including Newcastle, with its busy
business life, its keen cold air, the coal-dust begriming everything,
and its uncommonly stout people—the place to us coming from
the tropics was quite a marvel with what seemed to us to be its
unusually fat folk; and fat folk, too, who had not known
Cross's Indigestion Drops more than a month or two! Of all
these things it is not my purpose to write here. Let me,
however, in justice to the Steamship Company and to the
route, repeat what I have written before—the advice to tourists
seeking a three months' pleasure trip, to take the Barrier
Reef passage and the Northern Territory on the way to China.
From a short distance north of Brisbane till the northernmost
point of Australia there need not be the least fear of the dreaded
seasickness, and on the trip there is to be seen plenty that will
instruct and amuse. And now I have done.

www.ingramcontent.com/pod-product-compliance
Lightning Source LLC
Chambersburg PA
CBHW030836270326
41928CB00007B/1081